The World War II
Fact Book

The World War II
Fact Book

CHRISTY CAMPBELL

BLACK CAT

Copyright © Christy Campbell 1985

First published in Great Britain in 1985
by Macdonald & Co (Publishers) Ltd

Reprinted 1988 under the Black Cat imprint

Macdonald & Co (Publishers) Ltd
3rd Floor
Greater London House
Hampstead Road
London NW1 7QX

a member of Maxwell Pergamon Publishing
Corporation plc

British Library Cataloguing in Publication Data
Campbell, Christopher
    World War 2 fact book.
    1. World War, 1939–1945 – Dictionaries
    I. Title
    940.53'03'21   D740

ISBN 0-7481-0179-9

Printed in Hungary

Contents

Section 3: WEAPONS

Section 4: ORGANIZATIONS AND ARMED FORCES OF WORLD WAR II

Section 5: PEOPLE'S WAR

SECTION 1

Operations

Chronology

Prelude 1931–1939

18 September 1931 Mukden incident, beginning of Japanese conquest of Manchuria

12 December 1931 Saarland evacuated by French troops

30 January 1933 Adolf Hitler appointed German Chancellor

14 October 1933 Germany withdraws from the League of Nations

30 June 1934 'Night of the Long Knives' in Germany. SA leadership eliminated

25 July 1934 Austrian Chancellor Dollfuss murdered, Nazi Putsch in Vienna fails

19 September 1934 Soviet Union joins of League of Nations

19 December 1934 Japan renounces Washington and London Naval Treaties

13 January 1935 Voters in Saar plebiscite choose to rejoin Germany

16 March 1935 Hitler decrees universal military service for Germany, denounces Versailles Treaty disarmament clauses

April 1935 US Neutrality Act

2 May 1935 Franco-Soviet Mutual Assistance Pact signed (ratified by France 26 February 1936)

3 October 1935 Italians invade Ethiopia

Operations

7 March 1936   Germans reoccupy Rhineland

9 May 1936   End of war in Ethiopia as the country is annexed by Italy

June 1936   France begins rearmament

17–18 July 1936   Outbreak of Spanish Civil War

27 October 1936   Rome-Berlin Axis

25 November 1936   German-Japanese Anti-Comintern Pact

25 April 1937   Spanish town of Guernica razed by air attack

7 July 1937   Sino-Japanese War begins

13 December 1937   Japanese take Nanking

12 March 1938   German annexation of Austria

28 July 1938   Soviet and Japanese forces fight in Far East

29 September 1938   Munich Conference opens (to 30 September)

2 October 1938   Poland annexes Teschen

21 October 1938   Japanese take Canton

3 November 1938   Announcement of Japanese 'New Order in East Asia'

10–16 March 1939   Annexation of Bohemia and Moravia

15 March 1939   Germans enter Prague

15 March 1939   Hungary annexes Ruthenia

23 March 1939   Germany annexes Memel

28 March 1939   Madrid falls to Franco forces – end of Spanish Civil War

31 March 1939   British Government abandons appeasement policy, announces guarantee to Poland

1 April 1939   Italians invade Albania

4

22 May 1939   Germany and Italy sign 'Pact of Steel'

28 May 1939   New Soviet-Japanese fighting erupts at Khalkhin Gol

23 August 1939   Soviet-German Nonaggression Pact signed

23 August 1939   Japan renounces Anti-Comintern pact

The War 1939–1945

1 September 1939   Germany invades Poland – World War II begins
General Marshall becomes US Army Chief of Staff

3 September 1939   Britain, France, Australia and New Zealand declare war on Germany. *Athenia* sunk

5–17 September 1939   Battle of Warsaw, Lodz

15 September 1939   Soviet-Japanese Border Conflict ends

17 September 1939   Soviets invade Poland

27 September 1939   Warsaw falls

29 September 1939   Soviet-German Boundary and Friendship Treaty signed

3 November   US Congress passes 'cash and carry' amendment to Neutrality Laws

30 November 1939   USSR invades Finland – beginning of Soviet-Finnish (Winter) War

17 December 1939   *Graf Spee* scuttled in Rio de la Plata

12 March 1940   Finland capitulates, ending Soviet-Finnish War

30 March 1940   Japanese establish puppet Chinese government at Nanking

9 April 1940   Germans seize Denmark, invade Norway, Oslo captured

14 April 1940   British forces make landings in Norway

5

Operations

24 April–28 May 1940   Battle for Narvik

2 May 1940   Allies evacuate Namsos and Andalasnes, Norway, King Haakon VII escapes to Britain

10 May 1940   Germany invades Low Countries

10 May 1940   Fort Eban–Emael invested

10 May 1940   Chamberlain resigns as British Prime Minister, Churchill forms coalition government

13–15 May 1940   German armour crosses Meuse

14 May 1940   Netherlands surrenders, Queen Wilhelmina escapes to Britain. Rotterdam razed by bombing

26 May 1940   Allied evacuation at Dunkirk (to 4 June)

27 May 1940   Belgium capitulates

9 June 1940   Allied evacuation and Norway surrenders

9 June 1940   Germans reach Seine west of Paris

10 June 1940   Italy enters the war

11 June 1940   Italian air attacks on Malta

13 June 1940   Germans enter Paris

15–16 June 1940   Soviets occupy Baltic States, Latvia, Lithuania, Estonia

17 June 1940   Churchill offers indissoluble union with France

21 June 1940   France signs armistice with Germany

26–28 June 1940   Soviet Forces seize Bukovina and Bessarabia

3 July 1940   British neutralize French fleet at Oran

4 July 1940   Italians invade British Somaliland

18 July 1940   British close Burma road on Japanese demand isolating China

26 July 1940   First US embargo on war trade with Japan

15 August 1940   Eagle Day – Battle of Britain

24–29 August 1940   RAF bombs Berlin

3 September 1940   US-British destroyers-bases deal

7 September 1940   'Blitz' on London begins

13 September 1940   Italian Army advances into Egypt

15 September 1940   Hitler postpones Operation Sealion

15 September 1940   Mass bombing attacks on London

16 September 1940   Conscription begins in US

22 September 1940   Japanese forces move into northern Indochina

22 September 1940   British attack on Dakar

27 September 1940   Japan signs Tripartite Pact, Rome—Berlin–Tokyo Axis

18 October 1940   British reopen Burma road with US encouragement

28 October 1940   Italians invade Greece

29 October 1940   British land in Crete

3 November 1940   British land in Greece

5 November 1940   Roosevelt elected to third term as US President

11 November 1940   British attack Italian fleet at Taranto

14 November 1940   Greeks launch counterattack on Italians

15 November 1940   Blitz on Coventry

9 December 1940   British Western Desert Force attacks Italians – British Special Operations Executive established

11 December 1940   British capture Sidi Barrani

19 January 1941   British advance into Ethiopia and Eritrea

Operations

22 January 1941   British capture Tobruk
Luftwaffe aircraft arrive in Sicily

5 February 1941   British victorious at Beda Fomm

9 February 1941   Royal Navy bombards Genoa

12 February 1941   Rommel arrives in Tripoli

22 February 1941   Axis attacks at El Agheila

2 March 1941   BOAC begins 'ball bearing' run to Sweden

4 March 1941   British Commandos raid Lofoten Islands

7–27 March 1941   British troops arrive in Greece

9 March 1941   Italians attack Greece from Albania

11 March 1941   US Lend-Lease Act signed

24 March 1941   Rommel takes El Agheila
British complete clearing of British Somaliland

27 March 1941   Prince Paul overthrown in Yugoslavia

28 March 1941   Battle of Cape Matapan

3 April 1941   Rashid Ali coup in Iraq

4 April 1941   British capture Addis Ababa

6 April 1941   Germans launch Operation Marita, invasion
of Yugoslavia and Greece

9 April 1941   Axis captures Bardia

10 April 1941   US protectorate over Greenland

10 April 1941   Axis siege of Tobruk begins

12 April 1941   Belgrade falls

13 April 1941   USSR and Japan sign Neutrality Pact

17 April 1941   Yugoslavia capitulates

18 April 1941   British land at Basra, Iraq

22 April 1941   British begin withdrawal from Greece

23 April 1941 Greek Army surrenders to Germans

27 April 1941 Axis occupies Halfaya Pass

28 April 1941 Axis takes Sollum

2 May 1941 British complete evacuation from Greece

6 May 1941 British defeat Iraqi forces at Habbaniya

15 May 1941 British recapture Sollum

18 May 1941 *Bismarck* leaves Baltic

20–28 May 1941 Germans invade Crete

22 May 1941 British withdraw from Crete airfields

27–28 May 1941 *Bismarck* sunk

30 May 1941 Rashid Ali flees Iraq

1 June 1941 British complete evacuation of Crete

8 June 1941 British and Free French troops invade Syria

15 June 1941 British launch Operation Battleaxe offensive in Western Desert, repulsed by Rommel

17 June 1941 British withdraw in Western Desert

22 June 1941 Operation Barbarossa, Germany invades USSR

1 July 1941 Wavell appointed British C-in-C India, Auchinleck C-in-C Middle East

5 July 1941 US forces begin occupying Iceland

9 July 1941 German Army Group Centre encloses 300,000 prisoners west of Minsk

12 July 1941 Vichy French surrender in Syria

5 August 1941 Germans eliminate Russian resistance in Smolensk pocket

9 August 1941 Roosevelt and Churchill meet in Atlantic Conference (to 12 August)

Operations

17 August 1941   Germans take Kiev

25 August 1941   British and Soviet troops occupy Iran

September 1941   Flying Tigers begin operations in China

15 September 1941   Germans complete investment of Leningrad

7 October 1941   Germans take 650,000 prisoners at Vyazma

15 October 1941   Army Group South reaches Don

17 October 1941   Tojo becomes Premier of Japan

19 October 1941   Stalin announces state of siege in Moscow

31 October 1941   US destroyer *Reuben James* sunk by U-boat

15 November 1941   Germans resume drive on Moscow

18 November 1941   British open Crusader desert offensive, Brooke replaces Dill as British CIGS

30 November 1941   British Eighth Army links up with Tobruk garrison

6 December 1941   Soviets begin counteroffensive before Moscow

7 December 1941   Pacific war begins with Japanese attacks on US Pacific fleet at Pearl Harbor. Japanese forces land in northern Malaya (8 December west of International Date Line)

8 December 1941   United States declares war on Japan

10 December 1941   Siege of Tobruk is lifted. Japanese sink HMS *Prince of Wales* and *Repulse* off Malaya. Japanese take Guam, make first landings on Luzon

11 December 1941   Germany and Italy declare war on United States, which takes reciprocal action

16 December 1941   Japanese invade Borneo

17 December 1941   Nimitz replaces Kimmel as C-in-C of US Pacific Fleet

19 December 1941   Hitler assumes personal command of German Army, replacing Brauchitsch

19 December 1941   Italian frogmen damage Royal Navy warships in Alexandria harbour

20 December 1941   King is appointed C-in-C of US Fleet

23 December 1941   Wake Island falls

24 December 1941   Arcardia Conference begins in Washington (to 14 January) British reenter Benghazi

25 December 1941   Hong Kong surrenders to Japanese. HMS *Barham* torpedoed in Mediterranean

31 December 1941   Allied ABDA Command established under Wavell

1 January 1942   United Nations Declaration signed. U-Boat offensive off US coast begins

4 January 1942   Japanese begin air attacks on Rabaul

7 January 1942   Siege of Bataan begins

11 January 1942   Japanese invade Netherlands East Indies

17 January 1942   Halfaya garrison surrenders to British

19 January 1942   Japanese capture Tavoy, Burma

22 January 1942   In new Axis offensive, Rommel retakes Agedabia

24 January 1942   US destroyers sink Japanese shipping in Macassar Strait

27 January 1942   British begin withdrawal from Malay Peninsula to Singapore

30–31 January 1942   Battle of Moulmein, British pushed back in Burma

11

Operations

30 January 1942 Japanese seize Dutch naval base at Amboina

2 February 1942 Stilwell designated chief of staff to Chiang Kai-Shek

1 February 1942 US carrier aircraft raid Japanese bases on Gilbert and Marshall Islands

11 February 1942 German warships *Scharnhorst, Gneisenau, Prinz Eugen* make dash up English Channel (to 13 February)

15 February 1942 Singapore surrenders to Japanese

19 February 1942 Battle of Lombok Strait, Dutch destroyer sunk

19 February 1942 Japanese carrier aircraft raid Darwin, northern Australia

22 February 1942 Roosevelt orders MacArthur to leave Philippines

25 February 1942 ABDA Command dissolved

27 February 1942 Fighting in Java Sea ends Allied naval resistance in Netherlands East Indies (to 1 March)

7 March 1942 Japanese land in New Guinea
British Burma Army evacuates Rangoon

9 March 1942 Japanese secure Java, completing conquest of East Indies

23 March 1942 Japanese seize Andaman Islands

27 March 1942 British raid Saint-Nazaire

2–8 April 1942 Japanese carrier aircraft strike Ceylon

3 April 1942 Japanese open final Bataan offensive

9 April 1942 Bataan surrenders

18 April 1942 US (Doolittle) B–25 raid on Japan

29 April 1942 Japanese take Lashio, Burma Road terminus

12

4 May 1942   Battle of the Coral Sea (to 8 May)

5–7 May 1942   British attack Diego Suarez, Madagascar

6 May 1942   Corregidor surrenders

8 May 1942   Germans begin preliminary offensives in Soviet Union

12 May 1942   Russians open Kharkov offensive

17 May 1942   Germans counterattack in Kharkov area, beginning Battle of Kharkov

20 May 1942   Japanese complete conquest of Burma

27 May 1942   Rommel attacks Gazala Line in large-scale Axis offensive

28 May 1942   Battle of Kharkov ends in Soviet defeat

30 May 1942   RAF mounts 1,000 bomber raid on Cologne

3 June 1942   Battle of Midway (to 6 June)

7 June 1942   Japanese invade western Aleutian Islands, seize Attu and Kiska

9 June 1942   Japanese conquest of Philippines completed

10 June 1942   Free French evacuate Bir Hacheim

17 June 1942   British withdrawal from Libya leaves Tobruk isolated

18 June 1942   Churchill arrives in Washington

21 June 1942   Tobruk falls to Rommel's forces

28 June 1942   Axis forces take Mersa Matruh in Egypt Germans open summer offensive in Soviet Union

June/July 1942   Destruction of convoy PQ17

1 July 1942   First battle of El Alamein begins (to 17 July)

2 July 1942   Sevastopol falls to German Army Group South

5 July 1942   Soviet resistance in Crimea ends

Operations

6 July 1942   Voronezh falls

9 July 1942   Germans open drives towards Rostov and Stalingrad

24 July 1942   Rostov taken by German Army Group A

7 August 1942   US 1st Marine Division lands on Guadalcanal

8 August 1942   Battle of Savo Island (to 9 August)

9 August 1942   Civil disobedience campaign proclaimed in India

12 August 1942   First Moscow Conference (Churchill–Stalin) (to 15 August)

13 August 1942   General Alexander made C-in-C Middle East, Montgomery commander Eighth Army

17 August 1942   US Eighth Air Force makes first attack on European target (Rouen-Sotteville)

19 August 1942   Canadian and British force raid Dieppe

22 August 1942   Brazil declares war on Germany and Italy

24 August 1942   Battle of the Eastern Solomons (to 25 August)

24 August 1942   German investment of Stalingrad begins

31 August 1942   Battle of Alam Halfa (to 7 September)

6 September 1942   Germans capture Novorossisk

7 September 1942   Japanese defeated in Milne Bay area, New Guinea

12 September 1942   Eisenhower appointed C-in-C Allied Expeditionary Force (for North-west Africa)
Fighting on Bloody Ridge, Guadalcanal (to 14 September)

16 September 1942   German Army Group B enters suburbs of Stalingrad

14

25 September 1942 Allied counteroffensive opens on Papua

11 October 1942 Battle of Cape Esperance (to 12 October)

23 October 1942 Second battle of El Alamein begins (to 4 November)

26 October 1942 Battle of Santa Cruz Islands

3 November 1942 Axis begins retreat at El Alamein

6 November 1942 Vichy forces on Madagascar surrender

8 November 1942 Allies land in North-west Africa (Operation Torch)

9 November 1942 Germans begin move into Tunisia

11 November 1942 Vichy French cease resistance in North-west Africa
Germans move into unoccupied France
Eighth Army takes Bardia

12 November 1942 Naval battle of Guadalcanal (to 15 November)

13 November 1942 British retake Tobruk

19 November 1942 Russians open counteroffensive at Stalingrad

22 November 1942 Red Army units meet at Kalach, encircling German Sixth Army in Stalingrad

30 November 1942 Battle of Tassafaronga

12 December 1942 Manstein opens counterattack to relieve German Sixth Army

13 December 1942 Axis begins retreat from Al Agheila

24 December 1942 Admiral Darlan assassinated in Algiers

14 January 1943 Allied Casablanca Conference begins (to 23 January)

15

Operations

15 January 1943 British Eighth Army opens drive on Tripoli

30 January 1943 Ernst Kaltenbrunner appointed head of SD

30 January 1943 Admiral Dönitz replaces Raeder as head of *Kriegsmarine*
14th Indian Division advances into Arakan

2 February 1943 Paulus surrenders VI Army at Stalingrad

8 February 1943 Chindits cross Chindwin into Burma (withdraw in April)

9 February 1943 US forces complete Guadalcanal campaign

14 February 1943 Red Army takes Rostov

18 February 1943 Axis breakthrough at Kasserine Pass

18 February 1943 Goebbels 'total war' speech at Berlin Sportspalast

1 March 1943 Battle of the Bismarck Sea (to 4 March)

6 March 1943 Rommel repulsed at Medenine

9 March 1943 Von Arnim replaces Rommel as Axis C-in-C in Africa

11 March 1943 Chennault's air task force in China enlarged as 14th Air Force

14 March 1943 Germans retake Kharkov

16 March 1943 Convoy battle is climax of Battle of the Atlantic (to 20 March)

26 March 1943 Eighth Army breaks through Mareth Line
Battle of Komandorski Islands, N. Pacific

18 April 1943 US aircraft shoot down Admiral Yamamoto

19 April 1943 Rising in Warsaw ghetto

28 April 1943 (to 6 May) RN Convoy ON5–2 fights off 51 U-boats, sinks 7

7 May 1943 Allied 18th Army Group captures Tunis and Bizerte

9 May 1943 Axis forces in north-east Tunisia surrender unconditionally, 270,000 POWs

11 May 1943 US 7th Division lands on Attu

12 May 1943 Trident Conference (Anglo-American) begins in Washington (to 25 May)
All Axis resistance in North Africa ends
Japanese retake Arakan

16 May 1943 RAF Dam Busters attack Möhne and Eder dams
Destruction of Warsaw ghetto completed

26 May 1943 Katyn massacre revealed
Dönitz moves U-boat operating areas

3 June 1943 French announce creation of Committee of National Liberation

11 June 1943 Pantelleria surrenders after a week of bombing

11 June 1943 US 8th Air Force attacks Wilhelmshaven

30 June 1943 Operation Cartwheel (Rabaul) launched in south-west Pacific

5 July 1943 Battle of Kursk (to 12 July)
Battle of Kula Gulf (Kolombangara)

10 July 1943 Allies invade Sicily

12 July 1943 Red Army opens major counteroffensive from Smolensk to Black Sea. Battle of Kolombangara

22 July 1943 Palermo falls to US Seventh Army

24 July 1943 Allied bombers incinerate Hamburg (to 3 August)

Operations

25 July 1943   Mussolini resigns; Badoglio becomes Italian Prime Minister

1 August 1943   US B–24s bomb Ploesti, Rumania

2 August 1943   Hitler orders hold fast order in East

5 August 1943   Red Army takes Orel and Belgorod

6 August 1943   Battle of Vella Gulf (to 7 August)

14 August 1943   First Quebec Conference opens (to 24 August)

15 August 1943   US Force invades Kiska

17 August 1943   US B–17s raid Schweinfurt and Regensburg
Axis resistance ends in Sicily

17/18 August 1943   RAF raid Peenemünde

23 August 1943   Red Army retakes Kharkov

24 August 1943   Mountbatten appointed Supreme Allied Commander in South-east Asia

3 September 1943   Allies land on Italian mainland; Italians surrender

8 September 1943   Eisenhower announces Italian surrender

9 September 1943   Allies land at Salerno

10 September 1943   German forces occupy Rome

12 September 1943   British forces land on Kos, Samos, Leros

21 September 1943   British midget submarines attack German battleship *Tirpitz*

6 October 1943   Battle of Vella Lavella

12 October 1943   US Fifth Army attacks across Volturno River

13 October 1943   Italy declares war on Germany

18

14 October 1943 US B–17s suffer heavy losses in raid on Schweinfurt

19 October 1943 Allied foreign ministers meet in Moscow (to 30 October)

31 October 1943 US 3rd Marine Division lands on Bougainville; Battle of Empress Augusta Bay

6 November 1943 Soviets retake Kiev

12–16 November 1943 British ejected from Aegean toeholds

20 November 1943 US forces land on Makin and Tarawa

22 November 1943 Allied Cairo Conference (to 26 November)

25 November 1943 Battle of Cape St George

28 November 1943 Roosevelt, Stalin and Churchill begin Teheran Conference (to 30 November)

1 December 1943 Allies begin assaults on Winter Line in Italy

3 December 1943 Allied meetings resume at Cairo (to 7 December)

5 December 1943 First P–51 escorts operational with USAAF

26 December 1943 *Scharnhorst* sunk off North Cape
US 1st Marine Division lands at Cape Gloucester, New Britain

5 January 1944 Allied drive to the Rapido, Italy

8 January 1944 Red Army takes Kirovograd

11 January 1944 Allied air forces begin Operation Pointblank against German aircraft industry and Luftwaffe

15–19 January 1944 Liberation of Leningrad

19

Operations

16 January 1944   Eisenhower assumes duties as Supreme Commander, Allied Expeditionary Force

22 January 1944   Allied Forces land at Anzio

27 January 1944   Leningrad-Moscow railroad opened

31 January 1944   US forces land on Kwajalein (secured 7 February)

3 February 1944   Soviet forces trap two German corps at Korsun

4 February 1944   Japanese launch offensive operation in Arakan

13 February 1944   Combined Chiefs of Staff order intensive bomber offensive against Germany

13–15 February 1944   British counterattack in Arakan

15 February 1944   Allies bomb Monte Cassino monastery

16 February 1944   Germans begin counterattack at Anzio

17 February 1944   US forces land on Eniwetok (secured 22 February)

20 February 1944   'Big Week' of air attacks on Germany opens (to 26 February)

29 February 1944   US Army force lands in Admiralty Islands

5 March 1944   Second Chindit expedition into Burma

6 March 1944   Japanese 15th Army opens offensive towards India

20 March 1944   Germans occupy Hungary

25 March 1944   Death of General Wingate in air crash

30 March 1944   RAF suffers heavy losses in raid on Nuremberg

3 April 1944   British carrier aircraft damages *Tirpitz*

5 April 1944   US Fifteenth Air Force bombers raid Ploesti, Rumania

9 April 1944   Japanese invest Imphal and Kohima, India

22 April 1944   US forces land in Hollandia area, New Guinea

7 May 1944   Japanese launch offensive in East China

9 May 1944   Soviets retake Sevastopol

11 May 1944   Allies open drive on Rome with attack on Gustav Line

17 May 1944   Cassino falls to Poles

18 May 1944   US forces land on Wakde, off New Guinea

21 May 1944   Allies begin massive pre-invasion air attacks on rail facilities on the Continent

23 May 1944   US Fifth Army breaks out from Anzio beachhead

27 May 1944   US Army forces land on Biak

4 June 1944   US Fifth Army enters Rome

6 June 1944   Allies invade Normandy (Operation Overlord)

13 June 1944   First V–1 cruise missile falls on England

15 June 1944   US marines invade Saipan

19 June 1944   Battle of the Philippine Sea (Great Marianas Turkey Shoot) (to 20 June)

22 June 1944   Japanese offensive defeated at Imphal

23 June 1944   Red Army opens huge summer offensive on central front, Operation Bagration

27 June 1944   Cherbourg falls

3 July 1944   US First Army opens 'Battle of the Hedgerows' in Norman *bocage* country

21

Operations

Minsk retaken

9 July 1944   Fighting ends on Saipan

17 July 1944   Rommel severely wounded in strafing attack, yields army group command in France

18 July 1944   British Second Army opens offensive in Caen area (Operation Goodwood)
Tojo resigns as Japanese Premier, is subsequently replaced by Ioiso

20 July 1944   German bomb plot attempt to assassinate Hitler

21 July 1944   US marines invade Guam

24 July 1944   US marines invade Tinian

25 July 1944   US Third Army breaks out at Saint-Lô (Operation Cobra)

28 July 1944   Soviets retake Brest Litovsk, cross the San River

1 August 1944   US 12th Army Group becomes operational in France
Warsaw Uprising begins
Organized resistance ends on Tinian
Patton's Third Army breaks through Avranches gap

3 August 1944   Myitkyina (Burma) falls to Allies

4 August 1944   British Eighth Army takes Florence

7 August 1944   Germans in Normandy begin counterattack towards Avranches

7 August 1944   Red Army reaches Vistula

8 August 1944   Japanese take Hengyang, China

9 August 1944   Eisenhower establishes HQ in France

10 August 1944   Organized resistance ends on Guam

22

12 August 1944   German counterattack at Avranches ends in failure

13–19 August 1944   Germans caught in Falaise-Argentan pocket

15 August 1944   Allies land in southern France (Operation Anvil Dragoon)

19 August 1944   US Third Army reaches Seine River

20 August 1944   Red Army strikes into Rumania (which capitulates 23 August)

23 August 1944   US Seventh Army fights Germans at Montelimar, Southern France (to 28 August)

25 August 1944   Paris liberated. Aitake operation (New Guinea) ends in Allied victory

26 August 1944   US Fifth Army crosses Arno

28 August 1944   Germans surrender in Toulon and Marseilles

3 September 1944   British Second Army force enters Brussels
Southern France forces take Lyons

4 September 1944   British Second Army takes Antwerp
Fighting ends between USSR and Finland

8 September 1944   First V–2 rocket falls on England

11 September 1944   Allied Normandy and Southern France invasion forces meet near Dijon

12 September 1944   Second Allied Quebec Conference opens (to 16 September)

15 September 1944   US Army units land on Morotai and marines on Peleliu

16 September 1944   Red Army units enter Sofia

17 September 1944   First Allied Airborne Army units dropped in the Netherlands (Operation Market)

Operations

21 September 1944   British Eighth Army takes Rimini

2 October 1944   US First Army assaults Westwall

10 October 1944   Soviet forces reach Niemen River – begin drive to Baltic

13–16 October 1944   Air-sea battle off Formosa

15 October 1944   Allies open offensive in northern Burma

20 October 1944   Belgrade taken by Soviet and Yugoslav forces, US Sixth Army lands on Leyte

21 October 1944   US First Army occupies Aachen

23 October 1944   Battle for Leyte Gulf (to 26 October)

7 November 1944   Roosevelt elected to fourth term as US President

12 November 1944   *Tirpitz* sunk by RAF bombers

16 November 1944   US First and Ninth Armies open offensive to clear Roer plain

19 November 1944   British cross the Chindwin at Sittang, Burma

23 November 1944   French armoured force enters Strasbourg

27 November 1944   Fighting ends on Peleliu

28 November 1944   First B-29 mission from Marianas

3 December 1944   Civil war in Athens

13 December 1944   US Third Army takes Metz

15 December 1944   US force invades Mindoro

16 December 1944   Germans attack in Ardennes (Battle of the Bulge)

24 December 1944   Red Army encircles Budapest

26 December 1944   US Third Army armoured relief column reaches Bastogne

1 January 1945 Germans launch offensive (Operation Nordwind) against US Seventh Army

9 January 1945 US Sixth Army invades Luzon

12 January 1945 Major Soviet winter offensive opens
First convoy starts on Ledo Road

16 January 1945 Allied counteroffensive reduces German bulge in Ardennes

17 January 1945 Red Army takes Warsaw

20 January 1945 Hungary signs armistice with Allies

30 January 1945 Anglo-American talks prior to Yalta Conference begin at Malta

3 February 1945 US forces reach Manila

4 February 1945 Yalta Conference begins (to 12 February)

9 February 1945 French First Army concludes Alsatian operations with victory at Colmar pocket

13 February 1945 RAF bombers raid Dresden (followed by US Eighth Air Force bombers next day)
Budapest falls to Red Army

19 February 1945 US marines invade Iwo Jima

25 February 1945 B–29 raid on Tokyo demonstrates effectiveness of incendiary bombs

3 March 1945 Japanese resistance in Manila ends

5 March 1945 US First Army units enter Cologne (secured 7 March)

7 March 1945 Troops of US 9th Armoured Division cross Rhine on bridge at Remagen

9 March 1945 US B–29s begin incendiary campaign against Japanese cities

11 March 1945 US Eighth Army units land on Mindanao

25

Operations

22 March 1945 In surprise action, troops of US Third Army cross Rhine at Oppenheim

23 March 1945 British Second Army begins crossing Rhine near Rees

26 March 1945 Fighting ends on Iwo Jima

27 March 1945 Last V–2 rocket lands in England

30 March 1945 Soviets capture Danzig
Meiktila (Burma) secured by British forces

1 April 1945 US forces land on Okinawa

5 April 1945 Koiso resigns as Japanese Prime Minister; Suzuki succeeds

7 April 1945 Japanese superbattleship *Yamato* sunk

9 April 1945 Allies begin attack on Gothic Line

12 April 1945 Roosevelt dies; Harry S. Truman succeeds as US President

13 April 1945 Vienna falls to Soviet Army

16 April 1945 Soviet Army begins final Berlin offensive

18 April 1945 US forces complete Ruhr operations, taking more than 300,000 prisoners, US Third Army troops enter Czechoslovakia

21 April 1945 Allies take Bologna

23 April 1945 Himmler makes surrender offer to Western Allies

25 April 1945 United Nations conference opens in San Francisco
US and Soviet forces meet near Torgau, splitting Germany in two

28 April 1945 Mussolini and his mistress Clara Petacci are executed by partisans

30 April 1945 Hitler marries Eva Braun, commits suicide

2 May 1945 Soviet Army completes capture of Berlin German forces surrender in Italy

3 May 1945 Rangoon falls to the British

5 May 1945 German forces in Netherlands, north-western Germany and Denmark surrender, German Army Group G surrenders in Bavaria

7 May 1945 All German forces surrender unconditionally (2:41 am at Reims)

8 May 1945 V-E Day

13 May 1945 Last German resistance ceases in Czechoslovakia, thus ending fighting in Europe

20 May 1945 Japanese begin pulling back from Chinese bases

22 June 1945 US Tenth Army completes capture of Okinawa

30 June 1945 Luzon campaign concludes

16 July 1945 Stalin, Roosevelt, Churchill begin Potsdam Conference (to 2 August). Atomic bomb successfully tested at Los Alamos

25 July 1945 Organized resistance ends on Mindanao, Philippines

26 July 1945 Potsdam declaration issued. Churchill resigns following Conservative Party defeat; Attlee succeeds as British Prime Minister

6 August 1945 Atomic Bomb dropped on Hiroshima

8 August 1945 USSR declares war on Japan

9 August 1945 Atomic bomb dropped on Nagasaki. Soviets invade Manchuria

14 August 1945 Japan surrenders

2 September 1945 Japan signs Instrument of Surrender

Codenames

ACCOLADE
Unfulfilled plan, 1943, for capture of Rhodes and other Aegean islands

ACROBAT
Planned British operation to advance from Cyrenaica to Tripoli, 1941

ADLERTAG
Mass German assault during Battle of Britain, 15 September 1940

A GO
Japanese plan for a counterattack against US recapture of the Marianas, 1944

ALARICH
First codename for possible German military takeover in Italy

ALPEN VEILCHEN (Alpine Violet)
Axis invasion of Albania, 11 January 1940

ANKLET
Lofoten Islands raid 26 December 1941

APOSTLE 1
Allied return to Norway 10 May 1945

ANAKIM
First Allied plan for reconquest of Burma

ANTON
German occupation of Vichy France, 11 November 1942, known first as Attila

28

AUFBAU OST
Build up East – German preparations, prior to Barbarossa

AVALANCHE
Allied landings at Salerno 9 September 1943

AVONMOUTH
Allied expedition to Narvik, May 1940

AXIS (ACHSE)
German military takeover of Italy, 8 September 1943. Disarming the defecting Italians extended to garrisons in the Balkans, Greece and the Aegean

BAGRATION
Soviet offensive, July 1944

BARBAROSSA
German invasion of the Soviet Union, 22 June 1941

BATTLEAXE
British offensive June 1941 which failed to recapture Tobruk

BAYTOWN
British landings at Reggio, 3 September 1943

BERNHARD
Secret German plan to drop counterfeit money over Britain and undermine UK economy

BIGOT
Security classification for Normandy landing planning papers

BIRDCAGE
Airborne leaflet drop on POW camps announcing Japanese surrender

BLAUE (Fall Blaue, Case Blue)
German contingency plan for military operations in the event of war with Great Britain

Operations

BLACKCOCK
XII (British) Corps attack at Roermond, 16–26 January 1945

BODENPLATTE
Luftwaffe offensive operation against Allied airfields in north-western Europe, December 1944

BOLERO
Code name for build-up of US troops and material in UK prior to European invasion

BRASSARD
Allied amphibious landings on Elba, 17 June 1944

CARTWHEEL
Allied operations in 1943 for the seizure of New Guinea, New Britain Solomon Islands area

CATHERINE
British plan for forcing a passage into the Baltic to aid Poland, before the country fell

CERBERUS
Code name for the Channel dash by the German warships *Scharnhorst, Gneisenau* and *Prinz Eugen*

COBRA
Code name for Allied breakout from Normandy bridgehead, 25 July 1944

COCKADE
Part of Allied deception plan to convince Germans that the invasion of Europe would be anywhere but Normandy in the summer of 1944. Brittany, Northern Norway, and the Pas de Calais were all phantom objectives

CORKSCREW
Allied operations against the Mediterranean island of Pantelleria, June 1943

CROSSBOW
Code name for Allied operations against V1 and V2 sites and development centres

CULVERIN
Unfulfilled Allied plan for recapture of north Sumatra

DIADEM
Allied spring offensive in Italy, commenced 11 May 1944

DRAGOON
Allied invasion of southern France, subsequent to Anvil, July 1944

DYNAMO
Evacuation of Anglo-French forces from Dunkirk, 26 May–4 June 1940

EDELWEISS
German Army Group A's operations against Baku area of the Caucasus, summer 1942

EINHORN
Anti-partisan drive, Greece, July 1944

EISENHAMMER
Planned Luftwaffe attack on Soviet power stations, February 1945

EXPORTER
British and Free French occupation of Syria, 8 June–12 July 1941

FELIX
German plan to capture Gibraltar, Spanish Canary Islands, Portuguese Cape Verde Islands

FIREBRAND
Allied occupation of Corsica, September–October 1943. Effected largely by Free French forces

FLASH
Codename for attempt on Hitler's life, March 1943

FLINTLOCK
US invasion of Marshall Islands, 31 January–7 February 1944

FORAGER
US invasion of the Mariana Islands, 11 June 1944

FRITZ
Initial plan for German invasion of Soviet Union, December 1940

GALVANIC
US occupation of Gilbert Islands, Tarawa, Makin, 20 November 1943

GELB (Fall Gelb, Case Yellow)
German attack on the Low Countries and France, May 1940

GEMBOCK
Anti-partisan drive, Greece, July 1944

GOMORRAH
RAF bomber command raid on Hamburg, July–August 1943

GOODWOOD
British offensive south east of Caen, 18 July 1944

GRANIT
US offensive operations in the Central Pacific, beginning March 1944

GRÜN (Fall Grün, Case Green)
German plans for war with Czechoslovakia

GYMNAST
Original code name for Allied occupation of North-West Africa, succeeded by Torch

HARDIHOOD
Projected Allied military aid to Turkey

HARRIER
Proposed Allied attack on Trondheim, central Norway, April 1940

HERKULES
Planned Axis descent on Malta, 1942, involving airborne and sea landings. The operation was never mounted

HORRIDO
Anti-Partisan drive, Yugoslavia, spring 1944

HUSKY
Allied invasion of Sicily, 10 July 1943

I GO
Japanese code name for naval counter offensive, April 1943

ILT1S
Anti-partisan drive, Greece, March 1944

INFATUATE
Allied operations to capture Walcheren Island, 1 November 1944

ISABELLA/ILONA
Unfulfilled German plans to militarily occupy Atlantic coasts of Spain and Portugal, 1941

IRONCLAD
British occupation of Diego Suarez, Madagascar, 8 May 1942

JAEL/BODYGUARD
Allied deception plans to mislead the Germans as to the reality of the Normandy invasion. Later referred to as Bodyguard when it was thought to have had its security compromised

JUBILEE
Anglo-Canadian raid on Dieppe, 19 August 1942

JUPITER
Projected Allied invasion of northern Norway

KA GO
Japanese reinforcement of Guadalcanal, August 1942, resulting in the battle of the Eastern Solomons

Operations

KONSTANTIN
German operation to seize control of Italian controlled Balkans, September 1943

KORALLE
Anti-partisan drive, Greece, July 1944

KREUZOLLER
Anti-partisan drive, Greece, August 1944

KUGELBLITZ
Anti-partisan drive, Yugoslavia, late 1943

KUTUZOV
Soviet counter offensive in the Kursk Salient, July 1943

LILA
German operation to seize French Fleet at Toulon. The Fleet was scuttled, 27 November 1942

LITTLE SATURN
Soviet south-west offensive against the German relief forces trying to break through to the encircled 6th Army at Stalingrad, December 1942

LUMBERJACK
US First Army's advance to the Rhine at Cologne and further south by US Third Army, February 1945

LUSTRE
British transfer of forces from Western Desert to Greece March 1941

MAGIC
Operation Magic was the name assigned to the overall US intelligence programme devoted to breaking Japanese codes

MAGNET
Arrival of US forces in Northern Ireland, February 1942

MAILFIST
Planned Allied recapture of Singapore

MANHATTAN DISTRICT
Cover name for atomic bomb project

MANNA
British intervention in Greece, October 1944. Air drop of food over Holland, April 1945

MARITA
German attack on Greece, 6 April 1941

MARKET GARDEN
Two phases of the Allied attempt to seize bridges across the Dutch rivers and outflank the Siegfried Line, September 1944. Garden was the ground phase, Market was the airborne operation in which Allied paratroops were to seize key river crossings in advance of British Second Army's tanks. US airborne forces captured the bridges across the Mass and Waal, but the British paratroops at Arnhem were overwhelmed by German counterattack before the link up could be made.

MASTERDOM
Allied occupation of French Indo-China

MASTIFF
Medical aid to liberated Japanese POW camps

MENACE
British operation against Dakar, September 1940

MERKUR (Mercury)
German airborne attack on the island of Crete, 20 April 1941

MILLENNIUM
RAF Bomber Command's thousand aircraft raid on Cologne, 30–31 May 1942

NEPTUN
German anti-partisan drive, Greece 1944

NOAH'S ARK
Allied plan to harry German withdrawal from Greece and Balkans

Operations

NOBALL
Allied air force operations against German V-weapons sites 1944

NORDLICHT (Northern Lights)
German operation against Leningrad, summer 1942

OLIVE
Allied attack on the Gothic Line, Italy, August 1944

OLYMPIC
Code name for Allied invasion of Kyushu, one of the Japanese home islands, the opening phase of Operation Downfall, the assault on Japan itself. Olympic was scheduled for November 1945 but was pre-empted by Japan's surrender after the dropping of the two atom bombs

OVERCAST
US plan established in July 1945, to spirit German weapon scientists away from Europe to work in US laboratories

OVERLORD
Code name for the Normandy invasion, June 1944

PANTHER
Anti-partisan drive Yugoslavia, spring 1944

PEDESTAL
Relief convoy to Malta, August 1942, of 14 merchant ships escorted by a large naval force. Five got through with vital supplies

PILGRIM
Cover name for projected Allied operations to seize Atlantic Islands

PLUNDER
21st Army Group's crossing of the Rhine, 23 March 1945

POINT BLANK
Code name for RAF/USAAF's combined bomber offensive against Germany

PUMA
Proposed British operation to seize Canary Islands, 1941

PUNISHMENT
German air attacks on Yugoslav capital of Belgrade, 6–8 April 1941

RANKIN
Allied plans for return to European continent. Rankin A was plan to return in advance of scheduled Normandy invasion, B plan to land in case of German withdrawal from France or Norway, C in case of German unconditional surrender

RECKLESS
US operation against Hollandia, New Guinea, April 1944

REGENBOGEN (Rainbow)
Scuttling of German U-boats at war's end. 231 scuttled, May 1945

RHUBARB
RAF Fighter Command sweeps over English Channel and occupied French coastline, late 1940 onwards

RICHARD
German plan for intervention in Spain in the event of a Republican victory in the Civil War

RING
Soviet operation to destroy encircled German 6th Army at Stalingrad January 1943

ROESSELSPRUNG
Attack on Tito's HQ, Hvar, Yugoslavia, 25 May 1944

ROT (Fall Rot, Case Red)
German plans for military operations in the case of takeover of Czechoslovakia being resisted

RUMYANTSEV
Soviet counteroffenvise following Operation Citadel, August 1943, mounted at southern end of the Kursk Salient

Operations

SALMON TRAP
German plan to cut Murmansk railway, 1942, unfulfilled

SCHNEESTURM (Snowstorm)
Anti-partisan drive Yugoslavia, late 1943

SCORCHER
British occupation of Crete after withdrawal from Greece, May–June 1941

SEELÖWE (Sealion)
German plan for invasion of England, to follow the successful outcome of the air assault on fighter command bases, summer 1940

SEXTANT
Cairo conference held just before and after the British–Soviet–US conference at Teheran. At Cairo were US, British and Chinese heads of state, November/December 1943

SHINGLE
Allied amphibious landings at Anzio, Italy, 22 January 1944

SHO GO
(Operation Victory) Japanese defence plan, summer 1944. Sho Go embraced several plans, which could be put into effect once the access of Allied advance was made apparent. Plan 1 provided for the defence of the Philippines, Plan 2 the defence of Formosa and the Ryukyus, Plan 3 the defence of Japan itself, Plan 4 defence of the Kuriles and Hokkaido. When it was clear the Philippines were the US objective, Plan 1 was put into effect. The Battle of Leyte Gulf ensued

SHRAPNEL
Unfulfilled British plan, 1940, to seize Cape Verde Islands in the event of Spain entering the war on Germany's side and investing Gibraltar

SICKLE
Cover name for build-up for US Eighth Air Force in Britain

SLAPSTICK
British 1st Airborne Division's landing at Taranto, 9 September 1943

SLEDGEHAMMER
Early US plan, for an Allied landing on French coast in late 1942 in the event of an imminent Russian crisis on the Eastern front

SPRING
Canadian breakout in Normandy July 1944, coinciding with Operations Goodwood and Cobra

STARFISH
British deception plan early in the war to simulate the effects of marker flares dropped by bombers, and lure German bombers away from real targets

STARVATION
US naval operation to mine waters round Japanese home islands commenced March 1945

STEINADLER
Anti-partisan drive in Greece, July 1944

STEINBOCK (Ibex)
Luftwaffe bombing attacks on Britain, spring 1944

STRANGLE
Allied air operations commencing March 1944 attacking communication targets in central Italy

SUNRISE
Negotiations with the German command in Italy in secret for surrender of German forces, May 1945

SUPERCHARGE
Attack in northern sector at second Alamein, 2–4 November 1942

SYMBOL
Anglo-US Casablanca Conference, 14–23 January 1943

TERMINAL
Allied conference at Potsdam, 16 July–2 August 1945

THUNDERCLAP
Allied air attack on Dresden, February 1945

TIDAL WAVE
USAAF bombing of Ploesti, Rumania, 1 August 1943

TIGER
British fast convoy loaded with war material which passed the Mediterranean May 1941, bringing supplies to the Eighth Army in Egypt

TORCH
Allied invasion of North-west Africa, 8 November 1942

TOTALIZE
Canadian First Army's attack towards Falaise, 8 August 1944

TRIDENT
Anglo-US summit conference, Washington, 12–25 May 1943

TAIFUN (Typhoon)
German army group centres drive towards Moscow, September 1941

U GO
Japanese drive on India, from Burma, March 1944

ULTRA
Security classification afforded by British to intelligence gleaned from breaking the German Enigma code

URANUS
Offensive at Stalingrad, launched 19 November 1942, which encircled the German 6th Army

VALKYRIE
Security operations in the event of a revolt by slave labour in Germany. Used as a cover by 20 July Bomb Plot conspirators for abortive takeover plan

VARSITY
Allied airborne crossing of the Rhine, 24 March 1945

VELVET
Unrealized plan made late 1942, to base 20 Anglo–US squadrons in Soviet Caucasus

VERITABLE
Canadian First Army's operations, 8 February 1945

VULCAN
Final Allied offensive in Tunisia, 6 May 1943

WACHT AM RHEIN (Watch on the Rhine)
German attack in the Ardennes region, December 1944

WEISS (Fall Weiss, Case White)
German attack on Poland, 1 September 1939)

WEISS 1 and 2
German anti-partisan drive in Bosnia, February 1943

WESERUBUNG
German invasion of Denmark and Norway begun 9 April 1940

WINTERGEWITTER (Winter Storm)
General Von Manstein's unsuccessful operation to relieve encircled Stalingrad, December 1942

WOLF
Anti-partisan drive, Yugoslavia, spring 1944

ZITADELLE (Citadel)
German code name for the attack on the Kursk Salient, Soviet Union July 1943

ZEPPELIN
Abortive German plot to assassinate Stalin, July 1944

Who Fought Who in World War II

Forty years since the end of the 1939–45 war it is only too easy to remember the conflict as a set piece battle of good and bad, of 'Allies' and Axis, of comic book 'Krauts', 'Nips' and 'Eyties' – versus the rest. Of course the reality was far more complex. It was not just embattled democracies versus the dictatorships, and for many countries it was not the 1939–45 war at all but that of 1941–45. More than a handful of countries fought on both sides or split under occupation into rival resistance groups which fought each other. Countries which changed sides or fought on both sides (excluding those which in addition raised military contingents to fight with the Wehrmacht or Waffen-SS) included France, Finland, Bulgaria, Rumania and Italy.

Austria

Independent republic from 1919. Taken over as part of Greater German Reich in 1938 and armed forces absorbed. Vienna captured by Soviet forces April 1945. Postwar, divided into occupation zones.

Belgium

Neutral 1939. Surrendered to German invaders 24 May 1940. Liberated September 1944.

Brazil

Declares war on Germany, Italy and Japan 22 August 1942.

Bulgaria

Joins Axis March 1941. Invades Yugoslavia and Greece March 1941. Declares war on Soviet Union, Great Britain and USA, 12 December 1941. Declares war on Germany 8 September 1944.

Canada

Declares war on Germany 10 September 1939.

Chile

Breaks off relations with Axis 19 January 1943.

China

At war with Japan from July 1937.

Colombia

Breaks off diplomatic relations with Germany and Japan 31 December 1941.

Costa Rica

Declares war on Japan 10 December, Germany 13 December 1941.

Cuba

Declares war on Japan, Germany and Italy 13 December 1941.

Czechoslovakia

Absorbed by Germany 1938–39. 'Reichsprotectorate' created in Bohemia–Moravia. Nominally independent Slovak

43

state fought on German side, rebels 1 May 1945. Soviet forces take Prague 8 May 1945.

Denmark

Neutral in 1939. Overrun by Germans in two days, April 1940. US protectorate over Greenland from April 1941. Nominally independent under German control until 1943. Liberated May 1945.

Finland

Winter War with Soviet Union 1939–March 1940. Declares war on Soviet Union (the 'Continuation War') 26 June 1941. Peace treaty with Soviets 20 September 1944. Finnish Army attacks Germans 1 October 1944.

France

Declares war on Germany 3 September 1939. Overrun May–June 1940, armistice 25 June. Rump 'Vichy' state established with nominal independence while Germans occupy two-thirds of country including Paris and Atlantic coastline. French overseas possessions in North and Central Africa, Caribbean, mid and far East remain loyal to Vichy although Free French banner is raised first in Chad. Vichy forces in Madagascar, Syria and Algeria resisted Allied takeovers.

After 'Torch' landings in North Africa, Vichy ceased to have any real power, and was dissolved finally in June 1944 after Normandy landings. Corsica was retaken from Italians by Free French September-October 1943.

Germany

Adolf Hitler Chancellor, 30 January 1933. Rome-Berlin Axis signed 25 October 1936. Anti-Comintern Pact with Japan, 25 November 1936 (Italy signs 6 November 1937). 'Pact of Steel', military alliance with Italy 22 May 1939.

Non-aggression pact with Soviet Union, 23 August 1939. Invasion of Poland September 1939, Scandinavia, April 1940, Low Countries and France, May–June 1940, Soviet Union, 22 June 1941. Declares war on USA 11 December 1941.

Great Britain

Declares war on Germany 3 September 1939. Coalition government led by Churchill 10 May 1940–25 July 1945. At war longer than any other combatant except China.

Greece

At war with Italy from 28 October 1940. Germans invade 4 April 1941. Greeks surrender 1 May 1941. Germans withdraw September–October 1944, civil war follows.

Hungary

Intervention against Yugoslavia 11 April 1941. Hungarian force join war against Soviet Union 27 June 1941. Declares war on USA 12 December 1941.

Italy

Rome–Berlin Axis 25 October 1936. Military alliance with Germany ('Pact of Steel') 22 May 1939. Neutral on the outbreak of war, declares war on France and Britain 19 June 1940. Armistice with Allies 25 July 1943, declaration of war on Germany 1 October 1943. Puppet Fascist regime (RSI) continues in north until end of war.

Japan

At war with China since July 1937. Tripartite pact with Italy and Germany 27 September 1940. Non-aggression pact with Soviet Union, April 1941. Attacks US, British, Dutch, positions in Pacific 7 December 1941. Soviet Union declares war 10 August 1945. Surrenders 15 August 1945.

Mexico

Declares war on Germany and Japan 30 May 1942. A Mexican Air Force squadron fought in the Pacific from February 1945.

The Netherlands

Neutral in 1939. Overrun by Germans, May 1940. *Reichs-kommissar* installed 19 May 1940. Capitulation of German-held 'Fortress Holland' 5 May 1945.

Norway

Neutral in 1939. Invaded by Germans 9 April 1940. Liberated at end of war in Europe.

Portugal

Neutral throughout war. Allied landing rights in Azores granted October 1943 for anti-submarine warfare patrol aircraft. Portuguese Timor in Pacific overrun by Japanese but the Portuguese governor nominally remained in charge.

Soviet Union

Non-aggression pact with Germany, August 1939. Invades Poland September 1939. Invaded by Germans and Axis forces 22 June 1941. Declares war on Japan 10 August 1945.

Spain

Neutral throughout war. Hitler met Franco post fall of France but Spain could not be persuaded to join war. Various German plans were prepared to invade Spain and close the Mediterranean but never undertaken. 'Blue Division' of Spanish volunteers fought with Wehrmacht on Eastern Front.

Thailand

Occupied by Japan, December 1941. Puppet pro-Axis regime installed.

Turkey

Declares war on Germany and Japan 1 March 1945.

Decisive Campaigns

The Battle of Poland 1 September – 5 October 1939

The Polish Army of 1939 consisted of 30 active infantry divisions, 12 cavalry divisions, two of which were motorized, and 10 reserve divisions. One tank and two motorized brigades totalled 225 modern and 88 obsolete tanks plus some armoured cars. The air force deployed 150 fighters, 120 recce bombers, 36 medium bombers and 84 army co-operation aircraft. Principal Polish fighter was the gull-winged PZL 11C, dating from the early 1930s, and completely outclassed by the Luftwaffe's Bf109. The small navy had four destroyers, five submarines plus some auxiliaries. Poland's total armed strength was 370,000 men with 2,800,000 reserves. Poland's troops were brave and their commanders pugnacious but their lumbering mass would be sliced open by the new kind of war an Italian journalist dubbed Blitzkrieg – 'lightning war'.

The German attack began at dawn. One and a quarter million men in 60 divisions, nine of them armoured, under the overall command of General Walther von Brauchitsch.

The Polish Army under the command of Marshal Rydz-Smigly concentrated in forward cordon defence, a third of them in the 'corridor' to the Baltic exposed to a double envelopment from the west and from General Kuchler's II Army in East Prussia. To the south, General von Rundstedt's group of three armies was poised to sweep across Galicia, past Cracow and envelop Warsaw from the south.

The Luftwaffe destroyed the Polish air force in the first few days and was able at will to practise its technique of precision co-operation with deep ranging ground forces. One by one the Polish armies were rolled up and surrounded. On 8 September Reichenau's X Army in the centre attempted to take Warsaw but was beaten off; meanwhile another pocket held out at Kutno-Lodz until the 17th.

On that day the Soviet Union invaded from the east, ending any chance of a last ditch stand in the south-east of the country in the hope of a relief offensive by Britain and France. From the 17th to 5 October, the pockets of Polish resistance fell one by one – Warsaw on the 27th, the naval base of Hela on the Baltic on the 1st and the last organized resistance ended at Kock, fifty miles east of Warsaw, on the 5th. Polish losses were about 66,000 dead and at least 200,000 wounded. Nearly seven hundred thousand of the army were captured. German losses were 10,574 killed, 30,322 wounded and 3,400 missing.

The destruction of the Polish state was the overture – the long agony of the Polish people was just beginning.

Norway and Denmark

Norway and Denmark in 1940 were both neutral countries with tiny armed forces. An important proportion of Swedish iron ore reached Germany via Narvik, the port in the north of Norway, threatened by British naval blockade. After the *Altmark* incident of 16 February in which the Royal Navy seized the *Graf Spee*'s auxiliary in Norwegian waters, and increased British minelaying operations off the coast, Hitler resolved to strike north. On 9 April Operation *Weserübung* began with the conquest of Denmark (*Weserübung Süd*). German forces crossed directly into Jutland sweeping aside opposition and a small sea borne landing force captured Copenhagen.

Simultaneously in Norway German forces under the command of General von Falkenhorst began to land from the sea at Kristiansand, Trondheim, Bergen, Narvik and Oslo and by air at Oslo and Stavanger. The airborne attack at Oslo seized the city, but Norwegian shore batteries held the seaborne attack off for a day and sank the cruiser *Blücher*.

From 10–19 April, with all six of the initial objectives

49

including the capital captured, Luftwaffe transports continued to fly in supporting troops. The Norwegian Army was still fighting and 30,000 Anglo-French troops (already assembled for a possible expedition to Finland) landed at Namsos and Andalasnes; another small force was landed at Narvik in the far north. The Allied toeholds in central Norway however were pounded by air attack and an attempt to recapture Trondheim was beaten back. Andalasnes was evacuated on 1 May and Namsos a day later.

Meanwhile the German attackers at Narvik were now the defenders and for more than a month, despite naval support, the Allies were unable to completely dislodge the Germans. Then on 8–9 June, because of the collapse in France, the Allies evacuated Narvik. The British aircraft carrier *Glorious* was sunk while the German battle cruisers *Scharnhorst* and *Gneisenau* were damaged by torpedo attack.

The Battle of Flanders, the Battle of France

With the Polish campaign scarcely over, Hitler ordered his generals to prepare for an offensive against the apparently passive western Allies that same autumn. OKH's *Fall Gelb* (Plan Yellow), the Army High Command's original operational directive for a campaign in the west aimed at little more than seizing the Low Countries, 1914-style. From within Army Group A, its commander General von Rundstedt and his Chief of Staff, General von Manstein, pushed forward a plan with the objectives not just of seizing ground but destroying the Allied armies themselves with a massive armoured push at the centre of the Allied line which would break through to the Channel coast far to the west and roll up either of the divided portions. After initial resistance and under Hitler's pressure, Generals Halder and Brauchitsch at OKH agreed to reinforce the centre – Army Group A, inflated now to 45½ divisions with seven of them armoured, shaving Army Group B in the north to 29½ divisions. After many delays, caused by weather, by the capture of documents describing aspects of the plan when two Luftwaffe officers crashed in Belgium, and then by the invasion of Denmark and Norway, the German Army was poised to strike westwards.

The German forces, some 2½ million men in 104 infantry divisions, nine motorized divisions and ten armoured divisions were organized in three Army Groups, General von Bock's Army Group B in the north, von Rundstedt's Group A in the centre with most of the armour in von Kleist's Panzer Group and General von Leeb's Army Group C facing the Maginot Line. In support were two Luftwaffe air fleets with some 3500 front line aircraft.

The Allies were organized in three Army Groups, General Billotte's First Army Group in the north consisting of five armies including the BEF, General Giraud's Seventh Army, General Blanchard's First Army, General Corap's Ninth Army and General Huntziger's Second. General Pretelat's Second Army Group consisted of three armies drawn up from Verdun to Strasbourg while General Besson had but one army between Colmar and the Swiss frontier. C-in-C of the three army groups on the North-east Front was General Georges and above him the Allied C-in-C, General Gamelin.

Allied manpower numbered over two million, organized in 63 French infantry divisions, 13 French fortress divisions, 7 motorized divisions, 3 light mechanized divisions and a number of separate tank battalions organic to other units plus the 9 divisions of the BEF and one Polish division. There were more than 3600 Allied tanks, a good proportion of them as combatworthy as the opposition. The Armée de l'Air, the French Air Force, disposed of some 1400 combat aircraft and the RAF had some 500 aircraft in France – 130 fighters, 220 bombers and 50 army co-operation aircraft. The Belgian Army nominally numbered 600,000 men in 22 divisions and the Dutch Army theoretically 400,000 but in reality considerably less.

The German assault on the Low Countries began on 10 May. Dutch and Belgian airfields were pounded by air attack and paratroops seized vital river crossings into the heart of Holland laying an airborne carpet for Army Group B's panzer spearheads. The Belgian fort of Eban Emael, holding the northern end of the defence line, was captured by glider troops and the Belgians fell back from the Albert Canal to the River Dyle. The Allied C-in-C, Gamelin, expecting a repeat of 1914 and a German drive through northern Belgium which would swing south and west of Paris, ordered the mobile forces of French First Army and the BEF to advance into Belgium and hold a line on the River Dyle while Giraud's Seventh Army should race to the succour of the Dutch with most of France's mobile reserves and lavish fighter cover. After skirmishes with the IX Panzer Division near Breda, Seventh Army regrouped on the Belgian Army's north flank.

Under threat of aerial bombardment, and with its proof in the destruction of Rotterdam on 14 May, the Dutch surrendered.

With 35 of France's best mobile divisions including the bulk of the British Expeditionary Force now in Belgium, General George's North-east Front had a powerful left flank in the north and the Maginot Line to the right – but in the centre, facing the 'impenetrable' Ardennes forest, were only some four light cavalry divisions, and ten second rate infantry divisions of the Ninth and Second Armies and the overall strategic reserve was down to ten divisions. The reaper's cut was about to swing.

It was here on the French centre that the German blow fell, delivered by General von Kleist's two Panzer corps. On 10 May seven panzer divisions pushed through the Ardennes – German pioneers crossed the Meuse in rubber boats, the Stukas pinned down French artillery and by the 13th General Hoth's XV Panzer Corps made up of the V and VII Panzer divisions were across the river defence line at Dinant, General Reinhardt's XXXXI Corps with the VI and VIII Panzer at Montherme and Guderian's XIX Panzer corps containing the I, II and X Panzer Divisions at Sédan.

By nightfall on 15 May Corap's Ninth Army was routed along a fifty-mile front. With the French defence line fatally pierced, too late Gamelin ordered what little reserves there were into a new Sixth Army in an attempt to plug the gap. Giraud replaced Corap in command of what was left of Ninth Army only to be captured on 17 May. As the German armour sped westwards towards the Channel the only riposte was made by Brig-General Charles de Gaulle's 4th Armoured Division which attacked the German south flank at Laon on 19 May. On 21 May British armour attacked the 'panzer corridor' from the north at Arras with some initial success but, as at Laon, neither attack was supported and both were beaten back. On 19 May Gamelin was dismissed and replaced by General Maxime Weygand.

The spearheads of Guderian's XIX Panzer Corps which had crossed the Meuse at Sedan on 14 May reached the channel coast at Abbeville a mere six days later. Boulogne fell on 27 May and Calais was invested – 60 Allied divisions in the north were trapped. The Belgian Army surrendered on 25 May making further resistance in Flanders futile. Hitler's orders on 24 May to halt the panzers south and west of the Allied pocket in the north allowed a defensive perimeter to be established around Dunkirk and a seaborne rescue (Operation Dynamo) to be mounted. Some 850 vessels of all sorts snatched 338,226 men from the beaches over eight days, 139,067 of them French and Belgian, while the RAF, flying from bases across the Channel, beat back the Luftwaffe's attempt to finish them off from the air. Cherbourg fell on 31 May, besieged Calais on 27 May and Dunkirk on 4 June. The BEF suffered 68,111 killed, wounded or taken prisoner. It had left 2,472 guns, 90,000 rifles, 63,879 vehicles, 20,548 motorcycles and over 500,000 tons of stores behind.

The triumphant German armies regrouped to complete the conquest of France; von Bock's Army Group B on the left flank, Leeb's Army Group C to the right and Rundstedt's Army Group A once again in the centre. Weygand attempted to regroup on the Somme and the Aisne rivers with 40 shaken French divisions attempting to hold a 225-mile front above Paris. The German attack opened on 5 June and by the 9th Army Group B was on the Seine west of the French capital. On the 8th Weygand ordered French

Army Group 3 to withdraw to the Seine. On the 9th Rundstedt's forces in the centre attacked breaking through at Chalons and surging eastwards. The French were now in headlong retreat: Paris was declared an open city on the 13th and the Germans marched in next day.

German forces fanned out west, south and east wheeling round to pin the remnants of the French armies behind the Maginot Line. On 21 June, 32 Italian divisions attacked in the south to be checked by 6 French alpine divisions. On 7 June Reynaud resigned and Pétain took his place. On the 17th de Gaulle flew to Britain. Pétain and Weygand sought an armistice and, in Foch's railway coach, where the armistice of 1918 had been signed, Hitler himself dictated the terms. It was signed on 22 June and at half past midnight on 25 June it was all over.

The campaign in the west cost the Germans 27,074 dead, 111,034 wounded, 18,384 missing. French losses for the six-week campaign are estimated at 90,000 dead, 200,000 wounded, 1,900,000 prisoners and missing. Total British casualties came to 68,111, Belgian 23,350 and Dutch 9779. The French Air Force lost more than 560 aircraft in combat, the RAF 931, 477 of them fighters. The Luftwaffe lost 1284 aircraft.

Battle of Britain

The triumph in France brought German airpower to the Channel coast. The bulk of the British Army might have been snatched from the Dunkirk beaches but if the bedraggled infantry had kept their rifles, they had left behind their tanks and heavy equipment.

The RAF had lost almost a thousand aircraft in France, 477 of them fighters. The Germans, however, had no ready-made plan to invade immediately and when OKH came up with a plan in July for the invasion of England, (Operation Sealion), time was already running out. But with the Royal Navy still intact and the *Kriegsmarine* unable to challenge it directly, the invasion would require complete air cover – the RAF would be the first target.

Through July harassing raids were made on British coastal targets and channel shipping in an attempt to bring the RAF up to battle while landing craft and barges were assembled and an invasion force put together.

By August Göring had gathered 2800 aircraft, 900 fighters and 1300 bombers grouped in 3 Air Fleets, Kesselring's Luftflotte II based in northern France, Sperrle's Luftflotte III based in the Low Countries and Stumpff's Luftflotte IV based in Norway. Air Marshal Sir Hugh Dowding's Fighter Command could put up 650 fighters in 52 Squadrons, 60 per cent of them being Hawker Hurricanes.

From 8 to 18 August the Luftwaffe mounted large scale raids on the airfields of the RAF's front line Groups, Nos 11 and 12. On 15 August, grandly dubbed by Göring *Adlertag*, or Eagle Day, the Luftwaffe mounted more than 1790 sorties in five major attacks on targets extending in a 500-mile arc from Newcastle to Weymouth, losing 25 to 34 RAF aircraft in the process. In spite of continued attacks, the defenders enjoyed the advantage of radar plus a gleaning of enemy intentions from Ultra intelligence, and were thus able to concentrate to meet the attacks. Also significant was the fact that lightly damaged machines and especially pilots fell on friendly territory and could be put back into the battle.

On 24 August the Luftwaffe switched to attacks on inland RAF fighter sector stations. By the end of the month the defence was close to cracking – the wastage both of aircraft and pilots was simply outstripping replacements. If the attacks on Fighter Command went on, the RAF would go down fighting but they would go down just the same – numbers would decide the issue.

On 25–26 August RAF bombers had made a feeble night raid on Berlin, repeating the attack on the night of 6 September. In a rage Hitler ordered the attack switched from Fighter Command airfields and control centres to London itself, a huge target but at least a single one on which the RAF could concentrate its defence.

On 15 September the Germans mounted a massive raid

55

on London in daylight. Fifty-six attackers were lost to 26 defenders.

Daylight raids on the capital continued to the end of September but the toll on the bombers was heavy. Bomber Command struck back with a raid on barges and lighters massed for a seaborne invasion and on the 17th Hitler decided to postpone Sealion indefinitely. The last daylight raid was on 30 September from which time German bombers switched to the night 'Blitz' on British cities.

In the month from 13 August to 15 September the Luftwaffe lost 1216 aircraft to the RAF's 688. From 1 July to 31 October the Luftwaffe lost 2848 aircraft to the RAF's 1446 to all causes. For each RAF aircraft actually shot down in combat, the Luftwaffe lost one and a half.

The Night Blitz on Britain

With Sealion postponed, the Luftwaffe abandoned its attempt to destroy Fighter Command and switched to night attacks on British cities and production centres. London was the prime target and between 7 September and 13 November 1940 there were raids virtually every night.

The devastating attack on Coventry on 14 November marked a change of policy from pounding the political target of the capital to long-term strategic attacks on provincial industrial centres, and particularly ports, as an extension of the U-Boat blockade. The bomber aircraft of Luftflottes II and III were primarily He 111s, Do 217s and Ju 88s, each with comparatively light bombloads, using the direction finding device called *Knickebein* (crooked leg) and later a more sophisticated device called *X-Gerät* fitted in special pathfinding aircraft to find their critical targets in the dark. By early 1941 the RAF were putting up in defence hastily adapted night fighter aircraft with primitive airborne intercept (A-I) radar.

In the early spring of 1941 the Luftwaffe began a new campaign – between 19 February and 12 May it made 61 attacks, the majority against ports including London. In two raids on 16 and 19 April, well over 2000 people were

Organization of British Air Defences: Summer 1940

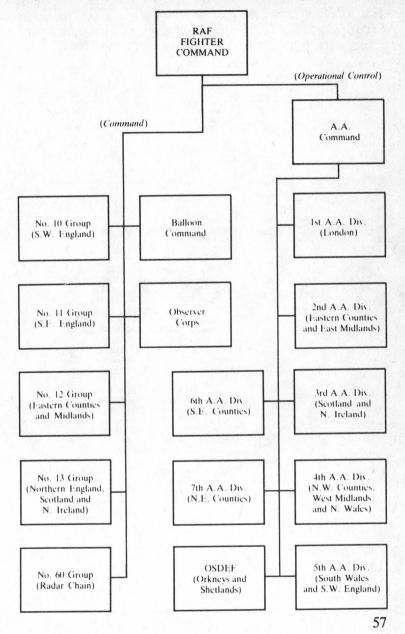

Night Blitz War Diary

The following is a *selection* of messages received in Home Security War Room from London Region No. 5 only during three hours of the attack on London of 11 May 1941

Time of origin	Form of message	In or out	Subject	Message No.
0036	Teleprinter	In	SOUTHWARK. H. E. Borough Road blocked. Mains damaged. WESTMINSTER 0004. H.E. Dolphin Square. No cas. LAMBETH 2325. H.E. Norwood Road blocked. BETHNAL GREEN 2350. H.E. Roman Road. Mains dam. ISLINGTON 2342. Heavy incendiary attack. H.E. at Stonefield Road. ST MARYLEBONE 2340. H.E. Wells Street. ST PANCRAS 2350. H.E. H.E. at HARROW and I.B.s at CAMBERWELL, TWICKENHAM, FELTHAM and HAMMERSMITH.	13
0040	,,	,,	POPLAR 2358. East India Dock No. 12. Half dock on fire.	14
0045	,,	,,	POPLAR 2359. South West India Dock Office wrecked by H.E.	15
0050	,,	,,	POPLAR 2359. Cootes Barge Road to right of S.W. India Dock entrance. 12 barges alight.	17
0055	,,	,,	STEPNEY 0020. Part of No. 9 warehouse boundary wall opposite No. 8 St Catharine Dock destroyed by H.E.	18
0055	,,	,,	WESTMINSTER. H.E. approx. 0027. Westminster Cathedral. Further details not yet available.	19
0102	,,	,,	HOLBORN report fire at British Museum, Gt Russell Street. No further details yet.	22
0116	,,	,,	CITY 0005. I.B.s on P.L.A. H.Q. Trinity Square. Fires extinguished. BETHNAL GREEN 2350. I.B.s. Fires. HAMMERSMITH 0018. 3 H.E. 20 casualties, including 18 trapped. WANDSWORTH 0015. 3 H.E. Wardens Post damaged. Casualties. LAMBETH 0005. H.E. 6 casualties. 0014. H.E. Westminster Bridge Road blocked. Bombing at CROYDEN, BERMONDSEY, BARNET.	28
0145	,,	,,	WEST HAM 2350. No. 25–27 Sheds, Royal Albert Dock fired by incendiaries. Fairly extensive damage to export goods.	38
0158	,,	,,	SOUTHWARK. H.E. River wall bank, side near power station; river wall damaged. Tide now rising. Possibility of flooding.	46
0200	,,	,,	WESTMINSTER 0024. I.B. Children's Hospital, Vincent Sq., Fire.	47
0230	,,	,,	WESTMINSTER 0155. 3 H.E. Chambers of Houses of Parliament.	59
0232	,,	,,	ST PANCRAS 0010. 3 H.E. Charlotte St area. 10 casualties. ISLINGTON 0037. 10 H.E. across borough. Property and mains dam. Many casualties. L.M.S. Railway Bridge at Corsica St dam. and in dangerous condition. No report of effect on Railway traffic yet.	61

0241	„	„	POPLAR 0055. P.L.A. report H.E. on mine-sweeper H.M.S. *Goatfell*. Believed direct hit.	64
0247	„	„	POPLAR 0115. P.L.A. report owing to damage to impounding station, S.W. India Dock, all power including high tension off.	67
0244	Telephone Fire Control	„	20-Pump fire at Railway Goods Yard, Silver-thorne Road, Clapham, WANDSWORTH. 60-Pump fire at Westminster Hall, WESTMINSTER	70
0300	Teleprinter	„	BERMONDSEY from 2358 onwards. Heavy attack by H.E. and I.B.s especially in Rotherhithe area. Much damage to dwelling houses and business premises. Casualties unknown. CHISLEHURST 0106. H.E. Val-liers Wood Road, casualties trapped. WESTMINSTER 0017. H.E. Bruton Street. Casualties. WANDSWORTH 0057–0123. 6 H.E. and many I.B.s. Damage to dwelling houses, flats and church. Casualties.	81
0325	„	„	H.M.S. *Tower* lying Cherry Garden Pier, BERMONDSEY, has received direct hit. Many casualties.	88
0326	„	„	ST PANCRAS. H.E. 0255. De Gaulle's Head-quarters, Gordon St, 10 casualties, some trapped. Headquarters partly demolished.	89
0334	„	„	ST MARYLEBONE 0040. 3 H.E. Fire and damage. ST PANCRAS 0035. 13 H.E. Widespread damage. At least 60 casualties. PADDINGTON 0055. 2 H.E. Casualties trapped. LAMBETH 0040 3 H.E. 18 casual-ties. Considerable damage.	93

Night Blitz on London: 7 October 1940–5 May 1941
Number of bombs dropped on London Boroughs

Borough	Number of H. Explosive bombs per 100 acres
Holborn	39.75
City	29.53
Westminster	28.85
Shoreditch	23.56
Southwark	23.35
Stepney	20.02
Finsbury	19.11
Chelsea	18.51
Bethnal Green	17.26
Bermondsey	17.16
Lambeth	17.14
Deptford	15.73

59

Tons of High Explosive aimed at United Kindom Cities in Major Night Attacks from Night of 7 September 1940, to Night of 16 May 1941

Target Area	No. of Major Raids	Tonnage
London (whole period)	71	18,800
London (after 14 November)	14	5,149
Liverpool–Birkenhead	8	1,957
Birmingham	8	1,852
Glasgow–Clydeside	5	1,329
Plymouth–Devonport	8	1,228
Bristol–Avonmouth	6	919
Coventry	2	818
Portsmouth	3	687
Southampton	4	647
Hull	3	593
Manchester	3	578
Belfast	2	440
Sheffield	1	355
Newcastle–Tyneside	1	152
Nottingham	1	137
Cardiff	1	115

killed and 140,000 dwellings destroyed. However, as these furious attacks were reaching a climax the Luftwaffe's bomber Gruppen were pulling out – heading eastwards under a cloak of secrecy to support another vast Blitzkrieg. By 21 May of the 44 bomber groups that had conducted the blitz on Britain, only four were left.

In nine months from 7 September 1940 to the end of May 1941 the Luftwaffe dropped some 46,000 tons of high explosive and 110,000 incendiaries, a total of 54,420 tons of bombs. British casualties amounted to over 40,000 civilian dead, 86,000 seriously injured and 150,000 slightly injured. Two million houses had been destroyed or damaged, 60 per cent of them in London. British industrial production and tonnage moving through the ports was not however seriously affected and internal communications were not disrupted.

War in the Desert
The First Campaigns

The fall of France not only isolated Britain, it brought Mussolini's Italy into the war scavenging for leftovers. The Mediterranean was vitally important to Britain, not only as the short sea route to India, Australia and the Far East, but as the gateway to the Middle East itself and the oil of the Persian Gulf. At sea the Italian Navy, six battleships and battle cruisers, seven heavy and fifteen light cruisers and 119 submarines confronted Admiral Cunningham's single aircraft carrier, three battleships and cruisers. The French of course were out of the picture. The RAF was weak, equipped with obsolete aircraft and numerically far inferior to the Italian opposition.

General Sir Archibald Wavell as C-in-C Middle East Land Forces had some 60,000 men to defend a colossal area, 36,000 in Egypt, 9000 in the Sudan, 5500 in Kenya, 1475 in British Somaliland, 27,500 in Palestine, 2500 in Aden and 800 in Cyprus.

Egypt was the vital position, because of the Suez canal and because it blocked the way to the Gulf. The Italians flanked Egypt from the west with the 200,000 strong Army of Libya and the 110,000-strong force in East Africa, Ethiopia, Eritrea and Italian Somaliland.

Operations began in earnest on 13 September when Marshal Graziani entered Egypt with five divisions from Libya. They halted after an advance of 60 miles, fortifying a series of camps, and waited for reinforcements – and water. The British Western Desert Force under the energetic command of Major General R. N. O.'Connor also

61

waited at Mersah Matruh. Recognizing how vital the defence of Egypt was, Churchill ordered 150 new tanks shipped to the Middle East even though Britain itself was faced with imminent invasion.

O'Connor made excellent use of these assets with just one armoured and one infantry division, two infantry brigades and a brigade of Matilda tanks to strike at Graziani's force without waiting to be attacked themselves.

The Italian camps were rolled up one by one, at Sidi Barrani, Nibeiwa, and Tummars while British tanks cut the coast road in their rear. By the end of the year the Italians were completely out of Egypt leaving 38,000 POWs and huge quantities of military stores in their wake while British forces were assaulting Bardia inside Libya.

Meanwhile at sea Cunningham's force had been reinforced and on 11 November a torpedo strike delivered by Swordfish aircraft from HMS *Illustrious* crippled the Italian fleet at Taranto. Wavell's 'neutralization' of the threat to Egypt from Libya had turned into a galloping offensive. On 3 January O'Connor took Bardia with another huge bag of prisoners and the windfall of over 700 trucks. With renewed mobility 13th Corps (as the Western Desert Force was renamed) rolled on to Tobruk which fell, like Bardia, in a single day. The British 7th Armoured Division now cut across the waist of Cyrenaica, reaching the coast at Beda Fomm and entrapping the retreating Italian X Army with the main British force still advancing along the coast road. After two days trying to break out, the X Army was effectively destroyed and its commander, General Bergonzoli, surrendered unconditionally.

In two months the Western Desert Force had advanced 500 miles, destroyed nine Italian divisions, taken 130,000 prisoners, 400 tanks and 1290 guns. British casualties amounted to 500 dead and 1373 wounded.

With the threat from the west removed (at least temporarily) Wavell was able to launch an offensive against the Duke of Aosta's 110,000 troops in Italian East Africa. As in Libya, a fast moving dashing British offensive launched from Kenya and Sudan ran rings round the inept Italian commanders, seizing huge tracts of territory, and many thousands of prisoners, for minimal losses. On 18 May 1941 Aosta surrendered.

It seemed that the threat to Egypt and the Gulf had been swept away. However, instead of allowing O'Connor's small but battle-hardened army to clear the rest of Italian Tripolitania (Tunisia to the west was under the control of Vichy France), 19th Corps was broken up and sent to Greece to face destruction by the Germans. From January, Luftwaffe aircraft began to arrive in Sicily, attacking Malta and harrying Benghazi. More significantly perhaps than the intervention of German medium bombers was the arrival on 12 February of Lt.-General Erwin Rommel in Tripoli with the advance detachments of what would become the 'Afrika Korps' with a brief from high command to conduct an 'aggressive defence'.

The impact of Rommel was anything but defensive. On 31 March he attacked, long before the British or OKH might have expected. With the best British troops now in Greece, Rommel drove back the covering force at El Agheila clearing Cyrenaica in a reverse of the original British offensive and O'Connor, architect of the earlier victory, was captured by a German patrol on the Barda-Derna road. Tobruk was besieged but, reinforced by sea, beat off an attack on 10 April.

Under pressure from Churchill to counterattack as soon as possible, Wavell launched a hastily prepared operation against the Sollum-Halfaya passes held by Rommel. Boldly named Operation 'Battleaxe', Wavell's offensive foundered after some initial success.

Within two months, the chance of clearing North Africa had been thrown away. British forces were summarily thrown out of Greece and Crete and now a vastly more competent and combatworthy Axis force was on the Egyptian frontier. After the failure of 'Battleaxe' Wavell was relieved by General Claude Auchinleck who also came under pressure from Churchill to launch an immediate offensive.

From July to October 1941 both sides drew up for battle.

Operations

The newly named British Eighth Army under the command of General Alan Cunningham was built up to seven divisions with over 700 new tanks brought in on the 'Tiger' convoy. The RAF Desert Air Force numbered more than a thousand aircraft, so critically did the British regard this theatre of operations, indeed the only theatre in which they confronted the enemy (however marginally) on land. Rommel regrouped his command (dubbed Panzer Group Africa on 15 August 1941) which now comprised the XV and XXI Panzer Divisions, the 90th and 164th Light Divisions and six Italian divisions, one of which was armoured. Tanks and aircraft strength was considerably less than the British, while the Royal Navy and RAF effectively harried Axis convoys at sea, choking Rommel's most vital commodity – fuel. Auchinleck launched his offensive, codenamed 'Crusader', on 18 November 1941. The plan was for the infantry of 13 Corps to attack the German line at Halfaya pass while the armour of 30 Corps with its new Stuart tanks would swing deep into the desert and relieve Tobruk, but swirling uncoordinated battles raged around Sidi Rezegh while a breakout from Tobruk was held.

With Crusader stalled, Rommel broke out towards the British rear and near panic resulted. Cunningham wanted to withdraw, believing his army would be destroyed, but Auchinleck insisted the offensive go on, appointing Major General Ritchie in Cunningham's place.

Rommel at last was held. After great effort Tobruk was relieved and the British slowly pushed Rommel back to his original start point at El Agheila. Axis losses were 24,500 killed and wounded and 36,500 prisoners. British losses were around 18,000.

By now Auchinleck was where Wavell had been a year earlier – but it proved no more possible for the British to push into Tripolitania than then. Meanwhile the strategic picture had been transformed with the German invasion of the Balkans, the airborne descent on Crete and the invasion of the Soviet Union. Although compared with the struggle in Russia it was a sideshow, German intervention in North Africa and a drive through Egypt could be part of a huge pincer movement around the whole Middle East, the other push clawing its way through the southern Soviet Union, to snap shut around the Gulf oilfields.

Meanwhile the Japanese had fallen on the British Empire in the Far East. Once again British divisions were diverted away from the western desert and once again Rommel was to fall on understrength defenders and this time push them all the way back to Egypt. On 21 January 1942 the Germans broke out from their defensive positions at El Agheila, pushing the Eighth Army back behind Benghazi to a line stretching from Gazala to Bir Hacheim, an old fort forty miles south in the desert, defended by a Free French light division. For four months each side stood still, building up their strength and fortifying their positions. The heavily mined British defence line ended in open desert. British armour, some 850 tanks including the first US supplied M3 Grants with a hull-mounted 75-mm gun, were deployed to cover the open flank but they were dispersed in brigades and positioned too far forward.

Rommel struck first, on 28 May 1942, sweeping round the south of the Gazala/Bir Hacheim line, meeting the British armour at a desert crossroads called Knightsbridge. A series of desperate battles raged in which the stopping power of the Grant's 75-mm was a vital asset for the defenders. Just as the panzers were running out of petrol, Rommel broke through back to his own lines through the rear of the British line, allowing supplies through to a defensive position actually within the British defences, dubbed by the troops that fought there the 'cauldron'. Ritchie's counterattacks bogged down and on 11 June Bir Hacheim fell. The Panzers now broke out of the cauldron sweeping north-east towards Tobruk once more and in a ferocious battle on 11–12 June the British lost a large part of their armoured reserve, leaving some 260 tanks smoking on the battlefield.

With the Eighth Army now in full retreat, Rommel was able to attack Tobruk from the south-east, taking it in a single day with 33,000 prisoners and vast supplies of stores.

On the day Tobruk capitulated, 21 June 1942, Rommel was promoted to Field Marshal.

The German high command now made a decision as critical as Churchill's intervention in Greece in 1940 had been. OKW was urging a halt, pending the capture of Malta by an air and sea invasion planned for August. Rommel meanwhile was urging that his advance should be continued and supported with the destruction of the Eighth Army as the potential prize.

Rommel won the argument and on 23 June Axis forces once again crossed the Egyptian frontier. By 25 June they were at the old defence line of Mersa Matruh. Then Auchinleck, having assumed personal command, fought a delaying action before falling back on the Alam Halfa ridge between El Alamein on the sea and the Quattarra Depression forty miles inland. There once again the lines congealed, the adversaries worn out and exhausted, but Rommel was only 60 miles from Alexandria and there was panic in Cairo.

Rommel's drive and the breakthrough at Gazala had been a brilliant piece of generalship. The British had lost 75,000 men including the 33,000-strong Tobruk garrison and all but 200 tanks. The Germans and Italians had lost 40,000 men but Rommel, in spite of being at the gates of Cairo, had stretched his supply lines to the limit, and was relying on captured stores and transport for survival. On 5 July the Germans had just 30 tanks in the front line ready for action.

Through July Rommel made several probes at the Alamein position, while Auchinleck counterattacked with some success from 14–27 July, but neither side was strong enough to do each other any real harm. On 13 August Auchinleck was removed as C-in-C Middle East by Churchill, replaced by General Alexander and by Lieutenant-General Montgomery appointed to direct command of Eighth Army.

By the end of August Rommel had managed to increase his armour strength to 203 German gun tanks and 243 Italian facing 480 British with more on the way. Meanwhile the attacks on the extended Axis supply lines were becoming critical while the British could only gain in strength as time passed. With fuel critically low, Rommel had to attack in one more attempt to destroy the British position in Egypt.

The second battle of El Alamein, known as the Battle of Alam Halfa, was to be the last chance. Rommel planned a repeat of the Gazala operation, an outflanking attack at the south, but Montgomery fortified the Alam Halfa ridge running at right angles to the rear of his main front. After three days of assaults in which the Germans had some initial success, the British tank brigade dug in on the ridge held their position.

Now the RAF showed their mastery in the air, breaking up the German set piece assaults; and on the ground the British were catching up with the qualitative superiority of the German armour although not yet with the formidable killing power of the 88-mm dual purpose anti-aircraft, anti-tank gun. The failure to break through at Alam Halfa marked not only the checking of Rommel 60 miles short of his prize but the end of his run of spectacular mobile offensive action.

Now it was Montgomery's turn. Reinforced by convoy with men and material, by October the British commander could muster 195,000 men, over 1000 gun tanks with 1000 more under repair, over 900 guns and nearly 1500 anti-tank guns. Half of Rommel's 100,000 men were Italian infantry, more than half the armour were worn out Italian vehicles, plus some 500 guns and 850 anti-tank guns. Much more critical than numerical inferiority was the fuel situation, down to three issues of petrol, or 180 miles of movement per vehicle, with only enough fuel to keep the supply traffic going between Tripoli and the front for three days.

The Battle of Alamein

Rommel, the master of mobile warfare, now dug in behind half a million mines and belts of wire with the four Axis armoured divisions grouped in two masses to plug the gap should the enemy penetrate the defence line. Against this Great War defence, Montgomery planned a set piece Great

War attack, a massive preliminary bombardment followed by a methodical infantry advance while the British tanks and anti-tank guns would be used to beat off German counterattacks and hold the flanks of any line of advance.

A tremendous British artillery bombardment on a six-mile front opened at 9.40 pm on the night of 23/24 October before the British infantry moved from their start lines twenty minutes later under a full moon to advance along the coastal road against the northern end of the Axis defence line.

The Italian infantry put up stiff resistance and a counterattack by the XV Panzer Division nearly stopped the British advance in its tracks. On 25 October Montgomery ordered the tanks of 10 Corps to force their own breakthrough, but still the Axis line held. On the 26th the second phase of the battle began as Montgomery remade his plan to get the bogged offensive moving again and, for a week, fierce fighting raged in and around the coast road as both sides raced to bring their armoured strength up from the south. Rommel meanwhile was running out of supplies and tank strength was being worn down fast without replacement. On 1 November Rommel extricated his infantry from imminent encirclement and pulled back three miles, while Montgomery launched another offensive move south of 'Kidney Ridge', 15 kilometres in from the sea. The 2nd New Zealand Division, under cover of a rolling artillery barrage, cleared a corridor through the minefields for British armour which beat off a German counterattack.

On 3 November Hitler intervened with a disastrous 'no retreat' order. It was rescinded two days later but the delay proved fatal. Rommel of his own volition extricated what was left of his forces, leaving behind the bulk of the Italian infantry. By 9 November the panzer army had a fighting strength of 500 Germans and 2500 Italians, a handful of guns and some 22 tanks. Some 10,000 Axis survivors were slouching westwards without equipment while more than 35,000 Axis soldiers had been left behind, dead on the battlefield or as POWs. The Eighth Army lost 13,000 killed, wounded and missing and 432 tanks, more than the Axis total at the start of the battle, as if to emphasize the British superiority in resources.

Montgomery pursued Rommel with caution and the RAF missed an opportunity to destroy the retreating Axis columns from the air. Rommel's retreat – from 5 November 1942 to 15 February 1943 all the way to the Mareth Line in Tunisia – was marked by stands at Mersah Matruh, El Agheila and at the Wadi Zem Zem but always Rommel managed to evade Montgomery's clumsy clutches. The great retreat stretched over 1500 kilometres without the forces disintegrating into a rabble but when Rommel heard on 8 November than an Anglo-American task force had landed in Algeria and were advancing on Tunisia he confided in his war diary: 'This spells the end of the army in Africa.' German power in Africa was down but not out – the battle for Tunisia was still to come.

The Battle of the Atlantic

The German Navy entered the Second World War with its major warship building programme five years off completion and only 48 ocean-going submarines (*Unterseeboot* = U Boat). For five years of war the submarine arm of the German Navy would wage a deadly, relentless war at sea, come close to squeezing Britain into submission, then cut the United States off from Europe. The crisis came in 1943 but the submarines went down fighting to the end.

The German Navy was unable to challenge the numerically far superior British Navy in direct fleet to fleet battle but immediately, on the outbreak of war, embarked on attacks on merchant shipping. The strategy came near to slashing Britain's Atlantic lifeline altogether and thus, without the fighting and winning of the Battle of the Atlantic, there would have been no Normandy invasion, no second front in north-west Europe and no decisive intervention by the Western Allies in the war.

The U-boat peril showed itself on day one of Britain's war when the liner *Athenia* was torpedoed 200 miles off the Hebrides on 3 September 1939. In response the Admiralty began a convoy system – east-west across the North Atlantic, and north-south to South America, to Gibraltar and to the Cape. The most immediate threat in the first months of war was from German surface raiders, either armed merchant cruisers or heavy surface units operating independently, preying on unarmed merchantmen. The pursuit and self-destruction of the 'pocket' battleship *Admiral Graf Spee* in the River Plate, 13 December 1939, was a timely boost to British morale but in fact the raider's tally was only nine ships in three months. The *Deutschland* accounted for two ships in two months before returning to Germany with engine trouble, covered by a sortie by the new battle cruisers *Scharnhorst* and *Gneisenau* (known in British popular demonology as the 'Salmon and Gluckstein' after a chain of chemists). The armed merchant cruiser *Rawalpindi* met the raiders, which had avoided Royal Navy patrols, east of Scotland off the Faeroes and radioed a warning before being blown out of the water. The German warships turned round and went home rather than wait for the Royal Navy to arrive in strength.

In October 1940 another major warship, the *Admiral Scheer*, broke out into the Atlantic. It met a convoy of 37 merchant ships escorted by the armed merchant cruiser *Jervis Bay* which engaged the attacker with defiant bravery, allowing the convoy to scatter. Nevertheless five ships were sunk and the *Scheer*'s cruise in the South Atlantic and Indian Ocean accounted for 16 more. The *Scharnhorst* and *Gneisenau* broke out again on 7 February 1941 sinking 22 ships in a six-week cruise, 16 of them in a two-day running chase. From February–April 1941 the *Hipper* undertook a successful raid into the North Atlantic but the most significant, the most dramatic and indeed the last of the *Kriegsmarine*'s surface forays was the cruise of the *Bismarck* in company with the heavy cruiser *Prinz Eugen*. On 18 May 1941 the task force began its journey from the Baltic to Bergenfjiord in Norway. Under cover of bad weather Admiral Lutjens slipped away heading for the Denmark Strait seeking to break out into the open Atlantic. On 23 May the Royal Navy finally caught up but the *Bismarck*'s excellent gunnery sent a 15-inch shell plunging into the British battle-cruiser *Hood*, which blew up with the loss of all but three of the 1500-man crew. The new *King George V* class battleship the *Prince of Wales* was forced to retire. Damaged in the exchange, and by a torpedo strike launched from the carrier *Victorious*, Lutjens turned for Brest, ordering *Prinz Eugen* to proceed independently. After losing contact for a day the *Bismarck* was slowed by another torpedo strike, launched from the carrier *Ark Royal*, until she was finally brought to battle and overwhelmed by the massed power of British battleships which had arrived to finish her off. Two torpedoes from the cruiser *Dorsetshire* sent the blazing hulk to the bottom.

In spite of the drama of the surface actions in the Atlantic, the U-boats posed a far deadlier threat. The fall of France brought the German Navy to the Atlantic Biscay seaboard, and Admiral Dönitz, commander of the U-Boat arm, moved his flag to Lorient within weeks of the armistice. German long range reconnaissance aircraft (Focke-Wulf Fw 200 Condors) could now fly deep into the Atlantic from their bases in south-western France and Norway.

Thus began the first 'Happy Time' of the German U-Boats. Dunkirk and the Norwegian débâcle had reduced the Royal Navy's destroyer strength while the threat of invasion and bombing of British ports further pinned down the Royal Navy. In the period July–October 1940, 144 unescorted and 73 convoyed merchantmen were sunk while the escorts accounted for only two U-Boats destroyed. Dönitz's commanders were learning to operate in 'packs', as many as fifteen strong, locating, trailing then converging on a convoy to attack at night and from the surface where the escorts' Asdic underwater detection gear was ineffective.

The release of more destroyers and aircraft as the invasion scare wound down plus bad weather caused a lull through the winter of 1940–41, but meanwhile Dönitz was commissioning twenty U-Boats a month, pushing them further into the South and western Atlantic and beginning to harden their bases in France, Germany and Norway in concrete bomb-proof pens. On a strategic level the Navy high command was urging operations to gain bases in the Iberian peninsula, the Canary and Cape Verde islands to further increase their reach. These were not forthcoming. The Royal Navy, too, had learned some hard lessons and had increased the quality and quantity of the escorts under the command of the newly-formed Western Approaches Command based at Liverpool.

A Newfoundland Escort Force based at St John's, Newfoundland, was established in May 1941. In September 1941 the first RN escort carrier HMS *Audacity* became operational, an extemporized flight deck on a merchant hull with six converted Hurricane fighters; nevertheless this improvised warship and its successors gave some air cover in mid-ocean and beat off the Condor menace in the eastern Atlantic.

The United States too was becoming quasi-belligerent – 50 old destroyers were handed to the Royal Navy in return for bases in the Caribbean, a US protectorate was placed over Greenland, US troops relieved a British garrison in Iceland (7 July 1941) and from September the US Navy began escorting convoys some 400 miles west of Iceland, allowing the British to concentrate resources in the eastern Atlantic. The U-Boats in fact sank one and damaged another US Navy warship on convoy duty in October 1941, six weeks before the German declaration of war.

Increasingly frustrated in the search for easy prey in the North Atlantic, Dönitz shifted operations south to the Freetown area off West Africa and at first rich pickings were had, 81 unescorted ships sunk. When the north–south route was given continuous escort, the U-Boats moved to the western and south-western approaches but again they were checked by surface escorts and land-based aircraft of RAF Coastal Command.

In September, however, operations in the western Atlantic paid off when a slow convoy was attacked by a 17-strong wolf-pack. The Royal Canadian Navy escort was overwhelmed and 16 merchantmen were lost before an escort group from Iceland came to the rescue.

Up to December 1941, shipping lost exceeded replacement by seven million tons. Britain was steadily losing the Battle of the Atlantic even if the tactics of the convoy system had slowed down the rate of losing. Now American entry into the war brought a new hope but a new Happy Time for the U-Boats with a new flock, tragically innocent of war, to prey on.

The German declaration of war on the USA laid open to attack the great throng of merchant traffic moving along the US east coast, in the Caribbean and into the Gulf of Mexico. The US Navy got it terribly wrong to begin with, adopting ambitious search-and-destroy tactics which allowed more than 200 merchant ships to be sunk until April 1942, many of them in sight of brilliantly lit coastal cities, without one U-Boat being destroyed.

Encouraged by this success, Dönitz sent the bulk of his force into the western Atlantic, using supply U-Boats to stage smaller 750-ton boats into action for a combined offensive from the Caribbean to the coast of New England. After appalling losses, 65 in February, 86 in March, 69 in April, 111 in May, the US Navy at last introduced a convoy system along the east coast. Momentarily checked, the U-Boats moved south into the Caribbean sinking 121 unescorted vessels in June. At the end of that disastrous month the US Navy now brought in convoys plus sea and air escort in these waters and at last ended the U-Boats' second 'Happy Time'. In July five submarines were destroyed in US waters.

Dönitz's response was once again to seek out the gaps in Allied coverage and in October long range U-Boats appeared off the Cape of Good Hope and in the southern Indian Ocean, mauling Middle East-bound convoys. In the North Atlantic the U-Boats wolf packs clustered in the 'air gaps' in mid-ocean where shore based air-cover ran out.

The second half of 1942, therefore, with the assault on US shipping and the second campaign on the convoy routes, went on balance in favour of the U-Boats whose own rate of production still far outstripped their losses (including not just machines but trained crews and skilful commanders).

There was one bright point, however; the Torch landings in North Africa were supplied by convoys which suffered no losses, but at the expense of regular convoys which had had their escorts transferred to protect the packed troopships.

Technology was also set to weight the scales of the battle. From the end of 1942 Royal Navy escorts were fitted with the newly developed Type 271 centimetric (working on a wavelength less than 10 cm) radar which could locate at least a U-Boat's conning tower in darkness, sometimes even a periscope. Then came High Frequency Direction Finding ('Huff-Duff') which could locate the very shortest burst of radio transmission from a surfaced U-Boat calling up a wolf pack, and fix its likely position. By the summer of 1942, airborne radar (ASV sets or 'Air to Surface Vessel') combined with airborne searchlights (Leigh lights) fitted to Coastal Command aircraft for making the final run in night attacks were making transits on the surface, particularly in the Bay of Biscay, near-suicidal. For a while a radar warning device called 'Metox' gave the U-Boats some respite until centimetric ASV (which they could not detect) became operational on Coastal Command aircraft in March 1943. Changing the settings on airborne depth charges to detonate in shallow water also brought greatly improved results in the battle between aircraft and submarine.

Escort vessels had their effectiveness and firepower greatly improved in spring 1943 with the introduction of 'Hedgehog', a device which threw a pattern of grenades ahead of the escort vessel, giving a U-Boat no chance to break sonar contact. New depth charge firing techniques brought improved results, while radio telephones allowed more effective co-ordinated action between escort groups who were becoming as skilled and battle-hardened as the U-Boats they hunted.

But the availability of new technology and new firepower in 1942–43 heightened the Allies' strategic dilemma. Should resources such as long-range bomber aircraft and centimetric radar be used to attack German industry or should they be committed to the Battle of the Atlantic? Churchill himself overruled the Admiralty and not until March 1943 did Coastal Command aircraft get centimetric ASV; the air gap was not closed until VLR (Very Long Range) B-24 Liberators were committed in strength.

A handful of Liberator 1s equipped with early model ASV radar in fact became operational with Coastal Command squadrons based in Northern Ireland in June 1941. US Army Air Force Liberators in the anti-submarine role operated from bases in Newfoundland, North Africa and Britain until in 1943 the US Navy took over these operational duties and USAAF Anti Submarine Command was disbanded.

By the beginning of 1943 the number of escort vessels available to Western Approaches Command had risen appreciably and the Royal Canadian Navy was beginning to find its feet. By March the Royal Navy was at last able to commit independent support groups as well as close escorts which could be sent to the aid of a threatened convoy, some of which included one of the new escort carriers. On 1 April 1943 the Royal Canadian Navy took over responsibility for convoy defence west of 47° West while the US Navy withdrew from its last North Atlantic base in Iceland, to concentrate on the mid-Atlantic, Gulf of Mexico-Gibraltar route. From this time until the end of the war the US Navy operated hunter-killer groups in mid-Atlantic composed of an escort carrier and between four and twelve destroyer escorts.

In March 1943 the crisis in the Battle of the Atlantic came, the point at which both sides came closest to winning and losing the battle on the convoy routes. That month Dönitz launched a 40 U-Boat strong offensive against a slow convoy from Sydney, Cape Breton Island (SC 118) and a fast convoy from Halifax (HX 229). The escorts of both were overwhelmed as they battered their way through the 'Black Gap' (the mid-Atlantic air gap) and out of 92 ships, 21 were sunk for the loss of only one U-Boat. In March 1943 sinkings by U-Boats shot up to 108 ships (627,377 tons), almost as bad as the worst months of 1942. The crisis had arrived.

In early May Dönitz concentrated the huge number of 60

75

U-Boats in four groups against the slow convoy ONS 5 (Outward North Atlantic Slow 5) but this time the escorts triumphed. The combination of radar, Huff Duff, the new *River* class frigates, the first effective use of support groups (one of which included the escort carrier *Biter*) plus VLR aircraft based in Iceland allowed the defenders to destroy seven U-Boats for the loss of twelve merchantmen. In mid-May the U-Boats were defeated again when support groups intervened decisively once more to defend convoys HX 237 and SC 129. Dönitz recalled the survivors on 24 May.

Forty-one U-Boats had been sunk in that one month, May 1943, and never again could the German Navy concentrate that same weight of firepower against the Allies' Atlantic lifeline. While Coastal Command scored remarkable success in the Bay of Biscay transit area (less so in the Faroe-Shetlands channel), the US Navy escort carriers mounted successful operations against 'Milchcow' supply submarines off the Azores – but the battle was by no means over.

In September Dönitz launched a new offensive. U-Boats were now equipped with new technical devices such as acoustic homing torpedoes. When attacked by aircraft, they were ordered to fight it out on the surface but, even with beefed up anti-aircraft armament, this proved an operational mistake. The phase from 1 September to the end of December 1943 has been judged to mark the final defeat of the open-ocean wolf packs as they accounted for an average of 22 ships per month for a loss of 62 U-Boats in the same period.

In the first months of 1944, with the huge build up of men and material in Britain for Overlord progressing, the U-Boats once again concentrated on the north-western approaches to the British Isles but, in contrast to the first campaign in these waters and the first 'Happy Time', the defenders were highly trained and well equipped. Captain F.J. Walker's 2nd Escort Group for example, operating with two escort carriers, had outstanding success sinking six U-Boats in a month. Between January and May 1944 merchant ship losses averaged 13.4 ships per month, pre-fabricated 'Liberty Ships' were pouring out of US shipyards and the U-Boat arm suffered 103 losses from all causes. While the defenders re-grouped their forces to protect the Overlord invasion, Dönitz pulled back to rethink tactics and to re-equip his vessels with the 'Schnorkel' breathing device which allowed a submerged U-Boat to run on diesels at periscope depth. When the invasion went in, some schnorkel-equipped boats got through to attack the mass of Allied shipping but far too few to have any real impact.

The German collapse in France meant the U-Boats lost their forward bases. Allied bombing pounded shipyards where U-Boats were assembled and minelaying in the Baltic denied crews their training areas. From September 1944 the U-Boats moved back to where they had started, inshore waters round the British Isles where the escort groups, used to operations in mid-Atlantic, had to learn new tactics all over again, hunting among shoals and wrecks in strong tidal waters. U-Boats appeared in the Channel, in the Irish Sea and off the mouth of the Thames where they had not appeared since 1940 and the Atlantic escorts were drawn in to hunt for them in the frustratingly difficult shallow waters.

There was a last card in the pack but it was played far too late. From 1943 the Germans had been developing a new generation U-Boat with a streamlined hull form, silent running electric motors, schnorkel, and auto-loading torpedoes plus very high underwater speed. This research resulted in 1945 in the type XXI long range U-Boat and type XXIII coastal U-Boat with an even greater threat emerging in the type XXVI Walter-engined vessel powered by hydrogen peroxide and capable of 22½-knots submerged and thus outrunning most escort ships, even underwater. Large numbers of the new vessels were on order and dispersed manufacture of prefabricated units meant that strategic bombing would not have stopped them getting to sea. By the time more than a handful were on the loose however, the war in Europe – and with it the last phase of the Battle of the Atlantic – was over.

Germany's Top U-Boat Aces

Name and final rank	U-boat	Type	Missions/ Days at sea	Period	ships/tons sunk
Lt Com. Otto	*U-23*	IIB	9/91	9.39–3.40	44/266,629
Kretschmer	*U-99*	VIIB	7/127	6.40–3.41	+ 1 destroyer
Capt. Wolfgang Lutl.	*U-9*	IIB	5/57	1.40–5.40	43/225,712
	U-138	IID	2/27	9.40–10.40	+ 1 submarine
	U-43	IX	5/192	11.40–1.42	
	U-181	IXD2	2/333	9.42–10.43	
Com. Erich Topp	*U-57*	IIC	3/34	7.40–9.40	34/193,684
	U-552	VIIC	10/291	2.41–8.42	+ 1 destroyer
Capt. Karl-F Merten	*U-68*	IXC	5/272	6.41–5.43	29/186,064
Capt. Victor Schütze	*U-25*	IA	3/98	10.39–5.40	34/171,164
	U-103	IXB	4/196	9.40–7.41	
Lt Com. Herbert Schultze	*U-48*	VIIB	8/202	9.39–4.40 1.41–6.41	26/171,122
Lt Com. Georg Lassen	*U-160*	IXC	4/329	2.42–5.43	28/167,601
Com. H. Lehmann-Willenbroch	*U-5*	IIA	1/15	4.40	
	U-96	VIIC	8/260	12.40–3.42	22/166,596
	U-256	VIIC	1/44	9.44–10.44	
Com. Heinrich Liebe	*U-38*	IX	9/319	9.39–6.41	30/162,333
Lt Com. Günther Prien	*U-47*	VIIB	10/225	9.39–3.41	28/160,939 + 1 battleship
Lt Joachim Schepke	*U-3*	IIA	3/24	9.39–10.39	
	U-19	IIB	5/58	1.40–4.40	39/159,130
	U-100	VIIB	6/101	8.40–3.41	
Lt Com. Werner Henke	*U-515*	IXC	6/337	8.43–4.44	25/156,829 + 1 depot ship
Lt Com. Carl Emmermann	*U-172*	IXC	5/365	4.42–9.43	27/152,656
Lt Com. Heinrich Bleichradt	*U-48*	VIIB	2/39	9.40–10.40	24/151,319
	U-109	IXB	6/363	6.41–10.42	+ 1 sloop
Lt Com. Robert Gysac	*U-98*	VIIC	6/183	3.41–2.42	25/144,901
	U-177	IXD2	2/310	9.42–10.43	
Capt. Ernst Kals	*U-130*	IXC	5/281	12.41–12.42	19/138,567
Lt Com. Joh. Mohr	*U-124*	IXB	6/262	9.41–4.43	27/132,731 + 1 cruiser + 1 corvette
Com. Klaus Scholtz	*U-108*	IXB	8/347	2.41–9.42	24/132,417
Lt Engelbert Endrass	*U-46*	VIIB	7/186	6.40–8.41	22/128,879
	U-567	VIIC	2/35	10.41–12.41	
Lt Com. Reinhard Hardegen	*U-147*	IID	1/25	5.41–7.42	
	U-123	IXB		2.41–5.41	23/128,412

Major U-Boat types: Technical Specifications

Type		VIIC	IXC	XXIC	XXIII	XXVI
Number completed		660	200	125	60	3
Displacement	surfaced	769	1,120	1,621	232	1,621
	submerged	871	1,232	1,819	256	1,819
Dimensions	length (feet)	220	244	252	112	252
	breadth	20	21	22	10	22
	draught	15¾	18¼	20	12	20
Machinery		diesel-electric	diesel-electric	diesel-electric	petrol-electric	hydrogen-peroxide
Shafts		2	2	2	1	2
BHP		2,800	3,000	4,000	600	
Fuel, tons		114	200	250	18	250
Speed	surfaced	16	18½	15½	9¾	20
	submerged	7½	7½	17½	12½	22½
Endurance	surfaced	6,500×12	11,000×12	11,150×12	2,800×8	
	submerged	80×4	63×4	285×6	113×6	
				110×10	43×10	
Guns		1 3.5"	1 37mm	2 twin 30mm	Nil	
		1 37mm	2 20mm			
		2 20mm				
Torpedo Tubes		5 21"	6 21"	6 21"	2 21"	6 21"
Torpedoes		14	19–22	20	2	20
Crew		44	50	57	14	50?

Operations

Total German U-Boat losses to all causes 1939–45

1 ON OPERATIONS

Period	On way to or from base	North Sea Baltic Arctic	N. & S. Atlantic	Mediterranean	Ind. Ocean	Total
Sept. 1939 to June 1940	2	11	10	–	–	23
July 1940 to March 1941	1	–	12	–	–	13
April 1941 to Dec. 1941	3	1	19	5	–	28
Jan. 1942 to July 1942	6	2	16	7	–	31
August 1942 to May 1943	31	5	90	19	1	146
June 1943 to August 1943	46	1	22	5	2	76
Sept. 1943 to May 1944	47	14	70	12	3	146
June 1944 to May 1945	50	24	85	2	6	167
1939–1945	186	58	324	50	12	630

2 BY OTHER CAUSES

(a) In home waters or at base by enemy action (air attack or mines)	81
(b) In home water or at base by accidents	42
(c) In evacuating forward bases or by scuttling/demolishing by own crews at end of war	215
	338
Brought forward	630
	968

3 REMAINDER

(d) Paid off during war owing to irreparable damage or obsolescence	38
(e) Captured by enemy or interned damaged in neutral barbours	11
(f) Surrendered at end of war	153
	202
Brought forward	968
Total Production	1,170

Barbarossa

By midsummer 1941 the Axis commanded or controlled the resources of fifteen European countries. One country remained defiant, but the U-Boats must surely see Britain off and pinch out the troublesome diversions in North Africa. The Balkans had been crushed by Blitzkrieg techniques as effectively and quickly as France had been – and German military power dominated Europe from the North Cape of Norway to the Aegean with a block of compliant satellites in the East.

Then there was the Soviet Union, the huge, sprawling land of 190 million, the ideological enemy to the east – the Bolshevik hordes who, for the time being at least by the terms of the non-aggression pact of August 1939, were quasi-partners in the New Order in Europe.

In fact formal planning for an invasion of the Soviet Union had begun in December 1940 and a military build-up in the east begun soon afterwards. Originally set for 15 May 1941, the timetable for Operation Barbarossa was postponed while the invasion of the Balkans swept the southern flank, kicking the British off the European mainland once more in the process.

The storm broke on 22 June 1941. Despite repeated warnings from the West to the Soviet leadership, and from their own sources, that invasion was imminent, the Germans had complete tactical surprise and along a 2000-mile front, the German armies began their advance. The Luftwaffe smashed the Red Air Force, droves of aircraft being caught on the ground.

The German plan was for Rundstedt's Army Group South to drive on Kiev and surround and destroy all Soviet forces between the Pripet Marshes and the Black Sea. Bock's Army Group Centre containing two Panzer groups was to drive along the axis Minsk-Smolensk to Moscow itself. General von Leeb's Army Group North was to drive north-east and take Leningrad, cutting off Soviet forces in the Baltic states in the process while the Finns would threaten Leningrad from Karelia. In the far north General

81

Falkenhorst would attack from northern Norway to cut the Murmansk-Leningrad railway. One hundred and sixty-two divisions of ground troops, approximately 3 million men, would be involved.

The essence of the German plan was not to seize ground but to destroy the Red Army; the tanks would slice through the defenders, surround them in huge 'pockets' for the German infantry to move in and mop up. Hitler believed the German Army would only have to 'kick in the door and the whole house would come crashing down', that the Soviet Union would be crushed by another, only bigger, Blitzkrieg which would be triumphantly over by the autumn. In the beginning it all succeeded brilliantly. In the centre, Hoth and Guderian's panzer groups punched through either side of Bialystok surrounding the Soviet armies drawn up on the frontier, once on 30 June and again at Minsk on 9 July, closing the net on 290,000 prisoners and huge numbers of tanks. Fending off counterattacks from the south by the newly appointed commander of the Western Front Marshal Timoshenko (General Pavlov was shot for incompetence), the panzer jaws snapped again around Smolensk on 16 July enclosing another 300,000 Russians. In the south the German target was Kiev, capital of the Ukraine. Spearheaded by Kleist's panzers, Army Group South battered through the frontier defences while the Rumanian Army moved on the Black Sea port of Odessa. The Soviet High Command fused the south and south-west fronts with Budenny in command but counterattacks floundered. Two German stabs pushed south-east and closed around Umlan on 4 August with another 100,000 prisoners, then pushed on deep south of Kiev into the Dnieper bend.

In the centre, meanwhile, Hitler ordered Guderian's panzer group to come wheeling south to close the huge Kiev pocket from the rear with five Soviet armies trapped inside. Kiev fell on 19 September and another 665,000 Russian troops surrendered. Meanwhile in the far south the Germans reached the Crimea where General von Manstein's newly formed XI Army sealed off the fortress of Sevastopol. After Kiev, Rundstedt's Army Group South reached the river Don on 15 October, threatening Rostov and Kharkov which fell on 24 October.

Army Group North's progress was just as spectacular. The first major obstacle was the Dvina River which was crossed by 2 July. The northern defences of the 'Stalin Line' were reduced and by 14 July the invaders were in the suburbs of Leningrad. By the end of August the Baltic had been cleared but Leningrad, although invested to the south and from the north by the Finns, held out with its only lifeline across Lake Ladoga. Hitler meanwhile had decided to take the city by blockade rather than frontal assault and switched all of Army Group North's armour except for one Panzer Corps to the centre for what, it was planned, would be the decisive drive on Moscow.

In the centre the Battle of Smolensk, 10 July–10 September, had shown the tenacity of the Soviet Army in defence after the disasters on the frontiers.

In the first few days, the Germans were advancing 30 kilometres every 24 hours. Smolensk blunted the drive on Moscow but, in spite of the strain on men and machines, Army Group Centre might still have driven clear to Moscow in August had Hitler himself not intervened to switch the punch out to the flanks, with the directive to Guderian's panzer group, for example, to drive south around Kiev.

After the annihilation of the Soviet armies in the Ukraine and with Leningrad under siege, the emphasis again switched to the Centre for what the Germans planned would be the final drive on Moscow and victory. Operation Typhoon, as it was called, opened on 2 October as 77 divisions including 18 armoured and eight motorized divisions struck east in three axes of advance.

Again the panzer jaws closed on Soviet pockets, at Bryansk and at Vyazma, capturing more than 650,000 prisoners. By 20 October the Germans were at Mozhaisk, a bare 40 miles from Moscow.

The Soviet Army had suffered colossal casualties, about 3 million men, half of them prisoners trudging west in huge columns to a captivity of appalling deprivation, but it had not been completely destroyed and space had been traded

83

for time. Time was against the invader; the dust roads of summer were turning to the mired tracks of autumn with the Russian winter looming. The German Army was unprepared to survive, let alone fight in sub-zero temperatures.

A new commander of the central Soviet forces barring the way to the capital, named General Georgi Zhukov, organized a new defensive front and held the German advance once more, buying time for Soviet reinforcements to arrive from the far east and for winter to bite deeper. Again the Germans stabbed at Moscow, on 15 November. Guderian's tanks broke through to Tula while II Panzer Groups tried to batter through to the north-west of the city. Both drives were checked as was a final lunge in the centre. German troops could glimpse the domes of the Kremlin glinting in the distance but the temperature was dropping to minus 40 degrees. Oil froze solid in tank engines, gun sights bloomed over, cylinder blocks cracked as did the morale of men used to winning who now began to shiver, then freeze in their summer uniforms. The drive on Moscow cost Army Group Centre 55,000 dead and over 100,000 wounded and frostbitten.

Under Zhukov's urging, Stavka, The Soviet High Command, withdrew the eight remaining intact tank brigades of the Red Army from the Far East and provided massive infantry reinforcements for his counterattack launched on 6 December 1941. With the Red Army making a general counteroffensive attacking at Rostov and attempting to relieve Leningrad, German Army Group Centre before Moscow could not be reinforced. Before Zhukov's divisions, riding in on the hulls of factory-fresh T-34s and clad in winter combat clothing, the invaders fell back from the gates of Moscow.

Japan's Triumph

The militarists who seized the political initiative in Japan in the autumn of 1941 devised a three-phase plan to emulate their partner in the Tripartite Pact, Germany, and seize an empire by military conquest. The colonial possessions of

France and the Netherlands were completely vulnerable and Britain's ability to respond effectively could be discounted. The military problem was whether Japan could take on the United States and win. First would be a devastating blow on the Forward US fleet base at Pearl Harbor in the Hawaiian Islands to cripple the ability of their main rival to respond. This would be part of a huge offensive to establish control over an area bounded by Wake Island, through the Gilbert Islands, New Guinea and the Dutch East Indies to Burma and the border of British India. Second would be the fortification of this perimeter and third would be the deflection of counterattacks until the enemy conceded defeat and acknowledged Japanese dominion over a vast 'Greater East Asia Co-Prosperity Sphere'.

On the morning of 7 December 1941 a Japanese naval task force under the command of Admiral Nagumo arrived at a point some 230 miles north of Pearl Harbor and began to launch waves of attack aircraft ('Kate' torpedo bombers and 'Val' dive bombers) plus the agile and effective Mitsubishi A5M Zero fighter to protect them in any air to air combat.

At Pearl, a radar report of approaching aircraft had been discounted and the detection of a midget submarine at 6.45 am had not fully alerted the defenders.

Without opposition therefore, the first Japanese aircraft swept in at 7.55 am, three waves of torpedo bombers, the first aimed at the US battleships lined up on the south side of Ford Island, the second a strike at warships lined up on the north side and a single strike at an isolated cruiser. Forty-five minutes later came high level bombers followed by dive bombers and strafing fighters. By 9.45 am it was over and five battleships were either sunk or badly damaged and several other major warships crippled. US Army aircraft were caught on the ground, fatally bunched together to 'protect them from sabotage' and could offer no riposte – out of an attacking force of 360 aircraft, only nine Zeros, fifteen Vals and five Kates were lost to whatever ground fire the defenders were able to put up.

The US Navy aircraft carriers *Enterprise* and *Lexington* were however out of the way, despatched to carry reinforcing Marine Corps Wildcat fighters to Wake and Midway Islands. The airstrike smashed the battleships but it had missed the carriers and Pearl's vital oil stocks. The attack united US political opinion around Roosevelt and, when Hitler declared war on the United States, it brought the world's greatest industralized power to the aid of embattled Britain and the Soviet Union.

The assault on Pearl was only one component of a huge co-ordinated offensive. Seven other attacks were launched simultaneously on British, US and Dutch controlled territory in the Pacific. On 8 December, US aircraft were caught on the ground in an airstrike on the Philippines. On 10 December the British capital ships *Prince of Wales* and *Repulse* were sunk by air attack in the open sea off the coast of Malaya. On Christmas Day Hong Kong surrendered with the loss of its 12,000-strong garrison. On 15 February 1942 Singapore capitulated with 138,708 British and Empire troops after the British had been pushed out of Malaya by a force half their size. In the battle of the Java Sea on 27 January a combined Dutch, US and Royal Navy fleet was crushed and on 9 March the whole Dutch East Indies was formally surrendered. The Japanese First Air Fleet sailed into the Indian Ocean with impunity, sinking the British carrier *Hermes* and other major warships off Ceylon, and seemed set to sail clear to Madagascar.

Having occupied Thailand, the Japanese Fifteenth Army began a rapid advance into Burma, besting British defenders at Moulmein and Sittang. The newly appointed British overall commander General Harold Alexander decided to abandon the Burmese capital Rangoon on 7 March. By May 1942 four-fifths of Burma was in Japanese hands and the British pushed back to the Indian border.

Of the US possessions, the island of Guam with a token defence was overrun after half an hour of fighting on 10 December. The garrison at Wake fought back, sinking two destroyers and inflicting heavy casualties on the invaders before being overwhelmed in a second attack on 23

December. After the disaster at Clark Field when US airpower in the Philippines was virtually wiped out in one blow, Japanese landings went in at Luzon from 10–22 December catching the US-Filipino ground forces under the overall command of General Douglas MacArthur in a pincer movement. Manila was evacuated on 26 December and US forces retreated into the Bataan peninsula. The defenders contested the Japanese advance for four months – MacArthur departed by PT-boat on 11 March on direct orders from Roosevelt. A month later resistance on Bataan was over and 64,000 Filipino and 12,000 US troops were taken prisoner. Between 7000 and 10,000 of these were to die of disease or starvation on the 'death march' to prison camps. The fortified island of Corregidor in Manila Bay held out until 6 May, under incessant bombardment when, with three days' supply of water left, General Wainwright surrendered and resistance on Mindanao and Panay formally ceased on 10 May and 18 May.

Between the attack on Pearl Harbor and the final US surrender in the Philippines, the Japanese advance had been made at astonishing speed over a vast area and for comparatively few losses in men, machines and warships. The Japanese had effectively seized the areas of natural resources and the 'island barrier' against counterattack dictated by the strategic plan, but they had failed to completely eliminate the strikepower in place of their most powerful enemy, the fast aircraft carriers of the US Navy. While the dispersion of forces at targets as separate as the Indian frontier, the Aleutian Islands, and the Solomons had thrown the defence in the first flush of Japanese conquest completely off balance, the failure to concentrate forces was yet to deny the Japanese the exploitation of their victories.

By May 1942, factions within the Japanese Army and the Navy conflicted as where to strike next – at Port Moresby in southern New Guinea thus cutting off Australia, perhaps at the Aleutian Islands, US territory in the northern Pacific or a thrust at Midway Island designed to bring the US Navy to battle and destroy it.

Operations

Rather than concentrate forces, all three operations were attempted – with disastrous results. Disturbed by the *Doolittle* carrier launched bombing raid on Tokyo, it was resolved in a 'revised strategic plan' to extend the defensive perimeter in the central and southern Pacific. Two naval task forces were assigned to the capture of Port Moresby, one moving through the Solomons towards Tulagi, the second and larger one including the carriers *Shokaku* and *Zuikaku* entering the Coral Sea from the east.

Fed by US 'Magic' intelligence (the decoding of Japanese high level secret communications), the US commander Admiral Chester M. Nimitz was able to concentrate a task force including two carriers, the *Lexington* and *Yorktown*, to bar the Coral Sea. When the rival carrier forces found each other on 7 May, they were not too disproportionate, two US carriers with 121 aircraft versus three Japanese carriers with 180 aircraft. In this first great carrier battle, when no surface ship on either side actually made visual contact with the enemy, the Japanese lost the carrier *Shoho* on 7 May. The *Lexington* in return was sunk the next morning and the *Yorktown* severely damaged. The *Shokaku* was badly damaged but, although some of her aircraft were lost, the *Zuikaku* was unscathed. Both fleet commanders withdrew after the drawn battle of the Coral Sea but the seaborne Japanese assault on Port Moresby was halted.

From Midway to Tokyo Bay

Midway

Believing that both *Yorktown* and *Lexington* had been sunk at the Battle of the Coral Sea, Admiral Yamamoto, commander of the Combined Fleet, prepared to carry out the next phase of the revised strategic plan by striking the US island base at Midway some 600 miles short of Pearl Harbor itself. Convinced that it would not be opposed by any US carriers, a huge Japanese fleet was assembled, 165 warships, but again they were split into separate groups scattered over the north and central Pacific. Vice Admiral Hosogoya's Northern Area Force, with two light carriers, was to make diversionary strikes on the Aleutian Islands. Other diversions using miniature submarines were mounted at Diego Suarez, Madagascar and at Sydney.

Three separate forces headed for Midway itself: Nagumo's First Air Fleet (missing the two carriers knocked out in the Coral Sea), the Second Fleet escorting the Midway occupation force of 51,000 troops and Yamamoto's main body with no fewer than seven battleships but only one light carrier. Meanwhile a screen of submarines was ordered to commence operating between Midway and the Hawaiian Islands reporting US Fleet movements.

On the US side Admiral Nimitz ordered Admiral Halsey's *Enterprise-Hornet* task force to steam at full speed to the area of action while the damaged *Yorktown* was patched up at Pearl in just 48 hours. In late May the US Pacific fleet assembled north of Midway, the *Enterprise-Hornet* force, now commanded by Rear Admiral Raymond Spruance, relieving the sick Halsey. Admiral Fletcher with his flag aboard *Yorktown* was in command at sea with Nimitz in overall command from fleet HQ at Pearl.

On 3 June the Japanese Northern Area Force began its diversionary attack on the western Aleutians, while, aware via 'Magic' of the actual thrust of the Japanese plan, Nimitz awaited the attack on Midway. Nagumo launched half of First Air Fleet's strength, 108 aircraft, against Midway, pounding the defenders but sparing the airstrip for future use. Meanwhile Midway's own landbased aircraft attempted to counter but were swatted down by the Japanese fleet defence fighters which lost just six of their own to 33 American.

At 17.00 hours on 4 June the second phase of the battle began. Aboard Nagumo's carriers, armourers were working feverishly to arm reserve strike aircraft with high explosive and fragmentation bombs for a second strike on Midway's defences rather than penetration bombs and torpedoes for attacking warships. Meanwhile the returning first strike wave was being retrieved, just as US attack aircraft from

89

Enterprise and *Hornet* were being launched. Half an hour later, at 07.30, *Yorktown* launched her aircraft, again timed to catch the Japanese on deck while being refuelled. The torpedo bombers of *Hornet* arrived first, Torpedo Squadron 8, equipped with Douglas Devastators which, flying low, slow and level were massacred by the Zero fleet air defence fighters. The torpedo force of *Enterprise* and *Yorktown* met the same fate in rapid succession and only six aircraft survived out of 41 without scoring a single hit.

While the Zeros were slaughtering the Devastators, high altitude cover was denuded and the US Navy Dauntless dive bombers found it. They nearly didn't, overshooting in the overcast weather. But the squadron from *Enterprise* made a crucial decision to turn round, finding Nagumo's fleet by luck through a break in the cloud just as *Yorktown*'s dive bomber squadron arrived on the scene. The Daunt-lesses from *Enterprise* began their attack at 10.22 on three Japanese aircraft carriers, just as their decks were crowded with aircraft, heading directly into the wind. In a matter of minutes the battle was decided – four bombs struck *Kaga* which went up in flames, *Soryu* and *Akagi* following, the mass of fuel and ordnance erupting on their decks ensuring their own self-destruction.

Hiryu broke away steaming north-eastwards, vengefully launching a dive bomber strike which scored three hits on *Yorktown*, followed by two torpedo strikes dooming the carrier. It was abandoned (the hulk stayed afloat for two days before being despatched by a torpedo from the Japanese submarine I–168). Meanwhile a 24 dive-bomber strong strike force from *Enterprise* found the *Hiryu* and sent her the way of her sisters. Even with Nagumo's First Air Fleet eliminated Yamamoto was still numerically far superior in surface ship strength and he pushed forward on Midway with the aim of forcing a surface battle in which his vast gunpower would tell. Spruance (to whom Fletcher had relinquished command after *Yorktown* was abandoned) withdrew eastwards. Realizing his trap had failed and now without air cover, Yamamoto broke off and ordered a general retirement.

For two days the US Navy pursued the retreating Japanese, avoiding night actions in which the Japanese were particularly adept. With fuel running low, Spruance abandoned the chase and turned back for Pearl Harbor having inflicted on the Japanese Navy its first clear-cut defeat in modern times.

Along with the carrier *Yorktown* the US lost 132 land and carrier based aircraft and 307 dead. The Japanese had lost four carriers, breaking their numerical superiority in the Pacific, plus 296 aircraft and 3500 dead, 114 of them naval airmen.

New Guinea and the Philippines

The first great bound of expansion carried Japanese power to the chain of islands running to the north of Australia – they held the northern half of New Guinea and the eastern Solomons but had been prevented at the Battle of the Coral Sea in seizing Port Moresby, the principal town of southern Papua. In May–July 1942 the Japanese strove to push south-east again, and consolidate an even wider defence perimeter, by establishing an airbase on Guadalcanal in the southern Solomons, and by moving again on Port Moresby across the Owen Stanley mountain range. Land operations were under the control of General Miamura's Eighth Army, fleet actions by Admiral Mikawa's Eighth Fleet, both with headquarters at the newly established big military base at Rabaul in New Britain.

Churchill and Roosevelt had agreed that the Pacific, including Australia, should be under American operational command, the Middle East and India remained a British preserve, the Atlantic and Europe a joint concern, but even within the unitary US Pacific command there was dissent.

It was divided into General Douglas MacArthur's Southwest Pacific Command and Admiral Chester Nimitz's Central Pacific Command. Each had control of all land, sea and air forces in their areas while Nimitz controlled all amphibious operations. Nimitz, backed by Admiral King in Washington, argued for a thrust through the central Pacific, the shortest route to the enemy heartland through the Gilbert, Marshall, Caroline and Mariana Islands. MacArthur, remembering the ignominy of defeat in the Philippines, urged a drive through the much more substantial land masses of New Guinea and the Philippines first. Meanwhile the renewed Japanese offensive had to be checked – Operation 'Watchtower' was formulated to deny the Japanese further advance south-east, to take the Solomons and the north-east coast of New Guinea followed by an assault on the main Japanese base at Rabaul.

On 7 August 1942 the US 1st Marine Division, supported by Admiral Fletcher's three-carrier task force, began landing on Guadalcanal and Tulagi in the southern Solomons, achieving tactical surprise until ferocious Japanese air and naval counterattacks were mounted. In a night action off Savo Island, superbly handled Japanese ships sank four out of five Allied heavy cruisers, forcing the US Navy to withdraw before the shore positions were consolidated. For six more months a prolonged and intensely destructive fight was waged for control of Guadalcanal with at least ten pitched land battles and seven major naval engagements until the Japanese finally evacuated their position in February 1943.

MacArthur meanwhile began the campaign to clear Papua and New Guinea, first by reinforcing Port Moresby, again under threat by the Japanese push over the Owen Stanley mountains and by an ampibious landing at Milne Bay at the eastern tip of the island, finally repulsed by the Australians on 5 September 1942. Through September and October US-Australian forces pushed the Japanese back through the mountains until, in turn, the Allied offensive bogged down in the jungle, short of supplies, and debilitated by disease. On 9 December the newly appointed ground forces commander General Robert L. Eichelberger got the stalled offensive going again, launching attacks on the fortified Japanese position at Buna-Gona on the shores of the Solomon Sea. Gona fell comparatively easily but Buna was taken only after vicious fighting in a malarial swamp, exemplifying the pattern of fanatical Japanese resistance with more than 7000 dead and only some hundred wounded prisoners surviving. The Allies lost 5700 Australian and 2783 US killed and wounded.

By mid-January the campaign in Papua was over but the fighting for the Solomons was still claiming the bulk of Japanese resources and the losses in aircraft and trained pilots was becoming critical. By the end of 1943, more than 3000 aircraft had been expended in the struggle for the Solomons alone.

Rabaul was now the primary US objective and the centre of Japan's defensive strategy and to eliminate it MacArthur received the lion's share of resources. Admiral Halsey's newly designated Third Fleet was shifted from Central to South-west Pacific command for a two-pronged offensive on New Britain, Halsey's forces driving north-westward through the Solomons and General Walter Krueger's US Sixth Army advancing northward through New Guinea and the island of New Britain itself towards Rabaul.

As preliminary moves the undefended Trobriand Islands, and Nassau Bay south of Salamaua, were occupied at the end of June 1943. In September US and Australian troops, now under the command of the Australian General Sir Thomas Blamey, took Lae and paratroops seized the Japanese airstrip at Nadzab. The port of Finschafen was taken on 2 October, opening the way for amphibious operations against New Britain.

The drive through the Solomons meanwhile, through October–December 1943, concentrated on Bougainville where the Japanese Seventeenth Army held an Allied perimeter established at Empress Augusta Bay. The tenacity of Japanese defence in place plus gradual mastery of sea communications meant that Japanese strong-points would be bypassed, sealing them off from air and sea supply until their military significance withered away. The isolation of Rabaul in June 1944 with its 100,000 strong garrison was a prime example – this, and the consolidation of the Solo- mons, virtually ended combat operations in the South Pacific theatre and Halsey's fleet was returned to Nimitz's command.

Operations

This was not before MacArthur's forces had cleared the northern New Guinea coast in a series of amphibious operations at Hollandia in April 1944, Wakde on 17 May, the coral atoll of Biak in June after a vicious fight in which the defenders lost more than 10,000 to 2700 US casualties, Wewak and Aitape, Noemfoor and Sansapor which marked the final set-piece fighting in New Guinea. The Japanese Eighteenth Army's remnants retreated into the jungle and isolated pockets of resistance remained but now MacArthur could look across the Celebes Sea towards Mindanao, southernmost of the Philippines.

The Central Pacific

The Central Pacific Command of Admiral Chester Nimitz had meanwhile been rebuilding its strength in warships and naval aircraft through the first half of 1943, preparing for a drive across the Central Pacific, dotted with chains of coral atolls, the long but most direct route to the heart of Japanese power. By October 1943 Nimitz could chalk up in his order of battle Admiral Raymond Spruance's Fifth Fleet with seven battleships and eight carriers almost equal to the pre-war strength of the entire US Navy, the Seventh Army Air Force based in the Ellice Islands and the 100,000 combat troops in the V Amphibious Corps plus Halsey's Third Fleet from June 1944 onwards. Against this array of strength, the Japanese Combined Fleet under the command of Admiral Koga (Admiral Yamamoto was intercepted in mid air between Rabaul and Bougainville and killed, 18 April 1943) with its main forward base at Truk in the Carolines, had now to defend a vast perimeter from the Aleutians to the Andaman Islands in the Indian Ocean. Despite the presence at Truk of the giant battleships *Yamato* and *Musahi*, Admiral Koga was outclassed and over-stretched when Nimitz began the US Navy's great drive across the Central Pacific. First to be attacked were the islands of Makin, where casualties in the actual assault were light, and Tarawa where the defence was much more tenacious. Inch by inch frontal assault supported by naval gunfire finally subdued the defence but at the cost of 985 dead US Marines and 2193 wounded. Out of 4700 defenders only seventeen combat soldiers were taken prisoner and Tarawa ranks one of the costliest battles in the history of American arms in the ratio of casualties to troops engaged. But the taking of Tarawa put the Marshalls within range and put Truk itself, the 'Japanese Gibraltar', under the threat of air attack.

Nimitz's next target was the Marshall group. After Admiral Mitscher's fast carrier task force, Task Force 58, had swept away local air opposition and pounded the defences in a three day naval and air bombardment, 40,000 men of General Turner's Fifth Amphibious Force landed on Kwajalein, Roia and Namur on 1 February. After a week of fierce fighting, Kwajalein was captured but at far less cost than at Tarawa: 372 dead and some 1000 wounded. The Japanese garrisons again fought to the death, 7870 killed out of 8000.

Now Mitscher's carrier air wings struck direct at Truk, failing to hit the bulk of the Combined Fleet which had already withdrawn in a replay of Pearl Harbor but sinking fifty merchant ships and showing the vulnerability of the base. Heavily fortified Truk was not seized outright therefore but left to 'wither on the vine' like so many other Japanese outposts, while US strikepower turned north-east towards the Marianas. The island of Saipan was taken after a month of fanatical resistance directed by General Saito the army commander, and Admiral Nagumo, veteran of Pearl Harbor, the navy commander, who both committed suicide. Tinian fell on 2 August and Guam on 3 August ending organized resistance in the Marianas. Meanwhile Vice-Admiral Jisaburo Ozawa's fleet had put to sea as the assault on Saipan went in, meeting Mitscher's carriers at daybreak on 19 June 1944. Disaster overtook Ozawa, the carriers *Taiho* and *Shokaku* were despatched by US submarines while his air wings, plus land based Japanese attack aircraft from Truk and Marianas bases, were shot out of the sky in droves by US fleet air defence fighters and or by massed anti-aircraft fire. 'The Great Marianas Turkey

95

Shoot' cost Ozawa 346 aircraft with their irreplaceable trained pilots, for the loss of 30 American. One bomb hit on the USS *South Dakota* was the only Japanese success.

Leyte Gulf and the Philippines

With MacArthur at Sanspor on the western tip of New Guinea and Nimitz in the Marianas, the tensions pulling at the two approaches to Japan had not been resolved. At a conference at Pearl Harbor in July President Roosevelt himself backed the MacArthur plan in outline and the two drives were given a common objective – Leyte in the Philippines. The plan was formalized by the joint Chiefs of Staff then brought forward without intermediate landings at Mindanao and Yap, to October 1944, so fast and effective had been the rate of advance of Halsey's Third Fleet with its new *Essex*-class carriers.

From 7–16 October the Third Fleet moved in to attack what remained of Japanese naval air power while the Fifth Army Air Force hit targets in the Philippines and in Formosa. Japanese aircraft on Formosa struck back fiercely and severely damaged several major US warships. Returning airmen vastly over-estimated their success, believing they had crippled the main US fleet, and further airstrikes were sent out to 'finish off' what was left. The result was another slaughter of Japanese aircraft, some 300 being shot down in two days, destroying the Imperial Navy's carefully reconstituted naval air wings.

The Philippines were defended by some 350,000 Japanese troops commanded by General Yamashita, the 'Tiger of Malaya'. Some 700 US warships were heading towards them, containing the 200,000 men of General Krueger's Sixth Army protected by a vast array of naval gun and airpower. This force landed on Leyte Island on 20 October as scheduled after a massive preliminary bombardment to be met by comparatively light resistance by the 16,000-strong Leyte garrison. Two days later General MacArthur waded ashore fulfilling his promise to return, accompanied by the Philippines President Sergio Osmena.

The Japanese High Command reacted to this major crisis by putting the 'Sho', the boldly named 'Victory' Plan, into effect, designed to lure off the US carriers, the main enemy striking force, away from a critical landing, allowing the remainder of the Japanese fleet, now denuded of airpower, to attack the transports, isolate and defeat the landing. The Japanese Chief of Naval Staff Admiral Soemu Toyoda disposed the Northern Force, or Third Fleet, with the four remaining carriers (in fact scantily equipped with aircraft and trained pilots) to steam from Japan towards Luzon and draw off the US carriers. Meanwhile Admiral Kurita's Centre Force with the enormous gunpower of two super-battleships, three other battleships and twelve cruisers, was to traverse the San Bernadino Strait. They would join Admiral Nishimura's smaller force to force the Sungao Strait between Mindanao and Leyte and smash the landing.

The battle opened on 23 October as Halsey took the bait and withdrew to chase Ozawa's decoy fleet. The smaller Japanese attack force was engaged by Admiral Kinkaid's Seventh Fleet and virtually wiped out in a ship to ship surface action. Meanwhile the Japanese Centre Force was engaged by aircraft of Admiral Mitcher's Task Force, part of Halsey's Third Fleet in the Suibuyan Sea, and the huge battleship *Musahi* was sunk. Halsey believed Kurita was now out of the fight and continued to chase Ozawa's decoy fleet northwards while the Centre Force turned round and sailed unopposed through the unguarded San Bernadino Strait, turning south and catching Rear Admiral Clifton Sprague's escort carrier group off the coast of the island of Samar.

Both commanders were taken off guard by this sudden encounter but Sprague reacted first, retreating into a provident rain squall while urgently recalling aircraft engaged on ground attack missions. Displaying outstanding seamanship, Sprague's force managed to hold off the powerful Japanese fleet until Kurita, fearing heavier air attack and not knowing how weak was the opposition, broke off and directed his scattered formations to regroup to the north. While Kurita and Sprague were duelling, Halsey's aircraft caught up with

Ozawa's decoy force, sinking four carriers (in fact virtually empty of aircraft), a cruiser and two destroyers. Halsey steamed on to bring the enemy within range of his massive battleship firepower and finish off the rest of Ozawa's fleet. At 20.00 hours Halsey picked up Kinkaid's report on Sprague's desperate fight, then at 10.00 came a strongly worded message from Nimitz at Pearl demanding explanation of Halsey's 'failure' to come to the rescue. Seething with frustration, Halsey raced south in time to catch a lone Japanese destroyer.

Kurita, believing himself to be confronting the main weight of the US fleet and informed of the destruction of Nisimura's Southern Force, had already turned back for the safety of Brunei Bay, negotiating the San Bernadino Strait once more without loss though harassed by returning aircraft from Halsey's Third Fleet. Meanwhile Sprague's escort carriers and the US Navy force returning from the fight in Surigao Strait were attacked by land based aircraft, including the first Kamikaze suicide attacks – which sank the escort carrier *St Lô* and damaged several other warships.

This Battle of Leyte Gulf (fought in fact entirely outside those waters) ended the Japanese Combined Fleet as a major fighting force – approximately 300,000 tons of warships were sunk and some 10,500 sailors and airmen of the Imperial Navy were killed. In this, the biggest naval battle ever fought, 282 warships were involved, 218 Allied (of which two were Australian) and 64 Japanese.

In spite of the shattering reverse at sea, there were still 60,000 troops on Leyte under the command of the formidable General Yamashita, victor of Malaya and Singapore. Resistance once again was fanatical, aided by the terrain and by tropical storms which turned dirt roads into cloying swamps. When the fighting on Leyte ended on 25 December 1944 the Japanese had suffered some 70,000 casualties, 48,000 of them dead, the Americans 15,584.

The strategy debate still had not abated. MacArthur wanted to land on the northern Philippine island of Luzon as soon as possible while Nimitz was arguing for a drive towards Formosa. Admiral King in Washington wanted to drive straight for the Japanese Home Islands. From November onwards, B-29 bombers based in the Marianas made direct raids on the Japanese mainland, the first daylight raid on Tokyo taking place on 24 November 1944. Navy, Army and Army Air Force each had their own route to victory. The Joint Chiefs of Staff directed that the two pronged attack should continue – Luzon would be the next target while Nimitz would attack Iwo Jima and Okinawa in the new year. Formosa and Japan itself were discounted for the time being.

In the struggle for Leyte, Japan had expended the mobile strikepower of her fleet and naval air force. However the Japanese grip on Burma had not been weakened and although the sea route to the 'Southern Resources Area', the oil rich East Indies still held virtually in their entirety, had been cut, a land route was still open through Indo-China. On the mainland of Asia Japan controlled a vast chunk of China, Korea and Manchuria garrisoned by the one million-strong Kwantung Army. The strategic offensive being waged by the long range B-29s from November 1944 was being faced by a dogged fighter defence inflicting a six per cent loss rate on the bombers.

It was clear therefore that, in spite of being battered back to the Home Islands, the ultimate assault on Japan would be appallingly costly; the invader would be met with even greater ferocity than that showed in the defence of a coral atoll a thousand miles from Honshu.

At the beginning of 1945 General Yamashita continued to show how deadly in the defence of Luzon. Lifted by the Seventh Fleet, the US Sixth Army moved from Leyte to land, on 9 January 1945, at Lingayen Gulf on the western coast of Luzon. Kamikaze attacks took a heavy toll of the US gunfire support ships but the ground forces got ashore without serious opposition. The Japanese retreated north making stubborn stands at Clark Field and fighting the northern mountains until the very end. When Yamashita surrendered on 2 September 1945 he still had an organized force of some 50,000 men. A naval garrison contested the capital Manila for two weeks of suicidal house to house fighting, finally subdued on 4 March. The Bataan peninsula was sealed off at the end of January while a task force seized the Subic Bay area on 30 January to prevent the Japanese repeating the US defence of the peninsula as in 1942. Corregidor, the fortified island in Manila Bay, held out in another suicidal defence, captured with most of its garrison sealed into the blown up tunnels of Malinta Hill. Four hundred and seventeen Japanese dead were counted – just 17 prisoners were taken. The campaign on Luzon cost the US 7933 dead and 32,723 wounded but the ratio of battle deaths was colossally in the attacker's favour, 24 to 1, with almost 200,000 Japanese killed.

Iwo Jima was to become another epic of ferocious resistance. Possession of this eight square mile dot on the map was deemed necessary as a forward air base but it was defended by 22,000 Japanese emplaced in an elaborate network of tunnels and bunkers. Total US Marine casualties were 6981 dead and 18,070 wounded. Only 212 of the Japanese garrison surrendered and many more lay uncounted sealed underground.

The final preliminary to the invasion of Japan was the possession of the Ryukus with Okinawa, the main island, the principal objective. Fighting continued for three months while Kamikaze attacks punished the Allied naval forces supporting the landings. A Royal Navy carrier force had meantime joined operations in the Pacific and their steel decked ships suffered less damage than the US wooden decked carriers. On 6–7 April the Japanese launched Operation 'Ten-Go', a co-ordinated naval and air suicide mission with a ferocious air assault by Kamikazes joined by the huge battleship *Yamato*, sailing south crammed with ammunition but without air cover and with only enough fuel for a one-way journey. Aircraft of Admiral Mitcher's Task Force 58 found the *Yamato* before her 18-inch guns could be brought to bear off Okinawa. Pounded by bombs and torpedoes, the superbattleship sank on 7 April with 2488 of her crew.

The defender of Okinawa, Lt. General Mitsuru Ushijima, committed suicide on 22 June as last resistance ended.

Japanese losses on Okinawa totalled 107,500 known dead and many thousands more sealed in caves. US casualties were 7374 killed and 32,056 wounded, the US Navy losing some 500 dead and 4600 wounded.

Okinawa was the end of the island hopping campaign. From the captured airstrips on Iwo Jima, P-47 and P-51 fighters could now operate as fighter escorts for the B-29s pounding Japan, the bombers themselves could use it as an emergency airfield and the loss rate fell dramatically. In March 1945 a new phase of strategic bombing opened; fifteen square miles of Tokyo were devastated in a firestorm raid on the night of 9–10 March, with 83,000 people killed and nearly 100,000 injured. In a protracted and deadly campaign the industrial areas of Japan's five largest cities, Tokyo, Nagoya, Kobe, Osaka and Yokohama, were completely destroyed.

The blockade of Japan had done more than militarily isolate the remaining garrisons on the defence perimeter. US submarines had sunk more than 4,800,000 ton of merchant shipping and 540,000 tons of warships. Now US submarines roamed inshore round the coasts of Japan itself, joined by aerial mining (starkly named Operation Starvation) carrier aircraft and US surface warships enforcing a total blockade of Japan's seventy million people.

On 26 July 1945 the Allies published the Potsdam Declaration drafted at the last meeting of the wartime Allies. Japan was warned that if they did not surrender immediately it would mean the 'inevitable and complete destruction of the Japanese homeland'. MacArthur and Nimitz's staffs meanwhile were drawing up plans for invasions of the Japanese home islands – Operation Olympic to strike southern Kyushu in November 1945 and Operation Coronet to be mounted in October 1945-March 1946 against Honshu with Tokyo as the target. Allied land sea and air forces were to be redeployed from Europe for the final assault on Japan – to face a still undefeated army of 4 million.

Of course it never happened. The war's greatest and most terrible secret was revealed on 6 August when Hiroshima was attacked with the first operational atomic

101

weapon. Two-thirds of the city were destroyed, 78,150 killed and as many injured. Three days later Nagasaki was attacked and 40,000 more civilians killed. Two days after the devastation of Hiroshima, the Soviet Union declared war and began an invasion of Manchuria, rapidly driving the Japanese across the Yalu river into Korea.

On 10 August the Japanese Emperor communicated the decision to surrender. On 15 August Japanese forces throughout Asia and the farflung bypassed garrisons in the Western Pacific laid down their arms. General MacArthur flew in on 28 August to begin the occupation while Allied ships anchored in Tokyo Bay. On 2 September, aboard Nimitz's flagship, the battleship USS *Missouri*, General MacArthur received the official Japanese surrender.

The Road to Stalingrad

After the failure before Moscow, Hitler sacked Brauchitsch, chief of OKH, and took personal command of the German Army. Between December and January 1942 the commanders of the Army Groups that had embarked on Barbarossa were all replaced and 35 other generals including Guderian and Hoepner were dismissed. Hitler believed it was his willpower and his 'no retreat' order after Moscow that had saved the German army from catastrophe and the bungling of defeatist generals. From henceforth OKH, Army High Command, would be concerned only with operations on the Eastern Front while OKW, Supreme Command of the Wehrmacht, became ground forces command in every operational area of German military power – no single organization possessed command over the army overall except in his – the Führer's – person. From now on Hitler's will, and Hitler's obsessions, would dominate operations on the Eastern Front and in the end contribute to the destruction of the German armed forces by the Soviet army.

At the outset of 1942 both OKW and the Soviet High Command planned ambitious offensive operations. The Soviets struck first, with the intent of relieving Leningrad and Sevastopol and of recapturing Kharkov. All three failed and at Kharkov in the south, the Soviets lost 600 tanks after Timoshenko's rigid and clumsy attack which drove smack into Kleist's Panzer Army at Kramatorsk, itself preparing for an offensive. After Kharkov and the loss of another 250,000 prisoners, the Soviet crisis was as grave as during the winter with the Germans at the gates of Moscow.

It was here, in the south, that Hitler planned a huge new summer offensive – 'Fall Blaue' (Case Blue), a drive through the Caucasus to the Caspian Sea to seize along the way the oilfields of Grozny and Maikop. Covering the flank of the main German drive was an industrial city and centre of key communication standing where the river Volga took a great bend. It was called Stalingrad.

Army Group South commanded by Field Marshal von Bock launched its attack on 28 June, smashing eastwards from the vicinity of Kursk to capture Voronezh on the upper Volga. Attempts to encircle and destroy the Soviet defenders 1941-style however failed and the Russian army was able to pull back in time.

On 13 July, Hitler recast the plans, dismissing Bock once again and dividing his forces into two new Army Groups, 'A' under General Weichs ordered to protect the flank by an active manoeuvre codenamed Operation Siegfried and Army Group 'B' under Field Marshall von List which would advance into the Caucasus (Operation Edelweiss). For both operations there were 68 divisions including nine armoured and seven motorized but one-third were Rumanian, Hungarian, Slovak and Italian. The plan involved lengthening the German front in the south from 500 miles (Orel to Taganrog on the Sea of Azov) into a huge bulging perimeter of 3000 miles. Simultaneously Hitler ordered the withdrawal of XI Army from the south to attack Leningrad and the withdrawal of two crack divisions to retrain with armour in the west.

Nevertheless the two army groups began their drive on 13 July, but the tug between Siegfried, the punch towards Stalingrad, and Edelweiss into the Caucasus, was stretching open the front and it allowed the bulk of the Soviet troops

103

caught in the Don bend to escape. The Caucasus drive had one armoured group, Kleist's I Panzer Army, to invade the Kuban area. Hoth's IV Panzer Army, to the north of von Paulus' VI Army plodding towards Stalingrad, was switched south on 9 July on Hitler's orders, transferring it to Army Group A's command on the 13th. The diversion was a fatal mistake. Without IV Panzer Army, Army Group B could make no progress towards Stalingrad. In the south, the extra tanks did little to help Kleist's Panzer Army coming east from Rostov and the transfer merely caused chaos on the inadequate Russian roads.

On 23 July Hitler changed the scope of operation yet again with Baku as the target in the south and Stalingrad in the north, with the aim of breaking the Soviet line of communication and then advancing on to Astrakhan along the line of the Volga. List's Army Group A captured Rostov on 23 July, crossed the Don on a wide front and burst into the Caucasus. Maikop with its oil fell on 9 August and within 12 days the foothills of the Caucasus mountains were reached. Then the pace slowed dramatically. It took another 85 days to advance a further 125 miles to Orzhonikidze, the most southerly point reached; List's armies were now drawing their supplies over four meagre cattle tracks. German mountain troops might swaggeringly plant the swastika on Mount Elbrus, but the mountain passes were blocked. There would be no further advance.

While Army Group A pushed deep into the Caucasus, the battle for Stalingrad was developing. It need never have taken place had Hitler adhered to the original plans as it would have fallen in mid July, but still the Russians had been badly mauled and all through August they simply fell back. Army Group B held an ever-lengthening north-eastern flank while its main element, von Paulus's VI Army, moved east across the Don to begin the direct attack on the city from the end of August. When Paulus began the attack, the defence of the city was in fact quite weak; the defending commander General Chuikov had something like one hundred thousand men to four times the German strength. The overall Soviet commander General Zhukov, who had directed the counter-offensive before Moscow, meanwhile built up a great offensive force on the German's exposed Don flank. In the embattled city the defenders of Stalingrad created an epic of resistance, fighting with ferocious tenacity to cling onto pockets on the west bank of the river, at the Krasny Octobyr factory, the Barikaddy artillery factory, at the southern railway station, at the 'tennis racket' marshalling yards, street by street, house by house, room by room until by 8 November all but a tenth of the city, now a monstrous wilderness of charred rubble and twisted metal, was in German hands.

By early November, as winter drew on, Paulus need have looked no further than his long exposed north-eastern flank, held by Hungarian, Italian and Rumanian 'allied' forces, and at the stalemate in the Caucasus to see how exposed his Army in Stalingrad was.

On 19 November Zhukov, commanding four Soviet fronts, launched Operation Uran, timed so that the first frosts would bring hard ground and thus mobility for the Soviets' 900 tanks. The Voronezh, South-west and Don Fronts punched out north of the city and Vatutin's Stalingrad Front from the south. On 23 November Soviet spearheads met at the Kalach bridge, which was seized intact, snapping shut on the 250,000 men of VI Army.

With a further million men in the Caucasus now imperilled, Hitler gambled again, ordering Paulus to stay put while a relief attack was mounted.

Manstein was hurriedly rushed from the Leningrad Front to command 'Army Group Don' hastily constituted out of part of Army Group A. Manstein finally managed to organize three understrength panzer divisions and launched a relief attempt (operation Winter Tempest) on 12 December. Paulus, doggedly obeying Hitler's no retreat order, refused to break out and meet it and the relief attempt collapsed 35 miles short of its goal.

Hitler ordered Paulus to fight on, to the last round and the last man. VI Army was dwindling fast – freezing, starving and running out of ammunition while the promised Luftwaffe airlift could not deliver more than a token 70 tons a day. When Paulus's last airfield was captured, VI Army's fate was sealed, but meanwhile seven Soviet armies were tied down at Stalingrad and could not prevent the Germans evacuating the Caucasus and saving something from the shambles of the Southern Front.

On 30 January the remnants of VI Army were cut in two. On 2 February Paulus surrendered. A hundred and fifty thousand were dead, over 91,000 went into a fearsome captivity from which only a few thousand would eventually return.

Kursk

After the catastrophe at Stalingrad, German Army Group South seemed broken and the whole German position in the southern Soviet Union shattered. Kharkov fell in February 1943 but Field Marshal Erich von Manstein, in one of the war's great feats of generalship, launched the hastily constituted IV Panzer Army in a brilliant 'backhand stroke' to deflect the Soviet onrush. On 14 March Kharkov fell to the Germans once again, the SS Panzer Corps with their new Tiger tanks attacking while further north the Grossdeutschland panzer grenadier division took Belgorod, both actions bringing the German line deep into a Soviet salient centred on Kursk. The third phase of Manstein's plan, to pinch out the salient, came to nothing when Army Group Centre proved unable to attack from the north and the spring thaw slowed movement down to a crawl.

As summer approached the commanders of both battered armies, Soviet and German, peered at that bulge on the map round Kursk and its strategic temptations. The new German Chief of Staff at OKH, Colonel General Kurt Zeitzler, proposed an attack first – General Model's IX Army from Army Group Centre would strike the salient's northern flank to meet Hoth's IV Panzer Army from Manstein's Army Group South moving up from the south in a vast double envelopment aiming to repeat the huge haul of prisoners and equipment that marked the first months of the German invasion. The Soviets had learned many lessons since then however and, as at Moscow, the hand of Zhukov would direct the defence – Rokossovsky's Central Front held the north of the salient, with the Bryansk (Popov) and the Western Front (Sokolovsky) stretching out on the flank to the north, while Vatutin's Voronezh Front held the southern face of the bulge with the South-western Front continuing its line south. The Reserve Front (renamed the Steppe Front) was also to be emplaced inside the salient.

Stalin possessed from 'Lucy' (the code name of Rudolf Roessler, the Swiss spy) very high grade intelligence appraisals of German intentions. Zhukov and his commanders pointed out the danger building up at Kursk and the fact that German forces would be too weak to attack anywhere else in strength. While Soviet strategic objectives were redefined, it was decided to reinforce the bulge and there to stand and fight – digging in on a huge scale in heavily mined deep defensive zones swept by massed anti-tank firepower.

Confronted with this kind of defence, the days of Blitz-krieg were over. Instead the German armour would attack frontally using a technique called 'Panzerkeil', an armoured wedge, to break through with the heaviest armour (Tigers and the new heavily armoured Ferdinand tank destroyers) at its tip and lighter Panthers and Mark IVs staged behind. Throughout June the forces on both sides grew, bringing together over two million men, more than 500 aircraft, 30,000 guns and over 6000 tanks and assault guns, all setting the stage for the greatest tank battle of the war.

Operation Zitadelle – 'Citadel' as the Germans code-named the attack on Kursk, began on 5 July. Model's IX Army punched into the northern face of the salient but broke down in Rokossovsky's defences. Large numbers of powerful German tanks were stranded helplessly in the second line of defences while the German infantry struggled to catch up and save them from close-in Soviet tank killing teams. At the village of Pnyri straddling the Kursk-Orel railway line, the Germans threw in everything down to the last reserves yet failed to break through. Along a 25-mile front in the north the battle raged but there was no German success, all for 50,000 German dead, 500 aircraft and some 400 tanks and assault guns destroyed. On 11 July, Model's attack ran out just a matter of hours before Operation Kutuzov, a counterattack by five Soviet armies, broke through north of Orel in a move which threatened to cut off the Germans' own salient.

In the south that same day, the greatest tank battle in history was taking place after a week of intense fighting in which the German armies had struck deep into the defence. The panzer wedges had advanced almost shoulder to shoulder, smashing through defensive lines and blasting Soviet armour out of their path. Hoth's IV Panzer Army now tried to break through to the village of Prokohrovka whereafter open country would allow full operational mobility. General Vatutin had already committed Central Front's armoured reserve by digging in the tanks of First Tank Army in an attempt to use their firepower hull down (just the turret showing) after a mauling in a confused tank battle south of Oboyan. With committed Soviet armour lacking now in numbers and mobility, Zhukov threw in two armies from the Steppe Front, including General Rotmistrov's Fifth Guards Tank Army.

On the morning of 12 July this force, 850 tank and assault gun-strong, met Hoth's panzers head on, coincidentally renewing their attack on Prokhorovka. There was no preordained plan; T-34s driven at full speed slammed into an SS Panzer Corps. More than a thousand tanks were milling on the dust-shrouded steppe, tearing each other with high velocity hardened steel sometimes at point blank range. By nightfall the slaughter was over – more than 300 German tanks burned on the steppe, more than half of Fifth Guards Army with them.

In spite of continued German stabs at the defences, Zitadelle was effectively over. On 12 July Hitler proposed withdrawing forces from the east to meet the new Anglo-American front in Sicily. Model's IX Army in the north was menaced by the Soviet counterattack and attacks in the south flickered out on 23 July. Now it was the Soviets' turn. On 3 August they counterattacked in the south, capturing

Belgorod on the 5th and Kharkov once again on the 25th. Twenty German panzer divisions had been ground down at Kursk. Soviet losses in men and material had been colossal but they would be made up.

Never again would the German Army have the strategic offensive initiative, never again would they choose where to fight. Some of the Soviet tanks that fought at Kursk bore crude propaganda slogans such as 'We will chase the fascist beast to its lair'. In that late summer of 1943 began the chase that would end in Berlin.

Tunisia, Sicily, Italy

At the December 1941 Arcadia conference in Washington, the new wartime allies, Britain and the USA, agreed on the long term strategic objective of 'closing the ring around Germany'. The southern component should be the Mediterranean, and that meant clearing North Africa first, where the British position was still in dire jeopardy. The British success at El Alamein in November 1942 was followed by the Anglo-American Torch landings in Vichy-French controlled north-west Africa beginning on 8 November 1942, which encountered significant but spasmodic resistance. The German reaction was to move into the unoccupied zone of France (Operation Anton) and to seize vital airfields in Vichy Tunisia. By December Axis forces had stabilized a western defence line and frustrated Allied plans of quick victory in North Africa. Rommel meanwhile had skilfully kept his forces intact during the long retreat from El Alamein. By 24 February 1943 the Afrika Korps was behind a strong defensive position called the Mareth Line and it had been able to detach forces to the rear to give the advancing Americans a bloody nose at Kasserine Pass and Gafsa.

On 6 March Rommel left North Africa, this time for good, General von Armin taking overall command in Tunisia and the Italian General Messe taking over the Mareth Front. Men and equipment meanwhile were flown in to the

109

Tunisian 'bridgehead' or arrived in ships running the Allied naval blockade.

The British assault on the Mareth defences began on 20 March with superior forces against an opponent who was still able to counterattack and escape encirclement. On 6 April Eighth Army crossed the Wadi Akarit after intense fighting and by 28 April it had reached Enfidaville, joining up with First Army. General Alexander, now in overall command of the Allied armies, called off these uncoordinated attacks, planning rather a joint operation by First and Eighth Armies. With this concentration of forces, the Axis defensive perimeter began to roll up – Tunis and Bizerta fell on 7 May, the Cape Bon peninsula was cut off on 11 May and Axis resistance ended, the Italian Navy making no attempt at evacuation. In total more than 275,000 Axis prisoners were taken, including the generals who led them.

In the 27 months of desert warfare since Graziani's attack on Egypt, Axis losses in North Africa in casualties and prisoners amounted to an estimated 620,000, one-third German. British losses amounted to 220,000 overall while from November 1942 to May 1943 US forces suffered some 18,000 casualties and the French around 20,000.

The Tunisian campaign blooded the US forces and provided the prototype for future Allied joint operations, but the clearing of North Africa posed new strategic problems. Where to strike next? – should landings be made in the Balkans, in Italy or should the Mediterranean front be held defensively while Allied power built up for an attack on north-west Europe, opening a 'Second Front' as Stalin insisted, where the main body of the enemy might be met and ground down?

Sicily

These tensions became clear at the Churchill-Roosevelt Casablanca Conference, which began on 14 January 1943 when 'unconditional surrender' became enunciated as the Allied war aim. First the enemy had to be brought to grips, but where? Sicily seemed a promising, if limited, objective completing the strategic intention of clearing the Mediterranean sea route and possibly gaining a springboard for a wholesale invasion of Italy itself. In fact Operation Husky, the invasion of Sicily, was a remarkably well planned and effective operation, bigger in its assault phase indeed than the Normandy landings the following year.

The seaborne invaders gained almost complete tactical surprise but the airborne component went badly awry. The plan was for Montgomery's Eighth Army, who had landed in the south-east of the island, to drive for Messina in the top left hand corner but the British drive was held by fierce German resistance at Catania. Patton's US Seventh Army meanwhile was sweeping through Western Sicily; it took Palermo on 22 July and began an advance along the northern coast road aided by small-scale amphibious operations. Those Italians who had not surrendered began an exodus across the Straits of Messina on 3 August, followed by the Germans from 11–17 August. US casualties were 7319 in the 38 days it took to capture Sicily, British 9353. Axis losses including prisoners were over 160,000 including 32,000 Germans.

The invasion of Sicily brought another result, in that it inspired the conspirators against the Italian dictator Mussolini finally on 24–25 July 1943 to act and remove him from power. The new head of government, Marshal Badoglio, began to put out secret peace feelers. If the Italians, with their position in the Mediterranean and Balkans, should indeed defect from the Axis, here was a major strategic opportunity. But there was no ready made plan for an invasion of Italy itself while already it was being relegated to a secondary theatre. Never again would the resources concentrated for Husky be available on that scale while the strategic intention of a campaign in Italy would progressively become to tie down German military assets which otherwise might resist the cross-Channel invasion of France.

Nevertheless Operation Baytown mounted on 3 September 1943 on the toe of Italy brought British troops back to the European mainland almost forty months since

111

Dunkirk. On 8 September Operation Avalanche was launched – General Mark Clark's US Fifth Army landed on the beaches of Salerno. The Italians meanwhile published the armistice on 8 September, the Italian fleet sailed from La Spezia to anchor under the guns of Malta while the German theatre commander, Luftwaffe Field Marshal Albert Kesselring, moved rapidly to disarm Italian land forces. Kesselring met the Salerno landing with all his available reserves and pinned the Allied forces down to four narrow unconnected beaches. By the 12th six German divisions had gathered to mount a ferocious counterattack which seemed set to throw the invaders back into the sea until naval gunfire, air support and air and seaborne reinforcements held the line.

Meanwhile Montgomery's Eighth Army was cautiously advancing through the mountainous Calabrian countryside harried by a single German battle group. Simultaneously with Avalanche, a British division had landed at Taranto (Operation Slapstick) sailing straight into the harbour on warships of Admiral Cunningham's battle fleet.

On 16 September Montgomery's army linked up with the south-eastern tip of the Salerno beach-head and Kesselring began disengaging. Through September and the first week of October, the Allies consolidated their grip on southern Italy; on 27 September, Eighth Army took Foggia with its strategic airfield, on 2 October, Fifth Army took the great port of Naples, and from 11 September to 4 October Free French forces cleared Corsica.

From 12 October to 14 November, progress bogged down as Fifth Army forced the Volturno and Eighth Army crossed the Trigano on the Adriatic side of the peninsula as autumn turned to winter and rains drenched the mountain trails. On 15 November, Alexander ordered a halt to rest and regroup.

By the time the Allied Fifth Army Group resumed its advance on Rome, Kesselring had now established a formidable defensive zone called the Winter Line or Gustav Line running along the rivers Garigliano, Rapido and Sangro. The Liri Valley leading through the hills was blocked by a mountain crowned by the famous Benedictine monastery of Monte Cassino.

While Clark's Fifth Army struggled forward, the British Eighth Army prepared to assault the eastern flank on the River Sangro but cold and bad weather which turned mountain streams into torrents, and determined German resistance, halted the Allies in a winter stalemate along the length of the Gustav Line.

With the narrow mountainous waist of Italy seemingly set to turn any Allied advance into a bloody crawl an obvious tactic was to mount outflanking amphibious operations but already the demands of Overlord, the planned Normandy invasion, were pulling men and amphibious lift away. In December both Eisenhower and Montgomery left the theatre while veteran divisions were pulled out of the line to be replaced by a polyglot variety of forces and nationalities, including Poles, Brazilians, Indian, French, Italian and New Zealand troops.

These were the forces which now invested Cassino, making attack after bloody attack without success. A huge aerial bombardment on 15 February 1944 reduced the monastery to rubble, to the advantage of the defenders who fought for every metre of churned stone.

Meanwhile an amphibious seaborne operation to turn the Gustav Line had been mounted at Anzio, 60 miles to the north of Cassino. Complete tactical surprise was achieved and within two days a seven-mile-deep bridgehead had been achieved – but the Allied commander, Major General John Lucas, with his commander General Clark concurring, did not strike out for the Alban hills, nor indeed for Rome itself, but waited for heavy equipment to be brought ashore. The delay allowed Kesselring to stage massive counterattacks with an extemporized XIV Army plus fresh divisions sent south on Hitler's direct orders. From March to May there was stalemate at Anzio. Lucas was replaced with General Lucius Truscott who was able to blunt a major German counterattack on 6 March. Anzio, which was meant to be a daring operational manoeuvre to abnegate a bloody frontal assault on the Gustav Line, turned into another

113

arena for deadly positional warfare. Not until 23 May was there a breakout and that after 23,860 US and 9203 British casualties had been taken off the beaches.

The Gustav Line was turned only after direct frontal assault. Alexander switched the bulk of Eighth Army from the Adriatic to the Cassino sector. French, Polish, British, US, and Canadian units made the assault on 11 May, the Poles planting their flag in the rubble of Cassino on 17 May 1944. On the 23rd, Truscott at last broke out of the Anzio beach-head linking with Fifth Army two days later. With their communications under heavy air attack (Operation Strangle March–May 1944) X and XIV German Armies were threatened with encirclement, but General Clark instead drove straight for Rome, entering it on 4 June as the main bulk of the retiring Germans slipped away.

In June 1944 there seemed to be every chance for the Allies to drive rapidly into northern Italy, even to break out into south-eastern Europe and the Balkans.

Alexander's forces however were depleted once again for the invasion of southern France (Operations Anvil and Dragoon) launched on 18 August and, as Fifteenth Army Group lost seven divisions, Kesselring gained eight more, drawn in from the Balkans and Germany. In a series of brilliantly directed delaying actions, Kesselring retired to a new defensive line astride the Apennines, the 'Gothic Line' extending across the peninsula south of Bologna.

The Allies planned to batter their way through with Clark's Fifth Army striking for Bologna in the centre while Eighth Army would roll up the Adriatic flank. The attack began on 25 August but Kesselring and the weather combined to deny the Allies a decisive breakthrough. General Leese's Eighth Army took Rimini on 20 September but the autumn mud slowed progress to a crawl. Clark stopped short of Bologna at the end of October having committed all his reserves and Eighth Army came to a dead stop in December with the capture of Ravenna. It was the second winter stalemate of the Italian campaign.

It lasted indeed until April 1945. Kesselring was succeeded in March by General Heinrich von Vietinghoff in command of German Army Group South-west holding the Gothic Line while the RSI (Repubblica Sociale Italiana, the rump of fascist Italy) 'Ligurian Army' held the Alpes Maritimes on the French frontier with some German stiffening.

In fact Alexander had only 17 against 23 German and four Italian divisions but after reorganization and re-equipment, a vigorous and skilful assault was launched on 9 April 1945. Eighth Army attacked using amphibious vehicles across Lake Comaccio, Fifth Army attacking five days later. By 23 April both armies were across the Po, Vietinghoff's X Army streaming north, abandoning their heavy equipment south of the river. From 20 April to 2 May the pursuit continued, US armour driving through Milan up to Lake Garda. On the far left the US 92nd division took Genoa on 28 April, meeting French troops advancing from Monaco. The Eighth Army's pursuit swept through Verona, Padua and Venice, crossing the Piave on 29 April. The Italian Resistance in the north rose in general revolt harassing the retreating Germans, stringing up the dead Mussolini by the feet in a Milan garage on 28 April. On 29 April Vietinghoff agreed a general surrender effective 2 May, without resort to Hitler, and US forces reached the Brenner pass on 4 May while New Zealanders of Eighth Army were already in Trieste.

The Italian campaign ended without a breakout by the western Allies into south-eastern Europe, and thus the Soviets reached Vienna first. But had it been a sideshow campaign as the bitter Song of the Eighth Army self-mockingly claimed – 'we are the D-Day Dodgers who fought in Italy'? It was certainly as ferocious and bloody as any other theatre of war but had the main body of the enemy been decisively engaged? Of the 127 divisions holding the front line of Fortress Europe from Norway to the Aegean at the time of D-Day only 22 were tied down in Italy and the 30 Allied divisions employed to do this might have seemed a poor investment of assets. However, on several occasions, the Italian theatre was bled of resources when a concerted Allied effort might have denied the Germans their two winters of resistance.

D-Day

The entry of the United States into the war, Roosevelt's 'Germany first' policy and the gradual mastery of the U-Boats in the Atlantic brought the prospect of Anglo-American power intervening on the continent of Europe in strength and opening a second front to relieve the beleaguered Soviets. But where?

Despite early optimism it was not until November 1942, against a soft target in Vichy North Africa, that US ground forces first met the European enemy in battle. Even at that stage it was hoped that a direct invasion of Hitler's 'Fortress Europe' would take place decisively in 1943. When Axis forces collapsed in North Africa, the German Army was still on the offensive in the Soviet Union, even after Stalingrad, though the great tank battle of Kursk would rob them of the strategic initiative on the Eastern Front forever. But politically the Soviets were still fighting for their lives and it was obvious in mid-1943 that the Western Allies could not just stand idly by. Hence the invasion of Sicily and thereafter Italy in summer 1943 which, if it did not bring the main body of the enemy to grips, did distract forces from the Eastern Front.

Through the spring of 1944 the clamour for a second front (Italy aside) grew ever greater but a mass sea and airborne opposed landing would, technically and operationally, always be a tremendous gamble. If the invasion failed on the beaches the ability of the Western Allies to intervene in the Russo-German war in Europe decisively could be discounted.

German indecisiveness certainly helped; there was disagreement in the High Command as to where the first blow would fall – in France almost certainly but would it be the Pas de Calais area or in Normandy – or might it come in Norway or the Balkans? The western European coastline was thus defended along its entire enormous length while there was further disagreement as to whether it was better to concentrate on smashing the invasion on the beaches or to keep powerful reserves inland. Meanwhile the efforts to fortify the coastline went on under the auspices of *Organisation Todt*, the German construction operation, and hundreds of thousands of workers, willing and otherwise, laboured to fashion millions of tons of steel and concrete into a continuous linear fortress.

Against this the Allies would pitch a great effort of preparation and planning, individual courage and operational boldness plus dramatic technical innovations such as specialized assault engineer tanks and the artificial harbours codenamed 'Mulberry'. Planning began in January 1943 when a skeleton Anglo-US staff was set up. The concept of a full scale invasion of France was agreed at the May 1943 Washington Conference, codenamed Operation Overlord, and set for May 1944.

In August 1943 COSSAC (Chief of Staff to the Supreme Allied Commander) submitted a draft plan to the Quebec conference which was approved. At the end of the year General Dwight D. Eisenhower was appointed Supreme Allied Commander of the whole operation, to be joined by Air Chief Marshal Sir Arthur Tedder as his Deputy, General Walter Bedell Smith as Chief of Staff, Admiral Sir Bertram Ramsay and Air Chief Marshal Sir Trafford Leigh Mallory as C-in-Cs Allied naval and air forces respectively. There was no parallel Allied land force supreme commander although General Bernard Montgomery, recalled from command of Eighth Army in Italy, would have operational control of land forces during the invasion opening phase as Commander of Twenty-First Army Group.

While the COSSAC plan set Normandy as the target, Montgomery manned it with more force applied on a broader front with two or possibly three airborne divisions holding the flanks of a five divisional assault frontage.

By May 1944 Eisenhower had shaped the final plans and Monday 5 June had been selected as the date for their execution. In essence the plan envisaged seaborne landings on five main beaches. Lt General Omar Bradley's First US

117

Army would land on Utah Beach north-west of the Carentan estuary, and on Omaha Beach to its west. US airborne forces would be dropped inland to secure the western flank. To the east General Sir Miles Dempsey's British Second Army (which included a Canadian Corps) would land on Gold, Juno and Sword Beaches west of the Orne river while airborne forces would land astride the Orne to protect the invasion's left flank. The front line combat strength of the invasion forces was 45 divisions, totalling with support units some one million men, with a further million in the logistic tail.

A massive and concerted air interdiction campaign in the weeks before D-Day (the 'Transportation Plan') had virtually cut the German forces in northern France in two for lack of communication. A skilful web of deception had spoon-fed German intelligence with misinformation as to where the invasion would fall and when. Of Field Marshal Rommel's Army Group B, VII army garrisoned the invasion area, four coast defence divisions, two infantry divisions, three panzer divisions and the Cherbourg garrison, while the bulk of XV Army with the mobile armoured reserve was in the Pas de Calais area tied down by Hitler's specific orders and by smashed communications.

On the night of 5–6 June, postponed for one day because of bad weather, British and US airborne troops took off for their vital destinations. Below them, into a stormy Channel, an armada of warships and landing craft was emerging from ports along the coast of west and south-east England. Minesweepers swept ten channels while naval escort groups kept what submarines that ventured near away from the packed troop transports.

The airborne arrived first. Men of the British Sixth Airborne Division, arriving by glider, seized bridges over the Caen Canal and the River Orne. Others landed east of the Orne with the missions of destroying the army artillery battery at Merville, the bridges over the Dives and of clearing an area north of Ranville for further air landings. On the bridgehead's eastern flank, the US 82nd and 101st Airborne Divisions landed in the south-east corner of the

Cotentin peninsula and, despite confused and bloody landings, managed to secure their objectives.

Thirty minutes before the first seaborne assault waves went in Allied warships opened a mighty big-gun bombardment of German shore positions, following up an equally ferocious aerial bombing. The great secret had been kept and the first the Germans knew the invasion was in progress was when the first shells fell on their bunkers. At Gold, Juno and Sword, the special assault armour of 79th Armoured Division proved very effective, clearing obstacles, and the British and Canadian troops of 1st and 30th Corps of Second Army got ashore and off the beaches with remarkably light casualties. On Utah Beach, Force U, the US 4th Infantry Division of First Army, made another swift and virtually bloodless landing but at Omaha Beach it was a different story. Amphibious tanks were launched too early and foundered. Without armoured support and pinned down by heavy defensive fire, the landings bogged down on the foreshore.

At last a combination of naval gunfire and bloody head-on assaults got Force O off the beaches at a cost of 1000 dead and 2000 wounded.

By nightfall on 6 June 1944, 156,000 Allied troops were ashore in Normandy and although Caen had not been taken in the first bound as planned, Fortress Europe had been cracked open.

Burma

Formerly a province of British India, Burma was detached administratively in 1937 and set up as a separate entity within the Commonwealth with a token self government. The first premier, Dr Ba Maw, resigned in 1939 over the Burma-China road, built to supply nationalist China. He escaped from British internment and was to head the collaborationist regime set up by Japan in occupied Burma.

Soon after the great offensive launched on 8 December 1941, a Japanese force moved into Thailand and the southern tip of Burma to cut British communications from

119

India to Malaya. On 12 January 1942, General Shojiro Iida's Fifteenth Army began operations in earnest, driving Lt General Thomas Hutton's force (the equivalent of two small divisions of British, Indian and Burmese troops) out of Moulmein with heavy losses. At the Battle of the Sittang, Japanese troops making outflanking moves through the jungle enveloped the retiring British from the rear causing them to lose their heavy equipment.

On 5 March Lt General Sir Harold Alexander arrived in the Burmese capital Rangoon to replace Hutton, but even with reinforcements from India, the new commander could do no more to hold the invaders. The newly arrived 63rd Indian Brigade was forced out of Pegu at the beginning of March and on the 7th Rangoon fell without fight. With their forces crumbling, the British accepted an offer of help from Chiang Kai Shek in the shape of the Chinese Fifth and Sixth 'Armies' under the command of the American Lt General Joseph Stilwell. Denied air cover the British and the Chinese were pushed back from successive defensive positions. Mandalay fell on 30 April, and, after a last desperate battle at Kalewa on 10 May, Major General William Slim now commanding the British Burma Corps led the remaining British troops across the Chindwin River and the hills of the Indian frontier while to the north and east the Chinese remnants were also scattering in full retreat.

For the rest of 1942 the Japanese consolidated their conquest – effectively four-fifths of Burma which cut off China from surface communication and menaced Britain's Indian Empire.

While preparing to meet an offensive in the dry season, General Sir Archibald Wavell as C-in-C India sought to mount a limited counter offensive as a morale boosting exercise. In the event the attempt to seize the port of Akyab on the Arakan coast was a disaster. The Japanese counterattacked, driving the British force back to where they started with heavy loss demonstrating once again the Japanese prowess in jungle fighting. On 8 February 1943 Brigadier Orde Wingate led his 77th Indian Brigade (later to be known as the Chindits) across the Chindwin River into Japanese controlled territory, the first long range penetration raid in Burma in an attempt to beat the Japanese at their own game of infiltration and encirclement. Militarily it was a failure – a few bridges were blown at the expense of one-third casualties and again the Japanese showed how tight was their grip.

In their frustration the Allied commanders could only disagree on what to do next. General Stilwell urged a re-invasion mounted by his rebuilt Chinese Army to reopen the land route (the air supply mounted over the 'Hump' could only supply a small proportion of China's logistic needs to stay in the fight). General Claire Chennault commanding the US Air Forces in China wanted the lion's share of 'Hump' supplies for his air fleets which alone he believed could push the Japanese back. Order was brought to these divergent interests on 15 November 1942 with the establishment of Allied South East Asia Command (SEAC) with Admiral Lord Louis Mountbatten as Supreme Commander. Stilwell was Deputy Commander but kept his other responsibilities as Chief of Staff to Chiang Kai Shek and C-in-C of US air and ground forces in S.E. Asia. The British Eastern Fourteenth Army was under the able command of Lt General Sir William Slim.

The Japanese meanwhile tightened their grip even further, building the 250-mile Burma Railway, and placed the country under Burma Area HQ, Lt General Masakazu Kawabe commanding who in turn was under the command of Field Marshal Count Terauchi with headquarters in Saigon, in overall command of the entire 'Southern Resources Area'. The Japanese Fifteenth Army including Subhas Chundra Bose's 'Indian National Army' held the Central Front, the Twenty-Eighth Army the Arakan Front and the Thirty-third Army faced Stilwell and the Chinese in the north. Kawabe directed Fifteenth Army to prepare a spoiling offensive into India, with the aim of seizing the Imphal-Kohima plain and cutting the railway into Assam which carried the supplies ferried to China over the Hump airlift and for Stilwell in north Burma. The first Japanese

121

blow however came in the south; General Sakurai launched an offensive in the Arakan against British XV Corps using the infiltration tactics that had worked so well in the first Arakan campaign. This time the British and Indian units stood and fought, supplied by airlift when cut off and eventually encircling the encirclers. Through March-April 1944 XV Corps fought its way towards Akyab when they were halted and forced to send reinforcements to meet the new crisis in central Burma as Lt General Renya Mataguchi's Fifteenth Army mounted its attack on India.

Already on the Central Front Wingate had launched the second Chindit expedition in March, flying into Japanese rear areas and establishing fortified blocking positions (code named 'Broadway', 'White City' and 'Blackpool') which were violently attacked by the Japanese who had initially been taken off balance. Wingate was killed in an air crash on 25 March at the height of the operation. Two brigades of the original five that had flown in were still combat-worthy and continued to fight with Stilwell.

Stilwell launched an offensive in the north with an American unit (Merrill's Marauders) operating in the Chindit fashion behind Japanese lines. His attack was a relative success, capturing Myitkina on 3 August, but disaster was looming.

The punishment meted out by Chennault's Fourteenth Army Air Force bombers led the Japanese to mount a new offensive in East China from May to November 1944 which overran seven out of twelve American airfields. As Chinese resistance crumbled, President Roosevelt urged Chiang to hand over full command authority to Stilwell. Chiang refused and to remove the political impasse Stilwell was recalled to the US and the China-Burma-India theatre dissolved, Major General Albert C. Wedemayer replacing Stilwell as commander of a new 'China Theatre'. Two divisions were airlifted back from the Burma front and revitalized the Chinese defence, holding any further Japanese advance. Lt General Daniel I. Sultan took over as field commander of the newly named 'India-Burma Theatre'.

The major crisis in the battle for Burma came on 8 March 1944 when the Japanese launched their offensive across the Indian frontier on the Central Front. Three Japanese divisions of General Mataguchi's Fifteenth Army crossed the Chindwin river on a broad front, heading for Kohima and Imphal, rapidly cutting off British outposts and investing the retreating British in their two objectives by 5 April. Keeping the besieged garrison supplied by air, General Slim began a drive with British XXXIII Corps to relieve Kohima, flying in reinforcements directly to besieged IV Corps at Imphal. Kohima was relieved on 20 April after a close run fight in which Allied air superiority had proved crucial. At Imphal the siege continued for 88 days, the Japanese holding off attacks from both the reinforced garrison and the relief column. Finally Fifteenth Army, unable to capture the supplies on which the plan depended, broke off – retreating across the Chindwin river leaving half their number dead in battle or of disease and starvation.

At the end of 1944 the Allies mounted a general offensive. To the south on the Arakan Front, Akyab was captured on 3 January 1945 and there was heavy fighting in the creeks and mangrove swamps of the coastal region – the so-called 'Chaung War'. On the Central Front the British Fourteenth Army crossed the Chindwin on 14 December, crossed the Irrawaddy on 14 January 1945 and finally took Meiktila on 4 March. A Japanese counterattack in an attempt to break out of the great trap Slim had sprung on the encircled Japanese Fifteenth and Thirty-third Armies was repulsed by 31 March by which time Mandalay had fallen.

On 1 May Rangoon fell without a fight and the battle for Burma was virtually over. The scattered remnants of several Japanese armies tried to fight their way back to Thailand only to be drowned in the Irrawaddy or Sittang rivers, swollen by the monsoon which broke at the beginning of May. While there were many small clashes, no more set piece actions occurred in the battle for Burma. Mountbatten's SEAC Headquarters now set to planning the reconquest of Singapore by amphibious landing, an operation that would be rendered unnecessary by Japan's surrender after the dropping of the atom bombs.

The Combined Bomber Offensive

Through the years running up to the outbreak of war a vigorous debate went on in military and political circles about the efficacy of strategic bombing, that is long range attacks on the enemy's heartland to attack his means to wage war and the will of his people to do it. Exaggerated fears about the power of the bomber and the threat to civilian populations contributed much to the climate of appeasement and to Hitler's bloodless conquests of 1936–9. When war finally came, it was thought that many thousands of civilians would be slaughtered in opening mass attacks on capital cities. In the event the Germans never developed an effective strategic bombing arm. The night Blitz on Britain was a failure, critical Soviet targets were out of reach, and the V1/V2 offensive of 1944–5 did little to alter the outcome of the war in Europe. In the event it was the Western Allies, Britain and the USA, who built up a massive bomber arm and used it to pound Germany by day and by night fulfilling those pre-war prophecies of massive civilian casualties, if not without cost to the men of RAF Bomber Command and USAAF, the United States Army Air Force who prosecuted this campaign. In the Far East, with Japan brought in range from November 1944, again the USAAF waged long range strategic warfare culminating in the atomic bombs attacks on Hiroshima and Nagasaki which ended the war and heralded a new, terrible kind of confrontation.

All the aircraft available to RAF Bomber Command in September 1939 were twin-engined, grouped in 17 squadrons totalling some 272 aircraft, and for the first eight months of war this force was aimed exclusively at military targets and severely mauled in daylight operations for its pains. Meanwhile Whitley bombers were operating at night on leaflet propaganda raids on population centres and although derided as useless, this groping around in the dark without radio navigation aid portended things to come. With the Germans on the Channel coast, leaflet raids became a thing of the past and bombers were the only means available to Britain to hit back at the enemy. At first attempts were made to hit critical targets, particularly oil targets at night, but the results were worse than disappointing. Unable to hit anything other than sprawling area targets, the emphasis began to shift to cities for cities' sake with the German will to make war as the target.

British experience in the Blitz showed that will to resist hardened rather than weakened under air attack but the War Cabinet, on the best economic and political advice, chose to believe that a full scale bombing policy was both justified and would prove effective. After 22 June 1941 it was the only way to bring direct military force to bear to bring aid to the British Commonwealth's only ally, the Soviet Union.

In the first months of 1941 Bomber Command was tied up trying to eliminate the German Navy's warships at Brest, and ports and harbours in northern Germany. Attempts to disrupt the transport system in the Ruhr and draw back some of the tactical airpower deployed on the Eastern Front were unsuccessful and a serious scientific study made in August 1941 revealed that only one bomber in ten was dropping its bombs even five miles from its prescribed target – navigation was the key problem.

On 22 February 1942 Air Marshal Arthur Harris became C-in-C RAF Bomber Command, an individual determined to prosecute a bombing offensive to the utmost. The diversion of Brest was now removed. New aircraft such as the four-engined Short Stirling, Handley Page Halifax and Avro Lancaster were coming into squadron service while the technological battle was about to have an impact with the appearance of the radio navigational aid called Gee. Bomber Command was now mounting raids with up to 250 aircraft on industrial targets but was still apparently unable to inflict any great degree of devastation. Under political pressure to divert bomber aircraft to the battles in the Middle East or in the Atlantic, Harris sold Churchill a plan for a thousand-bomber raid (drafting in all available aircraft and aircrew including instructor and training crews) on a German city – and Cologne was the chosen target.

125

Of the 1046 aircraft which made the raid, 910 reached and bombed the target and 39 were lost. They wrecked 13,000 homes and inflicted 5000 casualties including 469 dead but did not destroy Cologne entirely nor cripple any vital industry. Nevertheless the mass attack showed that the initiative of strategic air warfare had now passed overwhelmingly to the Allies.

At the Casablanca Conference of 21 January 1943 the future course of the Allied 'Combined Bomber Offensive' was mapped out. The RAF was by now joined by the confident USAAF, its commanders proud of the abilities of their heavily gunned B-17 Flying Fortresses and B-24 Liberators to make raids in daylight over defended targets. Through 1942 the US Eighth Air Force had been building up its bases in Britain and making attacks on targets in France and occupied Europe. At Casablanca the so-called 'Casablanca Directive' was drafted calling for the US to mount attacks by day while Bomber Command would operate at night; operational command devolved on Britain's Air Marshal Harris and US General Ira Eaker while broad target objectives such as U-boat construction, aircraft factories, transportation and oil plant were codified.

After Cologne had showed that even 1000 bomber raids could not paralyse a German city, the RAF stuck resolutely to night area bombing but now incorporating new navigational and radar devices such as 'Gee' and 'H2S', plus the Pathfinder Force, specialists in target marking flying high performance Mosquitos, to concentrate their destructive power. When it all worked it was devastating. The firestorm at Hamburg raised on the night of 24 July 1943, and maintained by a week long offensive, was set by aircraft using radar aids and 'window' electronic countermeasures. The raids killed perhaps up to 50,000 people. But the RAF's proven ability to 'rub out' German towns was not in itself proving a war winning weapon, however ferocious the attacks, and meanwhile RAF Bomber Command was being shot out of the sky by the ever more technically sophisticated, numerous and skilled German nightfighter force. In the four and a half months of the 'Battle of Berlin' from

126

November 1943 to March 1944, the RAF suffered 1077 bombers lost and 1682 damaged on 20,224 sorties. At this rate Bomber Command, not German industry, would soon cease to exist.

The American air commanders had expected as much. The RAF would be unable, however heavily it punished German cities, to materially affect the military course of the war by smashing German war production.

Through 1943 however the USAAF also suffered. Believing in daylight operations, using massed defensive firepower to drive off the enemy, the box formations of B-17s and B-24s were either driven too high by flak to bomb accurately or decimated by the Luftwaffe day fighters. Two thirds of a force despatched to attack a critical target, the ball bearing works at Schweinfurt, on 14 October 1943, were destroyed or damaged.

At the end of 1943 therefore it looked as if the bombing offensive mounted by the Allies had failed, beaten by the technical resources and determination of the German night fighter force just as the German U-boats were beaten by the Allied escort forces in the Atlantic.

Three factors came to the rescue – first was the introduction of the remarkable North American P-51 Mustang long range escort fighter able to fly to Berlin and back from British bases, which allowed the USAAF to rapidly gain daylight air superiority over western Europe and deep into Germany itself, allowing the Eighth Air Force from England and the Fifteenth Air Force operating from Italy to roam almost at will. Then in May 1944 the USAAF began a concerted offensive against the German synthetic oil industry. In June 1944, Bomber Command joined in by night with its immense bomb carrying capacity and improved navigational techniques. The oil offensive crippled the Luftwaffe's sortie rate, accelerating the winning of air superiority. Lastly the invasion of Europe pushed back the German night fighter defences with it.

Oil and communications were the priority targets in the last months of war. Cutting German communications in the area before the advancing Russians was the rationale behind

Bomber Command Casualties
1939–1945

Aircrew

Killed/presumed dead	55,435 all causes
Wounded	8,403
POW	12,844

Between September 1942 and September 1944, Bomber Command lost 30,500 aircrew killed.

Losses of the German Civil Population
in Air Raids, 1939–1945

Civilain Population	410,000
Non-military Police and	
Civilians attached to Armed Forces	23,000
Foreigners and Prisoners of War	32,000
Displaced Persons	128,000
	593,000

Wounded and Injured: 486,000

By comparison Great Britain lost approximately 65,000 civilians.

Losses suffered by the German Armed Forces amounted to 3.8 million killed.

Total number of dwellings destroyed *c* 3,370,000

Operation Thunderclap, the attack on Dresden made on the night of 14 February 1945.

This, the most destructive raid of the European war, ignited a firestorm in the old town packed with refugees while the Americans joined in the next day with over 400 aircraft of the Eighth Air Force. Estimates of those killed range from 50,000 to well over 100,000 dead.

From Normandy to the Baltic

With the D-Day Anglo-US-Canadian 'Army of Liberation' safely ashore in Normandy, Hitler was still convinced that another Allied attack would come in the Pas-de-Calais, which seemed to provide the shortest line to the heartland of German power. In choosing Normandy however, the Allies had avoided the heaviest defences and, except at Omaha Beach, had got ashore with remarkably few casualties. When the Germans at last realized that Cherbourg was the main objective it was too late for the powerful forces east of the Seine to be effective. The British investment of Caen absorbed German counterattacks and provided a shield for US exploitation farther west in the Cotentin Peninsula. By 12 June, a continuous bridgehead of over 60 miles long had been secured and in the second week the US First Army drove across the waist of the Peninsula wheeling up towards Cherbourg itself. On 27 June, the port was captured after five days of desperate resistance, with its harbour installations destroyed. The British meanwhile were bogged down before Caen and the Bocage country, a mass of small fields boxed in by high hedgerows which baffled attempts at an armoured breakout.

Through July the beach-head expanded, the artificial Mulberry harbours replacing demolished port installations. It was a month of tough fighting in which the Germans launched their most forceful counterattacks. Field Marshal Rundstedt was replaced by Field Marshal von Kluge who also took over Rommel's duties when he was seriously wounded by a strafing attack on his field car. SS General Paul Hausser now commanded the Seventh Army opposing the US First Army's advance, while General Eberbach's Panzer Group West barred the British advance in the east with seven armoured and two infantry divisions. On 8 July, General Dempsey's British Second Army at last penetrated Caen, but was held at the Orne crossings. On the 18th, Operation Goodwood was launched when three armoured divisions attempted to drive across the rear of the German defences but the attack was held. With the bulk of German armoured strength drawn to the British front, General Bradley's US First Army advanced their front eight miles during the first three weeks of July, bludgeoning their way into St-Lô on 18 July.

129

On 25 July, Operation Cobra was launched – after a massive air bombardment by strategic bombers, which cratered the ground to the advantage of the defenders, and killed or wounded more than 500 US troops. In the first two days only five miles were covered but then progress quickened towards Avranches at the base of the west coast of the Cotentin Peninsula. Meanwhile an attack by the British Second Army on the central sector south of Bayeux absorbed German reinforcements.

Through the gap opened at Avranches poured the tanks of General Patton's US Third Army, now brought across the Channel into the Allied order of battle. Patton's tanks surged southward and westward, scouring Brittany – then they turned east and swept through the country north of the River Loire towards Le Mans and Chartres.

Kluge launched a counterattack westwards at Mortain, towards Avranches, trying to pinch off Third Army, but Bradley shifted reinforcements and, with the aid of British tactical airpower such as rocket firing Typhoon ground attack aircraft, smashed this German riposte. This failed attack had drawn the bulk of German armour west, just as Patton was advancing eastwards behind their rear. US tanks wheeled north to Argentan, combining in a pincer move with First Canadian Army pushing south from Caen towards Falaise. Although this pincer movement did not close soon enough to completely cut off the German Seventh and Fifth Panzer Armies, 50,000 Germans were taken prisoner and 10,000 more killed within the deadly Falaise 'pocket', continually lashed by Allied tactical airpower.

The destruction of German combat power in France and the rapidity of Patton's wide flanking movement in fact had already forestalled the need for the landing in the South of France, codenamed Dragoon, but made just the same by General Patch's US Seventh Army on 15 August. Casualties in the assault amounted to just 183 killed and wounded, the subsequent advance was more like a peacetime manoeuvre than a wartime operation. French General Jean de Lattre de Tassigny's Second Corps drove on Toulon and Marseilles. US General Truscott's VI Corps thrust north in two columns up the Rhône valley and through the foothills of the Alps Maritimes, pursuing General Friedrich Wiese's German XIX Army, which was all but destroyed.

Meanwhile on 19 August the FFI (French Forces of the Interior) had begun a rising in Paris and street battles raged with the German garrison until US Fifth Corps with General Leclerc's French 2nd Armoured Division in the van arrived in the city on the 25th.

British Second Army crossed the Seine east of Rouen to trap the remnants of German VII Army reaching Amiens early on 31 August, having covered 70 miles from the Seine in two days. Second Army crossed the Somme driving past Arras and the rear of German XV Army still on the Pas-de-Calais coastline, reaching the Belgian frontier, entering Brussels on 3 September and Antwerp with its port facilities intact the following day. To the south, Patton's Third Army crossed the Meuse on 30 August, to be halted by lack of fuel as priority in supplies went to the British.

In the second battle of France from 6 June to September 1944, the Allies landed more than 2.1 million men, and had beaten the Germans back to their own frontier, at the cost of 40,000 Allied dead, 165,000 wounded, and 20,000 missing. The German armies had lost half a million men in the field and some 200,000 in the coastal garrisons, some of which still held out. The battered German Army was now behind the Siegfried Line, seemingly vulnerable to one more push into the Third Reich's heartland.

Both Montgomery and Bradley (commanding US Twelfth Army Group from August) had different plans as to where this final thrust should be aimed. Eisenhower approved Montgomery's plan to turn the northern flank of the defenders by seizing bridgeheads over the Maas (the Meuse), the Waal (Rhine) and Lek (Lower Rhine). This would be achieved by three airborne divisions clearing the way for a fresh drive by British Second Army. On 17 September 1944, air drops were made at Eindhoven and Nijmegen by the US 101st and 82nd Airborne Divisions, while the British 1st Airborne, with a Polish brigade attached, dropped at Arnhem. Ground forces linked with

131

the first two airborne bridgeheads on 18 and 19 September, but could not batter through to Arnhem, where the 1st Airborne had been forced into a dwindling perimeter by unexpectedly strong German defence. They held out for ten days instead of the two that had been planned – 2200 survivors were evacuated, leaving 7000 killed, wounded or captured.

Arnhem was a gamble that failed. German forces in the west now commanded by General Model and under the supreme command of Field Marshal Rundstedt, recalled by Hitler as *Oberbefehlshaber West*, performed an astonishing feat of recovery, preparing a stand along the fortified zone of the Westwall (Siegfried Line), the line of fortifications built along the line of Germany's pre-war western frontier. Through October–December, the Allies battered on the Westwall, Patton's Third Army closed in on Metz on 3 October, Hodge's First Army captured Aachen after bitter fighting on the 21st and through November, Bradley's Ninth and First Armies tried to enlarge the Aachen breakthrough at the Hurtgen Forest, but overall the general offensive brought disappointingly meagre results at heavy cost.

Now it was Hitler's turn to gamble with an offensive designed to split the advancing Allies in two and capture Antwerp, thus crippling their supply base. This was Operation Wacht Am Rhein, the Ardennes offensive popularly known as 'The Battle of the Bulge'. It began on 16 December during a period of bad weather which eliminated Allied air superiority. The striking force consisted of the V Panzer and VI SS Panzer Armies, 24 divisions-strong of which 10 were armoured with the latest and most formidable German tanks including some of the super-heavy Tiger II's.

With complete tactical surprise the German offensive slammed into unsuspecting Allied forces, the deepest thrust being made by Manteuffel's V Panzer Army, shattering two US infantry divisions. Two US airborne divisions were rushed by truck to the area, while Montgomery swung his reserves southward to forestall the enemy at any Meuse crossing. Meanwhile isolated US garrisons held out, blocking critical communications. Patton halted his advance in the Saar region on 18 December to shift his axis northwards to hit the southern flank of the German advance. By 26 December the German offensive had run out of steam, the US defenders of Bastogne were still holding out and the weather had cleared, allowing Allied tactical airpower to be unleashed.

German losses were some 120,000 men killed, wounded or missing, 600 tanks and assault guns, 1600 aircraft, and some 6000 tactical vehicles. Allied losses (mostly US), were approximately 7000 killed, 33,400 wounded, 21,000 captured or missing, plus over 700 tanks and tank destroyers.

The Ardennes offensive may have set back Allied operations in the west, but it expended the cutting edge of German offensive power. Meanwhile in the east in mid-January 1945, the Soviets after having remained virtually stationary in the centre launched a great offensive on 12 January, driving 300 miles to the Oder by the end of the month, where the advance halted. On 8 February, Eisenhower launched two offensives on Twenty-first Army Group and Twelfth Army Group sectors in an attempt to trap and destroy the German armies west of the Rhine. The opening attack was made by General Crerar's Canadian First Army but bad weather, water-soaked terrain, and deliberate flooding by the Germans, held up the advance and stalled the US Ninth Army to the south; as a result the Americans did not enter Cologne until 5 March, allowing the Germans to evacuate the bulk of their forces across the Rhine. While blocking the advance of the Allied left wing, the Germans had weakened their own left flank and created an opportunity for the US First and Third Armies to break through at Bonn, while a two-battalion task force of the US 9th Armoured Division seized intact a railway bridge over the Rhine river barrier at Remagen, on 7 March, before it could be blown up.

By 21 March the Allied Armies stood on the Rhine from Holland to the Swiss frontier, with a bridgehead at Remagen now 20 miles long and eight miles deep. Sixty thousand Germans had been killed in the Rhineland, and some quarter of a million taken prisoner – Allied losses were under 20,000. On the 22nd, Patton crossed the Rhine with minimal losses between Mainz and Worms and drove quickly into Northern Bavaria. One day behind Patton, Montgomery launched his set piece Rhine crossing, far downstream near the Dutch frontier. The river was crossed at four points during the night, and in the morning the two airborne divisions, the US 17th and British 6th, were dropped north of Wesel beyond the river to prise off the grip of the defenders. Montgomery's Twenty-first Army Group was soon pouring across twelve bridges and had broken a final German stand by 28 March. Hodge's First Army broke out of the Remagen bridgehead on the 21st, and reached Marburg, some 70 miles to the east, on the 28th.

A drive on Berlin seemed now in sight, but Eisenhower switched the effort to Bradley's Twelfth Army Group, driving east through central Germany towards Leipzig, concerned that the Nazis should make a last ditch stand in the Alps in the so-called 'National Redoubt'. (This turned out to be nothing more than a propaganda invention and the Germans unlike other defeated nations of the war did not spawn a resistance movement.) Meanwhile Montgomery's forces were to drive on Hamburg and the River Elbe, where they should wait for the advancing Russians. The offensives began on 28 March, with the objective of encircling the remaining German forces in the Ruhr, spearheads of Ninth and First Armies meeting at Paderborn sealing the huge pocket on 1 April. Inside were the disorganized remnants of Model's Army Group B – some 300,000 men. To the north, the British First Army reached the Elbe on 24 April, took Bremen after a week-long battle on 27 April, and Lübeck on the Baltic on 2 May; the great port of Hamburg fell on the following day without a fight. Meanwhile the US Third Army swept down the Danube Valley to occupy Linz on 5 May, reaching Pilsen in Czechoslovakia the next day, until halted on direct order from advancing on Prague itself. US Seventh Army, after a bitter

fight at Nuremberg, crossed the Danube, took Berchtesgaden, and met elements of the US Fifth Army moving
north from Italy at the Brenner Pass.

On 30 April, Hitler committed suicide. The next day,
Germany's military leaders began to negotiate with the
Allies. Dönitz, Hitler's designated successor, prevaricated
before sending emissaries to SHAEF at Rheims to negotiate
the final surrender of the Third Reich; meanwhile piecemeal
surrenders were taking place in Italy (2 May), in Holland (5
May), and on the Franco-US front in the south (4 May).

At Rheims, Eisenhower insisted on an immediate unconditional surrender, to which Admiral Hans von Friedeburg
and General Alfred Jodl agreed after Eisenhower threatened them with closing the Elbe crossings to the refugees
seeking to surrender to the Americans rather than face the
Russians.

The instrument of unconditional surrender was signed on
7 May, coming into force the next day. On 9 May, it was
ratified in Berlin in the presence of Soviet Marshal Zhukov.
The Second World War in the west formally ended at
midnight, 8–9 May 1945.

Russia Strikes Back

The Battle of Kursk marked the end of the Germans' ability
to take the offensive initiative on the Eastern Front. While
the Tiger tanks still burned at Prokhorovka, on 12 July the
Soviet Western and Bryansk Fronts launched Operation
'Kutuzov' aimed in turn at destroying the German position
around Orel from where Citadel had been launched. Three
days later the armies of Central Front joined the battle,
forcing General Model to withdraw from the Orel Salient
on 26 July. On 16 July, the Germans began a pull-back in
the Belgorod–Kharkov sector, and on 3 August the Soviets
launched Operation Rumyantsev, joint attacks by the
Voronezh and Steppe Fronts, the result of which was the
recapture of Kharkov once again. Only north of Velikye
Luki did the German line remain stable; elsewhere Soviet
forces rolled forward jabbing at the German line wherever

they encountered weakness. On 13 August, the forces of the South-western Front commanded by General Malinovsky forced their way across the northern Donets, while General Tolbukhin's Southern Front advanced on Taganrog, these two fronts enveloping German Army Group South from the flanks. Ignoring Hitler's orders to stand in place, Manstein once again kept his lines intact by skilful counter-attacks as he fell back to the River Dnieper.

Through September–November 1943, the Soviets pressed forward on Army Group South and Army Group Centre's Front, pushing the latter back to the edge of the Pripet Marshes, and recaptured Smolensk on 24 September and Kiev on 6 November. On 10 September, the forces of the North Caucasian Front advanced on the Taman Peninsula, destroying this last German bridgehead in the Caucasus, and seizing a bridgehead for themselves in the Crimea, cutting off the German XVII Army. In October 1943, the system of Soviet 'Fronts' was reorganized and renamed, catching up with their new strategic and geographic realities. While the Kalinin was renamed the 'First Baltic Front', the Central became the 'Belo-Russian' (or White Russian) and the Voronezh, Steppe, South-western and Southern Fronts were now called the 'First', 'Second', 'Third' and 'Fourth Ukrainian'.

In the first month of 1944, the Soviets launched a concerted winter offensive, as frosts hardened muddy tracks into passable roads. Two Soviet Army Groups attacked the German XVIII Army in the north, still besieging Leningrad. General Govorov's Leningrad Front crossed the frozen gulf of Finland while General Meretzkov's Volkhov Front attacked in the south. On 20 January, Novgorod was recaptured, while General Popov's Second Baltic Front threatened further envelopment, pushing back German Army Group North in its entirety until General Model arrived on 31 January to block further advance, aided by the spring thaws. Leningrad was at last relieved after an 890-day siege, in which some 200,000 citizens had been killed by direct military action and at least 630,000 died of starvation and cold.

In the Ukraine, General Vatutin's First Ukrainian Front launched the main Russian winter offensive on 24 December 1943, and recaptured Zhitomir and Korosten. Second Ukrainian Front meanwhile advanced towards Kirovograd, enveloping German VIII Army. By the end of January, ten German divisions were encircled in the Korsun-Shevchenkovsky area. Manstein's immediate counterattacks bogged down in bad weather and the attempts of the encircled troops to break out were only partially successful, German casualties being around 100,000. The Soviet advance continued south-west across the Bug and Dniester rivers, virtually cutting Manstein's command in two. By 26 March, Soviet forces were in Rumanian territory, while the investment of German troops trapped in the Crimea began on 8 April. Enraged by these setbacks, Hitler sacked both his southern army group Commanders, Manstein and Kleist, replaced by Model and General Ferdinand Schörner respectively.

Despite enormous reverses, the German Army on the Eastern Front in summer 1944 was still a formidable fighting machine. Including satellites it numbered 228 divisions with over four million men, nearly 50,000 guns, more than 5000 tanks and 3000 aircraft. Hitler had already ordered no retreat in the east, demanding a defensive based on fortresses and strongpoints, while attempting to keep adequate forces in the west to beat off an Anglo-US invasion. In consequence, the German defence line, 1400 miles long, was thin spread, lacking reserves and depth when the Soviets launched their summer offensive.

At the start of their huge drive west, the Red Army amounted to some six and a half million men, almost 8000 tanks and over 13,000 aircraft. It began in the north when the Soviet Karelian and Leningrad Fronts began their counterattack against Army Group North, forcing it back to the Finnish frontier. On 20 June, Viipuri fell and the Eastern Finnish defensives in the Lake Onega region were overrun. Hostilities between the Soviet Union and Finland ceased on 4 September, while the German XX Army hung on in the far north around Petsamo and Kirkenes.

137

The main Russian blow fell on the German centre, Operation Bagration, launched on 22 June 1944. One hundred and forty-six infantry and 43 Soviet armoured divisions attacked on four fronts, General Bagramyan's First Baltic, and General Chernyakhovsky's Third Belorussian punching out to the north and south of Vitebsk, taking the city on 27 June. The German Field Marshal Busch had had his forces depleted and was harried by Soviet partisans. On 3 July, Minsk was taken, trapping 50,000 Germans, on 13 July the Polish frontier was reached at Grodno, and in the north Bagramyan turned to the Baltic states taking Vilnius in Lithuania and Daugavpils in Latvia on 13 July. Army Group North was effectively cut in two with the bulk of its forces trapped in a huge pocket in the Baltic States.

Meanwhile, Busch had been replaced by Model, who scraped up sufficient reserves to counterattack and halt the advance of Rokossovsky's First Belorussian Front just east of Warsaw. But to the south Konev's First Ukrainian Front had attacked to capture Lvov on 27 July and reached the Upper Vistula and Baranov on 7 August. On 1 August, the Polish Home Army rose in revolt in Warsaw though the Germans who had been defeated in Belorussia had not yet been routed, and were reinforcing their positions west of the Vistula just as the Soviet offensive in Eastern Poland petered out. The Soviets sat on their hands, denying US and British supply aircraft facilities to land and when sporadic attempts to aid the fighters were made in September, it was too late. The result was a disaster as General Bor-Komorowski's forces were invested by SS troops, who smashed the rebellion in vicious street fighting, reducing the city to rubble. On the Polish side, some 15,000 Home Army soldiers were killed, and at least 200,000 Polish civilians.

While the Soviet offensive in Poland was running down, a new offensive was launched in the south. On 20 August, the Second and Third Ukrainian Fronts under Generals Malinovsky and Tolbukhin punched out on the southern wing of the Soviet Front across the Prut River into Rumania. Two of the four armies in German Army Group

South Ukraine, the Rumanian troops, allied themselves with the Soviets when Rumania capitulated on 23 August, and the bulk of the German VI and VIII Armies were trapped. Between 20 August and 3 September, the Soviet forces took 208,000 prisoners, including 21 generals. The entire German right wing collapsed, pulling back on the Transylvanian Mountains.

The Soviets almost won the prize of cutting Field Marshal von Weich's Army Group F off in the Balkans, just preventing its move from Greece into Yugoslavia. On 20 October, however, Tolbukhin's Third Ukrainian Front with Bulgarian forces (Bulgaria had changed sides when Soviet troops crossed the Danube on 8 September) took Belgrade with Tito's partisan forces. Weich meanwhile slipped through Sarajevo to the west, joining Army Group South. The Soviets continued north-west, crossing the Danube on 24 November. By 26 December, forces under Malinovsky and Tolbukhin encircled 188,000 Germans in the Hungarian capital of Budapest.

On the Baltic Fronts, Estonia and Latvia had been cleared by the end of October, while in the far north XX Mountain Army had been driven back from Petsamo and Soviet forces were on Norwegian territory.

The Soviet Army's final offensive, reaching out for Berlin itself, was planned for 20 January 1945, but was brought forward by eight days to relieve the pressure caused by the Ardennes offensive in the west. From the Baltic to the Carpathians, five fronts struck at the enemy along a line 755 miles long. Konev's First Ukrainian Front led, the fronts stretching to the north jumping off in turn – Zhukov's First Belorussian, Rokossovky's Second Belorussian, Chernyakovski's Third Belorussian, Bagramyan's First Baltic, and Yeremenko's Second Baltic. Overwhelmed by sheer weight of men and armour, the Germans fell back, leaving pockets of resistance in their wake. Zhukov reached the Oder River near Kustrin on 31 January after an advance of almost 300 miles. Konev reached the Oder on 18 February, before the advance turned north pinning the remains of

139

Army Group Centre into East Prussia and Army Group North in a shrinking pocket in Kurland in Latvia.

In the south, the advance of three Soviet Fronts through the Danube Valley was blocked by the siege of Budapest for more than a month, the west bank of the city finally falling on 13 February. Hitler ordered a final offensive launched on 5 March. After five days the VI Panzer Army had slowed down to a crawl and a rapid counterattack by Tolbukhin ended this, the last concerted German offensive of the war. By 20 March, the Soviets had reached the Austrian frontier. Malinovsky's Second Ukrainian Front drove into Vienna on 13 April.

For the final assault on the capital of the Third Reich three Soviet Fronts were assigned, commanded by Marshals Rokossovsky, Zhukov and Konev, numbering some two and a half million men with more than 42,000 guns, over 6000 tanks and 7500 aircraft. On 16 April, First Belorussian Front attacked at dawn after a massive artillery barrage, First Ukrainian Front joining in at daylight. On 19 April, First Belorussian Front broke through, reaching the outskirts of Berlin, while Konev's First Ukrainian Front rounded the south of the city. By 25 April Berlin was encircled, and on the same day, Rokossovsky's Second Belorussian Front broke through the III Panzer Army's line near Stettin. While Hitler from his bunker still ordered phantom armies to the relief of his capital, eight real Soviet armies were smashing their way through Berlin's defences, meeting fanatical resistance from old men, 16-year-old boys and the motley remains of the vast forces once assembled to destroy Bolshevism. On 30 April, Soviet forces broke in to the Reichstag building, the same day Hitler killed himself and his mistress Eva Braun. On 1 May the Red Flag was hoisted on the Reichstag and the next day General Weidling, Commandant of Berlin, surrendered. On 8 May Field Marshal Keitel signed the document of unconditional surrender, ratified the next day by representatives of the wartime Allies. The war in Europe was over.

SECTION 2

People

War at the Top

Inter Allied Relations

The grand coalition that ground down the Axis powers to defeat were unlikely allies. Both the Soviet Union and the United States through the decades before the war had withdrawn (for very different reasons) into inward-looking isolationism within their vast continental boundaries. Republican Spain, in spite of Soviet aid, had been defeated. In August 1939 the Soviet Union signed a non-aggression pact with Nazi Germany.

Britain and France declared war wearily in 1939 to save Poland and were militarily smashed nine months later for their pains. In the crucial year from the fall of France to the German attack on Russia, Britain stood alone as a focus for resistance to Hitler and, at last, the Soviet Union and the United States, in June and December 1941 respectively, entered the war as the result of direct attacks by Germany and Japan. Thenceforth the coalition, made up of ideological opposites, would hold, their political command systems made, for a time at least, more in each other's image by the exigencies of total war but behind the common front, suspicions and mistrust rumbled. Hitler not only brought them together but only Hitler could have kept them together.

The US suspected British 'imperialism'. The Soviets were suspicious of Western capitalism, and of the western Allies' reluctance to open a 'Second Front'. The British suspected the Russians of planning a power grab in Eastern Europe. China's Chiang Kai Shek was suspicious of Anglo-American motives while de Gaulle suspected everyone.

These tensions underlay the course of Allied relations throughout the war and coloured military strategy and in

143

turn of course were coloured by the ebb and flow of the war itself. And yet it all worked, until, for a moment at least, in the ruins of the thousand-year Reich, it looked as if a new world order might be born out of the sacrifice and comradeship of war, and the high purpose of destroying fascism. The irradiated clouds of Hiroshima would blow it all away with the birth of the age of atomic weapons and the cold war.

The Anglo-US dialogue opened in earnest when Churchill became Prime Minister in May 1940. Roosevelt was re-elected President for a third term in November 1940 and felt politically secure enough to override the powerful forces of isolationism and push the 'Lend Lease' bill through Congress, authorizing the President to supply the Government of 'any country whose defense the President deems vital to the defense of the United States'.

Already British scientific and purchasing commissions were revealing British technological breakthroughs and eyeing purposefully the vast industrial potential of the United States, just beginning to get onto a war footing. In January 1941 US and British staff officers met in Washington in a conference codenamed 'ABC 1' and drew up outline plans for US military intervention in Europe while through the spring and summer of 1941 the US Navy became much more active in the battle against the U-Boats in th Atlantic. From June 1941 onward the embattled Soviet Union also got lend lease aid and a loan of a billion dollars.

The first wartime meeting of Churchill and Roosevelt took place in August 1941 in Placentia Bay, Newfoundland, with the US still at peace. The result was the 'Atlantic Charter', a declaration of high purpose proclaiming democratic ideals and the rights of nations postwar to exist free from the fear of aggression and that the signatories (including a Soviet endorsement) would not seek 'territorial aggrandisement'. The next meeting was the so-called Arcadia conference which took place in Washington in December 1941 with the US now at war.

As a result perhaps it was much more practical militarily, creating the all important Combined Chiefs of Staff (see chart on p. 148) which from Washington would take the key strategic decisions of the war. At Arcadia too the 'Germany first' intentions of the US were spelled out although, with the Axis still triumphant, there was little chance of getting US power in strength into Europe, in spite of bold talk of a 'second front in 1942'.

Molotov the Soviet Foreign Minister visited London and Washington in May and June 1942 to urge a direct invasion of the continent. The British Chiefs of Staff were gloomy, the US military commanders were more optimistic although held back by Roosevelt. When Churchill went to Moscow in August 1942 to tell Stalin there would be no second front that year or even in 1943 the coalition was put under maximum strain.

The next Roosevelt-Churchill summit was at Casablanca in Morocco begun on 14 January 1943 following the successful Torch landings. At Casablanca, Churchill won the argument for an invasion of Sicily first and thence Italy, the so-called 'soft underbelly' of Fortress Europe rather than the direct attack on France being urged by General Marshall, the US Army's Chief of Staff. At Casablanca Roosevelt proclaimed the doctrine of unconditional surrender announcing that peace would only come through the 'total elimination of German, Japanese and Italian war power'. But now once again the alliance would be stretched, not by the means of winning the war but by what to do with the spoils of peace. As a preamble to the first meeting of the 'Big Three', Roosevelt and Churchill met in Cairo in November 1943 with Chiang Kai-Shek to raise China's status as an allied power, and to set the stage for the meeting with Stalin.

At the Teheran Conference from 28 November to 1 December 1943 Churchill, Roosevelt and Stalin met for the first time with the future shape of Central and Eastern Europe first on the agenda. Roosevelt urged the atomization of Germany itself into five statelets, Britain wanted Prussia separated from the rest of Germany and the organization of the various chunks into a 'Danubian confederation'. Stalin mistrusted this as providing the bones of another

German dominated superstate. But the real spectre at the feast was Poland.

Stalin had already broken off relations with the 'London Poles' over the Katyn massacre allegations. (In 1943 4000 Polish officers were found in a mass grave, murdered by the Soviet NKVD in spring 1940). The 'discoverers' were the Germans, quite capable of this kind of barbarity themselves, who exploited it to the full for propaganda purposes – and it worked, putting the Alliance under renewed strain. Churchill and Roosevelt however already recognized the reality of the situation and eventual Soviet domination in Poland. Stalin had already told British foreign secretary Eden that the Soviet Union's western frontier would to all intents and purposes be that agreed with Germany in 1939. The western Allies also did not argue over Poland's western frontier – the River Oder. 'Poland' would migrate westwards at Germany's expense, the Soviet Union would travel in its wake.

After Teheran Churchill met Roosevelt again at Quebec in September 1944. The British offered to send a Pacific Fleet to aid the US Navy (who by that stage needed no help in defeating Japan) but more importantly this conference outlined a new world security and monetary order, codified at the subsequent Dumbarton Oaks and Bretton Woods conferences.

In October 1944 Churchill and Eden went to Moscow and reached a series of so-called 'spheres of influence' agreements with Stalin, carving up who would have what in postwar Eastern Europe and the Balkans. Britain would have an overwhelming voice in the future of Greece where Communist-led partisans now had *de facto* control, the Soviet Union in Rumania, Bulgaria and Hungary. Yugoslavia would be 'fifty-fifty' while Poland hung in mid air, where, in spite of Churchillian growling, Soviet military power was the only political reality.

When the 'Big Three', Churchill, Stalin and Roosevelt, met at Yalta, the resort on the Black Sea in February 1945, the Soviet Army was now not the only one that was winning as had been the case at Teheran. The Russians were set to take Berlin but the Anglo-Americans were on the Rhine and poised to drive into Central Europe – in spite of the setbacks of the German Ardennes counteroffensive the pressure of which Soviet attacks had done much to relieve. Yalta marked the high tide of Allied unity.

The imminence of German defeat exhilarated the participants and the planning for a new coalition against Japan. Stalin promised to declare war three months after the defeat of Germany. In fact it came on 8 August 1945, two days after the dropping of the atomic bombs and was by then militarily irrelevant.

The main outcome of Yalta was a reaffirmation of the Teheran agreements on Eastern Europe. The realities of Soviet domination in Poland and the Balkans were accepted while the British 'sphere of influence' in Greece was recognized, Stalin even proscribing the Greek communist ELAS partisans who were set to overthrow the British-backed royalist Greek government. All these deals and compromises sealed the fate of millions of people, from the Germans of Central Europe to the scores of thousands of Soviet citizens captured in the service of the Third Reich now in POW camps awaiting their fate. Finally the Big Three called from Yalta for the remaining neutrals to declare war on Germany before 1 March 1945 and thus gain a ticket of admittance to the founding conference of the United Nations at San Francisco.

Between Yalta and the next conference at Potsdam held in July 1945, (the atomic bomb was successfully tested in New Mexico the day the conference opened), the grand alliance began to unravel. First it was a matter of personalities – Winston Churchill lost the British general election and was replaced by Clement Attlee. Harry S. Truman replaced Franklin D. Roosevelt who died on 12 April as President of the United States. Secondly, the manoeuvrings of Teheran and Yalta were now real, German power was broken and Europe a vacuum which Soviet and American power filled with exhausted Britain and strident France given a voice at the table.

The Allied Combined Chiefs of Staff 1942–45

BRITISH CHIEFS OF STAFF

Chief of the Imperial General Staff
(*Chairman of the
Chiefs of Staff Committee*)
Field-Marshal Sir Alan Brooke

Chief of the Air Staff
Marshal of the Royal Air Force
Sir Charles Portal

*First Sea Lord and
Chief of the Naval Staff*
Admiral of the Fleet
Sir Andrew Cunningham

Deputy Secretary (*Military*)
*of the War Cabinet
and Chief of Staff to
the Minister of Defence*
General Sir Hastings Ismay

Chief of Combined Operations
Major-General R. E. Laycock

Secretary
Major-General L. C. Hollis

UNITED STATES JOINT CHIEFS OF STAFF

*Chief of Staff to the
Commander-in-Chief of the US
Armed Forces*
(*Chairman of the Joint
Chiefs of Staff Committee*)
Fleet Admiral William D. Leahy

Chief of Staff of the US Army
General of the Army
George C. Marshall

*Commander-in-Chief of
the US Fleet
and Chief of Naval Operations*
Fleet Admiral Ernest J. King

*Commanding General,
US Army Air Force*
General of the Army
Henry H. Arnold

Secretary
Brig–General A. J. McFarland

BRITISH JOINT STAFF MISSION IN WASHINGTON
Head of the Mission
Field-Marshal Sir John Dill
(until November 1944)
Field-Marshal Sir Henry Maitland Wilson
(from January 1945)

The British War Cabinet 1942–45

Note: Members of the War Cabinet are shown in Italics.

Prime Minister, First Lord of the Treasury, Minister of Defence	*Mr. Winston S. Churchill.*
Lord President of the Council	*Sir John Anderson.*
Lord Privy Seal	(a) *Sir Stafford Cripps.*
	(b) Viscount Cranborne. (from 22.11.42)
Chancellor of the Exchequer	Sir Kingsley Wood.
Secretary of State for Foreign Affairs	*Mr. Anthony Eden.*
Secretary of State for Home Affairs, Minister for Home Security	*Mr. Herbert Morrison.* (entered War Cabinet 22.11.42)
Secretary of State for Dominions	*Mr. Clement Attlee.* (Deputy Prime Minister)
Secretary of State for Colonies	(a) Viscount Cranborne.
	(b) Colonel Oliver Stanley (from 22.11.42)
Secretary of State for India and Burma	Mr. L. S. Amery
First Lord of the Admiralty	Mr. A. V. Alexander.
Secretary of State for War	Sir James Grigg.
Secretary of State for Air	Sir Archibald Sinclair.
Minister of Aircraft Production	(a) Colonel J. J. Llewellin.
	(b) Sir Stafford Cripps. (from 22.11.42)
Minister of Supply	Sir Andrew Duncan.
Minister of Production	*Mr. Oliver Lyttelton.*
Minister of War Transport	Lord Leathers.
President of the Board of Trade	Dr. Hugh Dalton.
Minister of Economic Warfare	Lord Selborne.
Minister of Food	Lord Woolton.
Minister of Labour and National Service	*Mr. Ernest Bevin.*
Minister Without Portfolio	Sir William Jowitt.
Paymaster General	Lord Cherwell.
Minister of State (Middle East)	*Mr. R. G. Casey.*
Minister Resident for Supply (Washington)	Colonel J. J. Llewellin (from 22.11.42)
Minister Resident (AFHQ)	Mr. Harold Macmillan. (from 30.12.42)

People

The direct practical results of Potsdam were first, agreement on the government of defeated Germany. They created the Allied Control Council but each of the powers, the Soviet Union, the USA, Britain and later France had full sovereignty in their respective zones of occupation. Formal partitioning of Germany, considered at Teheran and Yalta, did not take place. The conference approved the principle of reparation to the Soviet Union and other nations who had suffered at the hands of the German invaders although this agreement later broke down.

A council of foreign ministers was established to prepare draft with the defeated nations while the conference recognized Soviet *de facto* dominance in Central Europe. It also resolved disposal of what remained of the German Navy among the victors (except for the submarines which were scuttled). The International Military Tribunal to prosecute Nazi war criminals was established and a quadripartite government for Berlin.

Biographies

Hitler, Adolf (1889–1945)

Führer and Reichs Chancellor of Germany, dominant figure of the 1930s in European politics and the head centre of the Second World War – its instigator and presiding influence almost to the very end.

Through the 1930s Hitler consolidated his absolute power within Germany itself, first within the NSDAP removing any 'revolutionary' opposition in 1934, then within the German state and armed forces merging them with National Socialism then binding them by oaths of personal allegiance to his person.

He spelled out his anti-semitism in his book *Mein Kampf* (*My Struggle*) in 1925 and along with his belief in 'Aryan supremacy' and the German destiny of conquest in the East. It was Europe's terrible misfortune that such beliefs would become allied to a triumphant military machine with the concentration camps and extermination commandos travelling in their wake.

The weakness of Anglo-French diplomacy and the political fragmentation of Germany's eastern neighbours allowed Hitler to rebuild German power both militarily and territorially from 1936–39. When Britain and France declared war for Poland in September 1939 Hitler was genuinely surprised, and the German rearmament programme was in fact a long way off providing the means and the capacity for sustaining a long war. But the Blitzkrieg campaigns, with Hitler's personal intervention at crucial points, were brilliantly successful. First Poland, then Denmark, Norway, Belgium, Holland and France were smashed leaving Britain isolated and impotent. The success of these campaigns confirmed Hitler in his own belief that he was the presiding military genius behind Germany's victories. But the true turning point came before Moscow in the winter of 1941 when Hitler ordered the army to hold, in spite of the imminence of disaster. When the front did not collapse he was convinced that his own willpower had saved the situation. The doubters in the general staff were dismissed in droves and thereafter Hitler would act as his own commander in chief with OKW (*Oberkommando der Wehrmacht*) as his compliant tool. OKH, Army High Command, was meanwhile diminished in status to supervise ground operations on the Eastern Front.

As the coalition of powers ranged against Hitler grew greater, Germany's actual unpreparedness to wage total war became more apparent. Having failed to win in 1941, the options began to run out. Just as at Moscow, Hitler's prescription for further reverses in Russia and the Mediterranean was no retreat, 'fight to the last round' and that fanatical willpower would triumph. Tanks and shells in overwhelming numbers proved more effective than willpower, but as Germany began to lose there was still immense popular faith to be found both in the military and in the German people in their Führer. The Germans fought for him more in rapture than in fear. After Stalingrad Hitler became more withdrawn making fewer and fewer speeches and public appearances; he refused to visit bombed cities but walled himself up in underground command bunkers where day and night lost their distinction. But still his reputation as the miracle worker of 1940–1 carried him along, plus hints of wonder weapons which would turn the tide.

In fact Hitler's health was deteriorating rapidly, his rages made even more intense and unpredictable by the prescriptions of the quack physician Morell. And yet still he held his commanders in awe. Even when at last a military resistance movement made its move in July 1944 it was after the Western Allies had successfully landed in Normandy yet was rapidly snuffed out by the military loyalists in Berlin aided by the SS in the aftermath.

The effects of the bomb blast in which Hitler miraculously

escaped death contributed to his further decline in health. Henceforth Hitler withdrew himself into a world of self delusion, raging at anyone who dared point out military reality and declaring his 'sleep walker's assurance'. His insistence on holding ground again and again threw away military resources until, at the very end, in the Berlin bunker itself he still clung to the idea of staying put while a miracle (such as the death of Roosevelt) would split the alliance and set the Soviet and the West at each other's throats. On 29 April 1945 he married his mistress Eva Braun and the following day they committed suicide. It was his final command that the German people who had proved 'unworthy' of him should be destroyed along with their Führer.

Churchill, Winston S. (1874–1965)

British Prime Minister 1940–45, symbol of defiance to Hitler and the will to win. Aged 64 on the outbreak of war, Winston Churchill already had a full but not entirely successful political career behind him. He had been First Lord of the Admiralty in the First World War but had resigned over the failure in the Dardanelles. He held various cabinet posts in Conservative governments of the '20s but on several issues had isolated himself into an eccentric, back bench wilderness through the '30s, particularly denouncing Chamberlain's appeasement policy. He was First Lord again in September 1939 and although the Royal Navy once again suffered, it was Chamberlain who took the blame for the fiasco in Norway. As Prime Minister of the coalition government from 10 May 1940, Churchill immediately made the first of his many blunt but brilliant morale-raising speeches. He acted as his own Minister of Defence and set his policy as 'victory at all costs' but promised only blood, toil, tears and sweat along the way. His relationship with Roosevelt was crucial and broadly successful and, in spite of being an anti-Bolshevik to his marrow, the military alliance with the Soviet Union was actively embraced in the cause of defeating Hitler. His relations with British military

153

and Allied political leaders were quirky and sometimes tempestuous but his leadership and conduct of the war were fundamentally unquestioned. When the British people rejected him in the election of 5 July 1945 for Clement Attlee and the Labour Party, he was genuinely piqued.

Roosevelt, Franklin Delano 1882–1945

President of the United States from 1933 to 1945. Roosevelt was a patrician and a Democrat, the only US President to be re-elected three times and its leader through its most severe economic crisis and biggest military conflict. From 1939 to 1941 he tried to steer the US people towards material help for the embattled European democracies if not actual military assistance. After winning a third term in November 1940, Roosevelt pushed the Lend Lease act through Congress, which underwrote US arms for Britain and, from June 1941, to the Soviet Union. From August 1941 when he and Churchill met to frame the Atlantic Charter, he either met or conversed with Churchill frequently.

Relations with Stalin were always more austere but nevertheless Roosevelt was resolved to seek amicable relations with the Soviet Union.

After the Japanese attack on Pearl Harbor and the German declaration of war, Roosevelt was able to lead a united nation to war and to steer it towards the 'Germany first' policy of victory in Europe before Japan.

Roosevelt was crippled by polio, although the extent of his disability was successfully concealed from the public who always saw a big-framed and apparently energetic leader. However he died of sudden cerebral haemorrhage on 12 April 1945, a few weeks before victory in Europe, a few months before the atomic bomb (the research programme for which he had set in motion) was successfully tested and shortly before the founding conference of the United Nations by which he set so much store.

Stalin, Josef (1879–1953)

Born in Georgia as Josef Dzhugashvili, 'Stalin' was a cover name from the days of Bolshevik insurrection. Stalin was editor of *Pravda* in 1917 and was in Petrograd during the October revolution and defender of Tsaritsin (later Stalingrad) during the Civil War. During Lenin's last illness, Stalin as secretary of the Communist Party formed a power group against Trotsky, driven into exile and eventually assassinated. From 1928 Stalin turned the Soviet Union inwards rather than attempting to export revolution and through the 1930s, fascism triumphed in Europe. Soviet military power was severely weakened by Stalin's purges and aid to Spain could not reverse the nationalist victory. In spite of vast numbers, the fighting ability of the Red Army was questionable. In August 1939 Stalin concluded a pact with Hitler and while Germany overran Poland the Soviet Union moved into Eastern Poland, the Baltic states and attacked Finland where Soviet military inefficiency was further shown up. Stalin expected a final showdown with Germany but was totally unprepared when the attack came in June 1941.

Initial political paralysis and military collapse turned just in time to dogged resistance, and through the GKO or state defence committee which Stalin headed, commanders of great ability were at last set against the invader with vast resources of men and material. Stalin made mistakes, ordering the Red Army to hold too long in the Ukraine in 1941 and urging the disastrous Kharkov offensive of 1942 which met the German drive on the Caucasus coming the other way, but vast human resources and a timely psychological pitching of the struggle as one for the Russian motherland rather than for Soviet communism, held the line plus a ruthless use of internal terror and the cult of Stalin's own personality.

Stalin was successful too in the politics of the wartime alliance. From 1941–44 with the Red Army the only force engaging the bulk of German power he had an enormous psychological advantage while his demands for a second front convinced Churchill and Roosevelt that Soviet war aims were simply to win the war rather than make a grab for the spoils in Central Europe and the Balkans. In the end military reality dictated the result and Soviet power entered the heartland of Europe to stay. Postwar Stalin sought to retain as rigid a grip on the new Communist states as he had on the Soviet Union itself. Only in Yugoslavia did he fail. Stalin died in 1953.

A–Z Biographies of WW2 Personalities

Anders, Lieut.-General Wladyslaw (1892–1970)
Polish military commander and reluctant political figure,
Anders was captured by the Soviets at the fall of Poland.
After the German invasion of Russia, Anders led now freed
Polish POWs via Iran to Palestine and a period of intensive
training under British tutelage. The Polish forces were
integrated with the British Eighth Army and fought with
distinction in Italy. Ander's Polish II Corps took Monte
Cassino after bloody hand to hand fighting on 18 May 1944,
and went on to fight at Pescara, Ancona and to take
Bologna.

After the death of General Sikorski, Anders became the
political focus for the 'London Poles'. At the war's end
Anders' 112,000 strong army was disbanded but only a
small percentage chose to return to a Poland under Soviet
control. Anders became the figurehead for Polish exiles in
Britain until his death in 1970.

Antonescu, Marshal Ion (1882–1946)
Rumanian dictator executed for war crimes in 1946. Defence
Minister Antonescu took power with the aid of the Iron
Guard fascist movement on 5 September 1940, signing the
Axis pact soon afterwards. Rumanian divisions fought with
the German Army Group South during the invasion of the
Soviet Union and the 1942 Caucasus offensive, fighting at
Stalingrad. As the Soviet counter offensive swept nearer
Rumania, Antonescu fell from power, dismissed by King
Michael in August 1944.

*Alexander, Field Marshal Sir Harold, 1st Earl Alexander of
Tunis (1891–1969)*
Considered by many the greatest British field commander
of the war, 'Alex' was a tough and resilient soldier, a

157

military 'fireman' called in by Churchill when the going was especially tough, and a gifted strategist on the grand scale. Alexander was an aristocratic Anglo-Irishman, a product of Harrow and Sandhurst; he served in the Irish Guards through the Great War, pursuing a professional army career thereafter, serving in the Baltic and in India.

In 1940 he commanded the BEF's First Division, covering the retreat to Dunkirk, personally commanding the last corps to get off the beaches. In 1941 and early 1942 he was in Burma, again conducting a fighting retreat into Assam.

With the crisis of August 1942 in the Western Desert, Churchill appointed him Supreme Commander in the Middle East in place of Auchinleck while Montgomery took over command of Eighth Army, Alexander framing the strategy underlying Montgomery's victories. After the Torch landings in Algeria, Eisenhower was appointed supreme Allied commander in North Africa with Alexander as his deputy and commander of Eighteenth Army Group. In May 1943 the last Axis forces in North Africa surrendered in Tunis and the Allies prepared to attack Sicily and Italy itself.

The invasion of Sicily was carried out under Alexander's overall command on the ground. When Eisenhower returned to England at the end of 1943 to prepare for Overlord, Alexander became the Supreme Allied Commander in the Mediterranean and was now set to oversee the protracted and bloody Italian campaign, facing ferocious German resistance, hostile terrain and constant bleeding of men and material resources for the assault on France, and the campaign in the West, while holding together the multi-national forces of Fifteenth Army Group.

Alexander received the unconditional surrender of German forces in Italy on 29 April 1945.

Aosta, Amadeo, Duke of (1898–1942)

Italian military commander, colonial governor member of Italian royal family. As C-in-C of the Italian armies in Eritrea and Ethiopia, Aosta led the invasion of British Somaliland in August 1940. After initial Italian success, the

British Commander General Wavell launched a pincers offensive against Aosta's 110,000 strong force rapidly over-running Italian East Africa. Aosta surrendered at Amba Alagi on 19 May 1941. He died in captivity in Kenya in 1942.

Arnim, Colonel General Jurgen von (1889–1979)
German general, last commander of the Axis forces in North Africa. Arnim commanded a Corps during Barbarossa and at the end of 1942 was appointed commander of V Panzer Army then in north-eastern Tunisia. When Rommel smashed through the American sector at Kasserine Pass on 18 February 1943, Arnim did not make a supporting attack in the north as was expected. A week later V Panzer Army attacked British First Army and gained some ground at high cost. On 6 March 1943 Rommel left Africa and was replaced by Arnim as Commander of Army Group Africa, who was now to preside over the retreat into the shrinking Tunisian bridgehead while Hitler was ordering a fight to the last round. With supplies rapidly dwindling and the Luftwaffe withdrawing to Sicily, Arnim was unable to stem the tide and went into the bag along with some 275,000 Axis POWs on 12 May 1943.

Arnold, General Henry Harley 'Hap' (1886–1950)
US general overall commander of the United States Army Air Force. Arnold was chief of the US Air Staff from 1938 and oversaw the huge wartime expansion of US airpower in both industrial and operational aspects, responsible from his desk in Washington for US air forces in all theatres of war.

Within the US Joint Chiefs of Staff Committee he was a leading advocate of airpower and like Harris and Spaatz was able to put the theories of airpower prophets like Mitchell and Douhet into effect. Arnold favoured precision bombing against critical industrial targets rather than Harris's insistence on area bombing. He resisted advice to turn the US Eighth Air Force over to night bombing while himself urging a single commander for the joint RAF/USAF

USAAF bombing commands. Arnold was the first five star
general of the United States Air Force created in 1947.

Auchinleck, Sir Claude (1884–1980)
British field marshal, C-in-C Middle East June 1941 to
August 1942, C-in-C India until 1947. A commander greatly
respected within the British and Indian armies, the 'Auk'
nevertheless suffered from Churchill's animosity and was
replaced as commander in North Africa in August 1942
after riding out Rommel's offensives. His reputation rests
on halting the German drive on Cairo at the First Battle of
Alamein, July 1942, and stabilizing the defence line from
which Montgomery would launch the decisive counter
offensive.

Auchinleck made his career in the Indian Army, coming
to Britain to command the newly raised IV Corps in 1940.
He was briefly C-in-C northern Norway, C-in-C India in
1941, then sent by Churchill to replace Wavell in Cairo.
His offensive codenamed Crusader relieved besieged
Tobruk but Rommel's counterstroke pushed the British
back to Gazala and Tobruk finally fell. In spite of the July
1942 success, Auchinleck was replaced by Alexander who,
it seemed to Churchill, would tackle Rommel more pugnaciously. Auchinleck returned to India and served as
Commander-in-Chief until independence and partition.

Aung San, General U (1915–1947)
Commander of the Burmese Independence Army (later
Burmese National Army), anti-British independence leader
who collaborated fitfully with Japanese. Negotiated with
post-war by British government but assassinated July 1947.

Bader, Group Captain Sir Douglas (1910–1982)
British fighter pilot and air combat tactician. Bader over-
came the disability of losing both legs in a 1931 flying
accident but cajoled his way back into the RAF commanding 242 Squadron from June 1940 and five squadrons thereafter, developing the successful 'Big Wing' tactics. Bader

crashed in France in August 1941 and spent the rest of the war as a POW.

Badoglio, Field Marshal Pietro (1871–1956)
Distinguished soldier and signatory of Italy's unconditional surrender in September 1943, Badoglio was the first prime minister of post-fascist Italy.

Badoglio fought in Italy's colonial wars and as a colonel in the First World War rising to deputy Chief of Staff. Governor of Libya and viceroy of Ethiopia, he was appointed Chief of Staff for the third time in 1940 but resigned after the fiasco in Greece. Badoglio was a key conspirator against Mussolini from 1942 onwards and took over the government from 25 July 1943. He announced surrender over Rome radio on 8 September but already the Germans were moving to disarm the disaffected Italians and claim Italy as a country under military occupation.

Beaverbrook, Lord Maxwell Aitken (1879–1964)
Press magnate, political ally of Winston Churchill and British cabinet minister, Minister of Aircraft Production 1940, Minister of Supply 1941–42, Lord Privy Seal 1943–45.

Benes, President Eduard (1884–1948)
President of Czech government in exile. President of Czechoslovakia from 1935, Benes resigned after the Munich agreement of September 1938 and taught briefly at Chicago University before forming the Czech National Committee in Paris. From London Benes led Czech Free Forces and a government recognized by Britain from July 1941. Benes signed a treaty with the Soviet Union in December 1943 and became President in 1946. He died soon after the 1948 Communist takeover.

Beveridge, Sir William (1878–1963)
British academic and administrator. Author of Beveridge Report published December 1942 which laid out foundations for postwar British state welfare system.

161

People

Bevin, Ernest (1881–1951)

British politician, Minister of Labour and National Service in War Cabinet. Bevin rose through trade union politics (dockers, TGWU, TUC Chairman, 1936) in Labour Party, elected MP in 1940. As a minister in the coalition government he used the Emergency Powers act to mobilize labour, proscribing strikes and, from 1941 onwards, directly conscripting men and women into industry.Foreign Secretary in Attlee's government July 1945–1951. He attended the Potsdam conference and presided over Indian independence and the establishment of the state of Israel.

Billotte, General Gaston (1875–1940)

French general, commander of First Army Group in 1940. Billotte was responsible for the crucial area of operations in May–June 1940 with two French armies and the BEF under him. He supervised the Allied advance to the River Dyle on the invasion of Belgium and the subsequent withdrawal and was planning a counterattack when he was killed in a motor accident.

Blaskowitz, Colonel-General Johannes von (1883–1948)

German general, tried at Nuremberg, committed suicide. Commander VIII Army during invasion of Poland and subsequently commander of Army of Occupation. Commander of 1 Army during Operation Anton, the occupation of Vichy France. Commander of Army Group G briefly from end of 1944 and in last weeks of war the commander of 'Fortress Holland', surrendered 5 May 1945.

Blomberg, Field Marshal Werner von (1878–1946)

Defence Minister in Hitler's first cabinet from January 1933, the regime's first *General Feldmarschall* (April 1936), Blomberg played an unwitting role in the subjection of the army to Hitler's will. In the Blomberg-Fritsch crisis of 1938, Blomberg was stripped of office for having 'married a prostitute'. Hitler used the episode to abolish the war

162

ministry as such and subordinate it to the new *Oberkommando der Wehrmacht* (OKW) with himself as head. Blomberg was captured by US troops at the end of the war and died while waiting to become a witness at Nuremberg.

Blumentritt, General Gunther (1892–1967)
A diligent staff officer and field commander in closing months of war, Blumentritt was chief of planning and operations on Rundstedt's staff during Polish and French campaigns. From January 1942 he was Chief of Staff to Field Marshal von Kluge's V Army. Back on Rundstedt's staff in France he was an important figure in counter-invasion planning. October 1944 he was appointed commander of XII SS Corps, from January 1945, commander of XXV Army, March Commander of 1 Parachute Army, April Commander of 'Army Group Blumentritt', finally surrendering to the British at Lübeck.

Bock, Field Marshal Fedor von (1885–1945)
A Pour le Mérite bearer from the First World War, Bock rose through the *Reichswehr* to command by 1938 one of the three Army Groups into which the peacetime army was divided. Commander of Army Group North during the Polish campaign, Army Group B during the invasion of the West, and Army Group Centre during Barbarossa. Commander Army Group South January–July 1942, replaced by von Weichs after incurring Hitler's wrath and killed at the end of the war in attack by British aircraft.

Bradley, General Omar Nelson (1893–1982)
US general who commanded four field armies during the drive into Germany, the largest number of troops ever commanded by a US field commander – over a million and a quarter men. He showed his talents in Tunisia, taking command of II Corps from Patton, taking Bizerte in 1943 with 40,000 Axis prisoners. He then led II Corps during the invasion of Sicily.

In October 1943, Bradley set up HQ of First Army at Bristol, beginning planning for Overlord. First Army went ashore at Omaha and Utah beaches, cleared the Cotentin Peninsula, captured Cherbourg and participated in Operation Cobra, the breakout battle of 24 July 1944. On 1 August Bradley took command of Twelfth Army Group, commanding its four armies until the war's end. His troops bore the brunt of and held the German Ardennes attack, taking the Remagen bridge, sealing the Ruhr pocket and finally meeting the Soviets on the Elbe. Of US generals Bradley especially earned the respect and affection of the men he commanded.

Brauchitsch, Field Marshal Walther von (1881–1948)

German field marshal, Commander-in-Chief of the German Army 1938–41. After the dismissal of Fritsch, Brauchitsch was appointed C-in-C of the German Army largely because he was more pliable to Hitler's will. From there on, as the German Army achieved more and more military success on the battlefield, in fact politically it was in steep decline. After the failure before Moscow in December 1941, Hitler himself assumed supreme command, the first civilian to command the German Army. Brauchitsch remained on the active list, but saw no more active service during the war. He died in Hamburg before the start of his war crimes trial.

Braun, Wernher von (1912–1977)

At the age of 25, Braun, a trained rocket engineer, was appointed technical director of the German Army's research centre on the Baltic coast at Peenemünde, and by 1938 he had developed the prototype A-4, 'Aggregat-4', a ballistic missile which could carry a high explosive warhead over a short distance.

With the Luftwaffe pressing for research funds for their V–1 cruise missile, the V–2 army programme was not given the full go-ahead until 1943 when Hitler demanded mass production. The first V–2 was fired against Britain in September 1944 and in the following months more than three and a half thousand were aimed against Britain and Antwerp.

Braun surrendered himself and his research to the Americans in 1945. He and his team were installed at Redstone Arsenal, where their work contributed greatly to the development of US inter-continental ballistic missiles and the space programme.

Brooke, Field Marshal Sir Alan (1883–1963)
Chief of the Imperial General Staff (CIGS), 1941–46. Field Marshal Brooke, later First Viscount Alanbrooke, was Britain's most important professional soldier during the war.

In France in May 1940 he commanded the British II Corps and played a vital role during the BEF's retreat to evacuation from Dunkirk. As Commander-in-Chief Home Forces, Brooke had to build up anti-invasion forces in Britain on slender resources, succeeding Sir John Dill as CIGS in December 1941.

In this command he played a vital role right at the head centre of the Allied prosecution of the war, turning Prime Minister Churchill's ideas into practical plans.

Budenny, Marshal Semyon (1883–1973)
Budenny was a veteran of the First Cavalry Army of the Civil War, membership of which was enough to secure Stalin's lack of enmity and to have survived the purges of the 1930s. Blessed with this good fortune, Budenny was unfortunate enough to be facing Guderian and Kleist's panzer armies in the Ukraine and Bessarabia in June 1941.

Budenny's forces were rapidly encircled by the advancing German armies and in spite of desperate counterattacks, could not hold the line. Budenny was removed from command on 13 September 1941, but his old associations were to save him from disgrace. He was transferred to a reserve front before Moscow and in 1942 a quiet Caucasian front until January 1943, when he was made the titular commander of the Soviet Army's Cavalry.

Chamberlain, Neville (1869–1940)
British statesman, Prime Minister, 1937–1940. Very important figure in the run up to the outbreak of war.

Born into a political family, he left Rugby school early to concentrate on business and later local government in Birmingham. In 1918 became a Conservative MP; no other PM entered Parliament so late. Minister of Health 1924–29 and in 1931 Chancellor of the Exchequer. In May 1937 he became Prime Minister in succession to Stanley Baldwin and quickly took charge of foreign policy although he had little previous experience. Here he relied strongly on the advice of Sir Horace Wilson, a career civil servant who in fact had more influence on the direction of foreign policy than the Foreign Secretaries, Anthony Eden, who resigned in protest February 1938, and Viscount Halifax.

Chamberlain genuinely believed Hitler could be 'appeased' by a mix of direction discussion and concession. During the Czechoslovak crisis of 1938 Chamberlain flew to meet Hitler at Berchtesgaden and Godesberg followed by the four-power conference at Munich. When Chamberlain returned with a 'piece of paper' bearing Hitler's signature and promising 'peace in our time' he was hailed as a hero by one section of the nation, as the arch appeaser who had betrayed Czechoslovakia by the other. On 15 March 1939 when the Germans occupied Prague even Chamberlain, under pressure from Halifax, began to see that Munich had opened the way for German domination of Central Europe.

Chamberlain still spoke of the possibility of negotiation on 2 September 1939 as German armies were pushing into Poland. At last at 11.15 am on the morning of Sunday, 3 September, Chamberlain told the nation by radio that Britain was at war with Germany. Chamberlain's hesitancy was evident through the first winter of the Phoney War and he resigned after the disaster in Norway in April 1940 to be succeeded by Churchill. He resigned from Churchill's coalition war cabinet on 3 October 1940 and died on 9 November 1940.

Canaris, Admiral Wilhelm (1887–1945)
Head of the German *Abwehr* (Armed Forces Intelligence, literal meaning 'defence') from January 1935, Admiral Canaris flirted throughout with resistance to Hitler and the Nazi

regime. Although he did not become actively involved in the military resistance, he used the apparatus of the *Abwehr* to provide cover and assistance to its members.

After the July plot collapsed, Canaris was arrested on 23 July 1944. Control of military counterintelligence passed entirely to the RHSA. After interrogation, Canaris was executed on 9 April 1945, only a few days before its liberation, at Flossenbürg Concentration Camp.

Chiang, Kai-Shek (1887–1975)

President of Nationalist China from 1943, Chinese General-issimo, and Allied Supreme Commander of the China Theatre of Operations. Chiang became Commander-in-Chief of the Kuomintang Army in 1925 and broke with the Communists two years later. In 1928 he established a nationalist government at Nanking.

After the Japanese attacks on Shanghai at Nanking, Chiang set up a seat of government at Chungking. After Pearl Harbor, Chiang was greeted by Roosevelt and Churchill as an Allied national supreme commander and treated as such at the 1943 Cairo Conference. In fact, on the ground, all the Chinese armies could do was tie up Japanese strength which might have been deployed elsewhere in Asia, while he himself feuded with his own commanders, and fitfully fought the Communists. Operationally there were problems, particularly with General Joseph Stilwell, his US Chief of Staff, who called Chiang 'The Peanut'. Recognized in 1945 by the West as Chinese Head of State, Chiang's power was on the wane and he was to be driven to Formosa by the Communist offensives in the Civil War of 1948.

Chuikov, General Vasili (1900–   )

Chuikov was commander of the Soviet 62nd Army during the defence of Stalingrad, holding the right bank of the Volga throughout the siege. This command fought through all the Soviet counteroffensives to Berlin itself.

167

People

Ciano, Count Galeazzo (1903–1944)

Italian Foreign Minister from 1936, appointed for the fact that he was Mussolini's son-in-law rather than his brilliance as a career diplomat. After the Axis reverses, he resigned in February 1943 but remained as a member of the Fascist Grand Council. Soon after the Council voted to depose Mussolini, the Duce was rescued by the Germans and set up a new Fascist republic. Reviled by the new government in Rome, Ciano was tricked by the Germans into fleeing north. He was tried and shot by his former Fascist cronies on 11 January 1944.

Clark, General Mark (1896–1983)

Able and successful US commander. The captor of Rome 4 June 1943, and at the war's end commander 15 Army Group in Mediterranean and after 1945 commander of the US occupation zone of Austria.

Clark's Fifth Army took part in the Anzio landings of January 1944, but this operation did not cut German communications to Rome from Cassino. Clark bowed to military pressure to have the Cassino Benedictine monastery bombed, but turning it into rubble just stiffened the defences.

After the capture of Rome, forces were diverted from the Italian Front to the landings in the South of France, code-named Anvil and Dragoon. Clark argued in private for a continued drive through Italy, and ended his operations there. Clark was commander of UN Forces in Korea in May 1952. He retired from military service in October 1953.

Clay, General Lucius (1897–1977)

US logistics expert, he was sent to France in 1944 following the Normandy landings to command the base section. After the German defeat he became, under General Eisenhower, Deputy Military Governor of the US zone responsible for military government and for the US voice in the whole of the Western Allied occupation zone. As such he was an important figure in the establishment of the new post-war federal republic.

Crerar, General Henry (1888–1965)
Canadian general. From 1942–44 Crerar was GOC, 1 Canadian Corps, UK and Italy. From late 1943 he was Commander, Canadian First Army. In February 1945, eight British divisions and most of 21st Army Group were assigned to Crerar in the operations to clear the mouths of the Rhine.

Cripps, Sir Richard (Stafford) (1889–1952)
Socialist politician, member of the wartime coalition cabinet. Cripps swung from pacifism to opposing appeasement in the late thirties, and was expelled from the Labour Party in 1939. From 1940 to 1942 he was British Ambassador to Moscow, and in 1942 headed the Cripps Mission to India, which swung Indian nationalists to a policy of cooperation with a promise of independence post-war. In November 1942, he was made Minister of Aircraft Production. Cripps became Chancellor in the post-war Attlee government in 1947 in succession to Hugh Dalton and was responsible for a policy of austerity.

Cunningham, Admiral Sir Andrew Browne (1883–1963)
Admiral Cunningham, later Viscount Cunningham, was one of the outstanding naval commanders of the war.

At the outbreak of war, Cunningham was British commander in the Mediterranean. When Italy declared war, Cunningham saw his main fleet base at Malta compromised but realized the strategic importance of seizing the initiative in the Mediterranean. In November 1940, three battleships were put out of action at Taranto by air-delivered torpedo attack, and the night battle of Cape Matapan in 1941 ended the Italian naval challenge in the Mediterranean.

The intervention of German airpower, however, brought a new crisis, and Cunningham's command was severely depleted in the actions off Crete, during the siege of Malta, and bringing supplies to embattled Tobruk.

169

In June 1942, Cunningham was sent to Washington as British Naval Representative on the combined Chiefs of Staff Committee, and was then appointed Eisenhower's deputy for the Torch landings. He was also naval commander for the Sicily landings, but succeeded Pound as First Sea Lord in October 1943.

Darlan, Admiral Jean François (1881–1942)

At the fall of France, Darlan was Commander-in-Chief of the French Navy. He had assured Churchill the fleet would not fall into German hands, but accepted the position of Minister of the Navy in Pétain's government, becoming Vice-Premier in the Vichy government, February 1941.

Trying to lean both ways, in 1942 he lost his political power when Laval returned and was appointed High Commissioner in French North Africa. Meanwhile, the US authorities recognized Darlan as Head of the French government, in direct opposition to the British recognition of de Gaulle. Any potential inter-Allied political problem was removed when Darlan was assassinated by a French monarchist on Christmas Eve, 1942.

de Lattre de Tassigny, General Jean (1889–1952)

Commander of the French 14th Division on the Ain in 1940, de Lattre was sent by the Vichy regime to Tunisia before being recalled for his Allied sympathies. He escaped from prison to Britain, where he was received by de Gaulle, becoming Commander of the First French Army in North Africa. He led this command in the liberation of France and was the French signatory of the German surrender document.

de Valera, Eamon (1882–1975)

Taeshoch (Premier) of Ireland from 1937, he was the backbone of Eire's neutrality policy and refused Britain the use of bases in Southern Ireland and other forms of military cooperation.

Dietl, Colonel General Eduard (1890–1944)

Commander of the German 3rd Mountain Division which took Narvik in the Norwegian campaign of 1940. Dietl was later commander of Army Group North and of the German mountain and ski troops operating in Finland, 1942–44. He was killed in an air crash.

Dietrich, General Josef (Sepp) (1892–1966)

An SS *Gruppenführer* from 1933, Dietrich played an important part in the blood purge of Röhm's SA in June 1934, as head of Hitler's bodyguard SS unit. In 1938 this unit, now the 'Leibstandarte SS, Adolf Hitler,' became a motorized infantry unit. It later became a panzer division, remaining under Dietrich's command until 1944. As a general of the Waffen-SS, Dietrich commanded the First SS Panzer Corps on the Eastern Front and in December 1944 led the VI SS Panzer Army in the Ardennes offensive.

In 1946, Dietrich was tried for responsibility in the Malmédy massacre, in which American POWs were slaughtered, convicted and sentenced to life imprisonment.

Dill, Field Marshal Sir John Greer (1881–1944)

Commander 1 Corps, British Expeditionary Force in France, Dill was appointed General in October 1939, and in April 1940 he returned from France as Vice-CIGS to succeed Ironside as CIGS in May. Dill's cautious personality clashed with Churchill's impetuousness at this most difficult stage of the war, and he was replaced by Brooke as CIGS at the end of 1941. Dill accompanied Churchill to Washington, heading the British Joint Staff Mission, remaining as Senior British Officer on the Anglo-US Combined Chiefs of Staff, building up significant relationships with Roosevelt, King and Marshall. Upon his death in 1944, he was buried in Arlington National Cemetery, Washington.

Dobbie, General Sir William (1879–1964)

A retired Royal Engineer general in 1939, Dobbie was appointed Governor of Malta in the spring of 1940, holding the island through the siege until replaced in May 1942 by Lord Gort.

Dönitz, Grossadmiral Karl (1891–1984)

Successively commander of the German Navy's U-boat force, Commander-in-Chief of the German Navy, and last head of German government in May 1945.

Dönitz was assigned to the new U-boat arm of the German Navy in 1935, being responsible for its technical and manpower build-up. With the French Atlantic coast in German hands post-1940, Dönitz established his HQ at Lorient, from where he prosecuted the U-boat war which nearly severed the Atlantic lifeline to embattled Great Britain. The entry of the US into the war offered merely a new crop of easy targets rather than a sustained counter-offensive, but the Allies seized the technical initiative with developments in radar and radio direction finding, closing the mid-Atlantic air gap by mid-1943. From here on the U-boat offensive was in decline. Meanwhile Dönitz had been appointed Commander-in-Chief of the German Navy as from 30 January 1943, succeeding Eric Raeder, and Dönitz switched production from surface units to U-boats and E-boats. On 30 April, Dönitz received instructions from Bormann via radio that Hitler was dead, and he was the new Head of State. Dönitz was arrested on 23 May 1945, and sentenced at Nuremberg to ten years' imprisonment at Spandau Prison in Berlin. He was released in October 1956.

Donovan, William J. (1883–1959)

'Wild Bill' Donovan was a World War I hero, a peacetime lawyer who was appointed by Roosevelt to head the Office of Strategic Services (OSS), forerunner of the CIA or Central Intelligence Agency. The OSS had three branches; Operations, Intelligence and Research – with an assorted group of talents working for it in the field or behind the scenes in Europe and the Far East. At the Nuremberg Trials, Donovan acted as an aide to the Chief Prosecutor.

Douglas, Air Marshal Sir William Sholto (1893–1969)
Assistant Chief of the British Air Staff at the outbreak of
war, Sholto Douglas succeeded Dowding as Commander,
RAF Fighter Command, in November 1940. He was suc-
cessively C-in-C RAF Middle East, and then C-in-C Coastal
Command. Post-war, he was the British member of the
Allied Control Council for Germany.

Dowding, Air Chief Marshal Sir Hugh (1882–1970)
The commander of RAF Fighter Command during the
Battle of Britain summer 1940, he lost the doctrinal battle
within the RAF and retired from active service in 1942. His
single-mindedness secured the withdrawal of the remaining
British fighter squadrons in France during its collapse, and
his resolution and abilities as a commander were a vital
asset during the critical battle in the skies above southern
England, especially during the large-scale Luftwaffe offensives of July/September 1940.

From November 1940 to 1942 he served on a mission for
the Ministry of Aircraft Production to the US and Canada.

Eaker, General Ira C. (1896–   )
Commanding General, US Army Air Forces in the United
Kingdom from October 1943, Commander-in-Chief Mediterranean Allied Air Forces from January 1944, Eaker
was an exponent of strategic bombing. At the Casablanca
Conference he convinced the Combined Chiefs to allow his
Eighth Air Force to continue daylight precision bombing,
and the combined bomber offensive with the RAF operating
at night was also known as the Eaker Plan.

From his Mediterranean command he continued a strategic bombing offensive from Italy against southern Germany, and in March 1944 planned the air assault on the
monastery at Monte Cassino.

He became Deputy Commander USAAF in the spring of
1945, later he served as its Chief of Staff until retirement in
1947.

People

Eden, Anthony (1897–1977)
Foreign Secretary in Churchill's coalition government from 23 December 1940, to 27 July 1945. Eden had been Foreign Secretary from 1935 to 1938, but resigned because of Chamberlain's appeasement policies. Recalled to the Chamberlain Cabinet as Dominions Secretary in 1939, he became Secretary of State for War when Churchill took over in May 1940.

Eden travelled extensively to Greece, to Moscow, to Washington, to Algiers and to virtually all the major wartime Allied Conferences, where his charm and persuasiveness were at a premium.

In spite of his Conservative politics, he was able to accommodate relations with the Soviet Union, but tried to dissuade Churchill from making concessions to Stalin in Eastern Europe. Churchill always regarded him as his natural successor in the event of his own death.

Falkenhausen, General Alexander von (1878–1966)
Commander-in-Chief of German occupation troops in Belgium and France. From early 1942, Falkenhausen became involved in the opposition to Hitler, but was dismissed from his post five days before the July plot attempt on the dictator's life. Arrested and imprisoned by the Nazis, he was released by the Americans but was sentenced in 1951 to twelve years in prison because of the shooting of hostages in occupied Belgium. He was in fact released shortly after being convicted.

Falkenhorst, Colonel General Nikolaus von (1885–1968)
Commander-in-Chief of German troops in Norway during the invasion of May 1940, he stayed in Norway as military commander until the end of the war.

Fatch, Rear Admiral Aubrey Wray (1883–1978)
Fatch commanded a task force in Nimitz's Pacific Fleet. At the Battle of Coral Sea his Task Force 11 consisted of the carrier *Lexington*, two heavy cruisers, and five destroyers. In that, the first carrier battle of the war, he launched the

174

air attacks which sank the two Japanese carriers but the *Lexington* was badly bombed and sank soon after. In 1944 Fatch became Deputy Chief of Naval Air Operations.

Fletcher, Vice Admiral Frank Jack (1885–1973)
US naval commander whose most distinguished contributions to the outcome of the Pacific War were at the battles of Coral Sea and Midway. Fletcher's task force with his flag in the carrier *Yorktown* sighted the Japanese fleet heading for Port Moresby, fighting a four-day air battle, 4–8 May 1942. After the *Yorktown* was hit, Spruance directed the Battle of Midway. In August 1942, Fletcher commanded the carrier group off Guadalcanal, but withdrew when his flagship, the *Saratoga*, was hit and he himself was wounded. After action in the Eastern Solomons where the *Enterprise* was badly damaged, Fletcher was transferred to command the North Pacific forces, where he remained until the end of the war, retiring in 1947.

Franco, General Francisco (1892–1975)
Franco had defeated the Spanish Republic largely with the help of German and Italian military aid and personnel. In spite of this, Franco did not join the war on the Axis side even at the highest tide of German victories. Spanish neutrality ensured British control of the Western Mediterranean from Gibraltar.

Hitler and the Spanish 'Caudillo' met at Hendaye on the Franco–Spanish border on 23 October 1940, but the two dictators did no more to enter into a military alliance. Spanish volunteers however did serve on the Eastern Front in Wehrmacht uniform.

Frank, Hans (1900–1946)
Frank was a lawyer and early member of the Nazi Party, becoming Reich Commissioner of Justice in 1933. In 1939 he was appointed Governor-General of that Polish territory (called the Government General) which had not been annexed by Germany or the Soviet Union following the dual invasions of 1939. From Cracow in collusion with the

175

SS and the German military occupation forces, he supervised a brutal and repressive regime, enslaving the Poles and rounding up Jews for extermination in the concentration camps of Auschwitz and Treblinka. After German defeat, he tried several times unsuccessfully to commit suicide, surviving to face trial at Nuremberg, admitting his guilt in emotional terms and compiling a lengthy testimony in captivity.

Frank, Karl Hermann (1898–1946)
The leader, along with Konrad Henlein, of the Sudeten German Party and from 1939 Secretary of State for the Reich's protectorate of Bohemia and Moravia. After the assassination of Heydrich, he ordered the massacres at Lidice and Lazaky. He was publicly hanged near Prague in May 1946.

Fraser, Bruce Austin, First Baron Fraser of North Cape (1888–1982)
Commander-in-Chief of the British Home Fleet, who directed the action against the German battlecruiser *Scharnhorst* on 26 December 1943, off the North Cape. From August 1944 Fraser was Commander of the Eastern Fleet in the Indian Ocean, commanding the Pacific Fleet from November that year. Fraser was First Sea Lord and Chief of the Naval Staff from 1948 to 1951.

Freyberg, General Sir Bernard (1889–1963)
Commander of New Zealand troops in World War II. As a young soldier in the First World War, Freyberg had shown himself to be immensely tough and valiant, winning the Victoria Cross in 1917.

In 1939, Major General Freyberg became Commander of the New Zealand Division, which went on to become one of the élite units of the Allied Forces in North Africa, with Freyberg fighting successfully to keep them as a single cohesive unit.

After being diverted to Greece, Freyberg and his troops withdrew to Crete in May 1941, and he led the island's defence, inflicting heavy casualties on the airborne German invaders.

This was Freyberg's last independent command; henceforth his New Zealanders fought in the North African campaign, and in November 1942 they moved to Italy, transferring from the British Eighth Army to General Clark's Fifth Army. Freyberg led the attacks on Monte Cassino, urging the bombing of the Benedictine monastery. After the war, he was made Governor-General of New Zealand from 1946 to 1952.

Frick, Wilhelm (1877–1946)
Minister of Interior from 1933 to 1943 and then Reich's protector of Bohemia and Moravia, but Frank, his deputy, had real power. Frick, the early Nazi and faceless civil servant, was executed in October 1946, after trial at Nuremberg.

Fritsch, General Werner von (1880–1939)
Commander-in-Chief of the German Army in 1938, dismissed by Hitler for alleged homosexual conduct, Fritsch's aloof silence gave Hitler the opportunity to subordinate Army High Command, and 16 high-ranking generals were retired. Fritsch was killed by a stray bullet during the attack on Warsaw, September 1939.

Gamelin, General Maurice (1872–1958)
Chief of Staff for National Defence during the fall of France. Having failed to assist Poland in 1939 or prevent German victory in Norway, Gamelin failed to intervene decisively in the conduct of the battles of May 1940, even after it was clear that his subordinate, General Georges, had lost control on the North-east Front. He had to be removed from office on 19 May. In 1942 he was put on trial by the Vichy government for his role in the French defeat, and was jailed until 1943 before being deported to Germany. He was finally freed by advancing US troops in May 1945

People

George II, King of Greece (see *Monarchy*)

*George VI, King of Great Britain and Northern Ireland
(1895–1952)* (see *Monarchy*)

Georges, General Alphonse (1875–1951)
General Georges commanded the French troops on the
North-east Front in 1940 including the Seventh Army, Army
Groups 1 and 2 and the BEF. When the German attack
broke on 10 May, Georges delegated command to General
Billotte, commanding the French Army Group 1, while he
supervised the redeployment of the Belgian Army. When
the axis of German advance through the Ardennes became
apparent, Georges was unable to make effective counterattacks. He was relieved of command on 19 May.

Giraud, General Henri (1879–1949)
With the assassination of Admiral Darlan on 24 December
1942, General Giraud was appointed High Commissioner
for French Africa as well as French Army Commander-in-
Chief having been smuggled out of France by submarine on
the eve of the Torch landings. While the US backed Giraud
as a figurehead for French military participation, the British
were still backing de Gaulle. At Casablanca in January
1943, the two arrivals made a temporary reconciliation,
heading a central French Committee of National Liberation
on an equal basis. Over the next year, Giraud slowly lost
his US support and was outmanoeuvred by de Gaulle. In
August 1943 Giraud stepped down from his political position, devoting himself to the build-up of French military
forces. By April 1944, Giraud's role was totally eclipsed.

Goebbels, Josef (1897–1945)
Minister of Propaganda from 1933, Gauleiter of Berlin and
advocate of 'Total War', Goebbels was the nearest thing to
an intellectual in the Nazi leadership who understood that
ideas were as powerful as tanks or guns of the apparatus of
terror and coercion. He sold Hitler to the German people

178

as something to love rather than fear, and in this he was successful right up to the very end.

He joined the party in 1925, becoming Gauleiter of 'Red' Berlin in 1926 and became head of the party's propaganda section in 1929 where his talents as a huckster and political fixer flourished. From 1933 onwards all aspects of German cultural life were absorbed under his umbrella with total control of the mass media, newspapers, film and radio in which anti-semitism was pre-eminent. In the years of German triumph, Goebbels' job was relatively easy. In the years of defeat, his undoubted black talents showed themselves and the unity of the embattled Reich was maintained to the end. Goebbels played a particularly important part in the suppression of the July 1944 plot and continued his exhortations to 'Total War' begun with the Sportspalast speech of February 1943. He was loyal to Hitler to the end, sharing the last days in the bunker and committing suicide with his wife, having poisoned his children, on 30 April 1945.

Göring, Reichsmarschall Hermann (1893–1946)
Commander of the Luftwaffe, President of the Reichstag, Interior Minister, then Prime Minister of Prussia, Commissioner of the Four Year Plan, Plenipotentiary for Armaments, Warden of the Reich Forests. Göring rose as the Nazi party rose, accreting ever greater office and power to himself, driven by an ambitious and flamboyant personality. He fell from Hitler's grace only at the very end, having suggested by radio that he take over leadership of the crumbling Reich. Hitler, in the bunker, stripped him of all his offices but his decline had begun in 1942 paralleling that of the Luftwaffe itself, unable to stem the tide on the Eastern Front or protect Germany from the lash of Anglo-American bombing.

Göring was a hero of the First World War, who had taken command of the great von Richthofen's fighter group in 1918. He had fled to Scandinavia after the collapse, but returned to Germany to become an early member of the NSDAP. He briefly commanded the SA and was wounded in the Munich putsch of 1923. In the late 1920s Göring was politically useful to the Nazis by cultivating what remained of German society, especially sympathetic industrialists. After the seizure of power Göring became one of the most important figures in the Reich, collecting offices and rewards, relinquishing only one, control of the Prussian police, the Gestapo and the first concentration camps, to Himmler and the SS in 1934.

Göring concentrated on building the Luftwaffe which came into the open in March 1936, although subsequent misplanning was to sow the seeds of eventual defeat. By July 1940 when he was created *Reichsmarschall*, his air force was everywhere triumphant – that is until the Battle of Britain where his promises started to ring hollow. The failure in Russia showed up the lack of planning for a long war over long ranges. The promise to supply VI Army at Stalingrad proved as flimsy as his declarations that Germany would be immune from air attack. From 1942–45 the combined Allied bombing offensive wrecked German cities from end to end while Göring squabbled with and wasted the talents of his gifted subordinates such as Udet, Jeschonnek and Galland.

As the *Reichsmarschall* retreated into a life of sumptuous luxury, a drug fuelled fantasy world which did not extend beyond the borders of his estate Karinhall filled with looted art treasures, the real chief executive of the Luftwaffe became Field Marshal Erhard Milch who deployed its declining resources with some competence. Göring was captured alive and was the principal defendant at Nuremberg. Sentenced to death by hanging, he committed suicide on 15 October 1946.

Gort, Field Marshal John (Sixth Viscount Gort) (1886–1946)
With an outstanding record of valour in World War I, Lord Gort was promoted Chief of the Imperial General Staff (CIGS) in 1937, becoming Commander-in-Chief of the BEF in France in 1939. After Dunkirk, Gort became Governor of Gibraltar, and then Governor-General and C-in-C in Malta 1942–44. He was promoted Field Marshal in 1943,

serving as High Commissioner and C-in-C Palestine at the end of the war.

Graziani, Rodolfo (1882–1955)
Governor of Libya 1930–34, C-in-C Ethiopia 1936–37, Chief of Italian Army Staff 1939, 1940 C-in-C Italian Armed Forces in Libya.

Graziani became Minister of War in Mussolini's Fascist Government of 1943. He was captured by partisans in April 1945, sentenced to prison in 1950, and freed by amnesty that year.

Greim, Robert Ritter von (1892–1945)
An able Luftwaffe commander of the Second World War, Greim was summoned by Hitler to the bunker, then under Soviet siege, to be told in person that he was Commander-in-Chief of the Luftwaffe in succession to Hermann Göring. There was no Luftwaffe left to command, and Greim committed suicide on 24 May.

Groves, General Leslie (1898–1970)
US Army Engineer Officer, in 1941 he was Deputy Chief of Army Construction. In September 1942 Groves was promoted to Brigadier General in command of Manhattan District, the cover name for the A-bomb project. Groves urged the operational use of atomic weapons to end the war.

Guderian, Colonel General Heinz (1888–1953)
Guderian was a key figure in the build-up of Germany's armoured forces before the war and in their operational use in battle. He commanded a corps in Poland, showing the promise of his Blitzkrieg theories. The crossing of the Meuse at Sedan and the following thrust at Northern France showed just how right he had been. In June 1941 Guderian commanded II Panzer Army. After falling out with Hitler and his superior, Field Marshal von Kluge, he was removed from his command.

After the disaster at Stalingrad however, he was back

in favour, now Inspector General of Armoured Troops. Following the July Plot, Guderian replaced General Zeitzler as Chief of the General Staff, but again clashed with Hitler and was relieved on 28 March 1945.

Haakon VII (1872–1957) (see Monarchy)

Haile Selassie (Emperor of Abyssinia) (1891–1976) (see Monarchy)

Halder, General Franz (1884–1971)
Chief of the German Army General Staff through the period of military success until dismissed by Hitler in 1942. Having flirted with military resistance to Hitler prior to the invasion of Czechoslovakia in 1938, Halder advised against an invasion of the West in 1940, seeking a defensive posture only, but with the succession of German victories Halder became subordinate to Hitler's will. Halder led the planning for the invasions of Poland and the West, for Operation Sealion and for Barbarossa.

When in December 1941 the Army Commander in Chief, von Brauchitsch, was replaced by Hitler himself, Halder remained as Chief of General Staff but was finally replaced by Zeitzler in September 1942, after one of Hitler's rages.

Halder flirted with the anti-Hitler July Plot conspirators and was arrested after the failure of the attempt on Hitler's life. He was kept in Flossenbürg, but escaped death, meeting American troops in the Tyrol on 4 May and being able to give important evidence at the Nuremberg Trials.

Halifax, Edward Frederick, First Earl of (1881–1959)
British Foreign Secretary from 1938–40 in Chamberlain's government, Ambassador to Washington 1941–46. Halifax had been a supporter of Chamberlain's appeasement policy in the late 1930s; in spite of this in May 1940 it looked like he might become Prime Minister in place of Winston Churchill. He proved a very successful Ambassador to the US.

Halsey, Vice Admiral William Frederick (1882–1959)
US naval commander in the Pacific War. Halsey's carrier task force was at sea when the Japanese struck Pearl Harbor, but carrier aircraft under his command were to take the first US counteroffensives of the Pacific War. Halsey successfully struck the Gilberts, targets in the Marshall Islands, harassed the Japanese garrison on Wake, and Marcus Island.

He oversaw Doolittle's B-25 raid on Tokyo in April 1942, but missed the Battle of Midway when hospitalized in the US. He was appointed Commander of South Pacific Forces in October 1942, and was immediately involved in the Battle of Santa Cruz Island and the Guadalcanal operations, November 1942.

Halsey's forces were engaged through 1943 in climbing the Solomon Islands chain, until in June 1944 he became Commander of the Third Fleet engaged in the central Pacific, an operational command much to Halsey's liking.

Third Fleet's first operations in the central Pacific were the assault on the Western Caroline Islands, and at the beginning of October 1944 it steamed to support General MacArthur's landing at Leyte on 20 October. When Halsey was given the position of the Japanese carrier fleet, he set off in pursuit leaving the San Bernardino Strait unprotected. In fact the Japanese carrier force was a decoy, allowing Admiral Kurita's battleships to pass the Strait, where it was engaged by Vice Admiral Kinkaid's Seventh Fleet.

Harriman, William Averell (1891–1983)
US businessman turned diplomat, Ambassador to Moscow 1943–46.

Harris, Air Chief Marshal Sir Arthur (1892–1984)
Harris was the architect of the RAF's night bombing policy. The Commander of No. 5 Bomber Group in 1939, Harris was disillusioned with the early RAF precision attacks on military targets. Head of Bomber Command from February 1942, he advocated instead a policy of 'area' bombing of German population centres rather than industrial targets.

People

The effectiveness of this policy, aimed at both German civilian morale and at levels of war production, has been deeply questioned, especially when set against cost in lives of aircrew.

Henderson, Sir Nevile (1882–1942)
British Ambassador to Berlin from 1937, Henderson was a supporter of Chamberlain's appeasement policy.

Hess, Rudolph (1896–   )
A member of the Nazi Party from 1920, from April 1933 Hess was Hitler's deputy as Party Leader, but not Deputy Head of State.

Hess flew to Scotland on 10 May 1941, seeking a separate deal with the British without Hitler's knowledge. Hess was treated as a prisoner and tried at Nuremberg for crimes against peace. Against Soviet wishes, he was not executed but sentenced to life imprisonment, and remained in his ninetieth year a prisoner in Spandau in the British sector of Berlin.

Heydrich, Reinhard (1904–1942)
The most powerful figure in the SS after Himmler and the principal instigator of the attempted extermination of European Jewry. Heydrich was an athletic man of action compared to the desk bound Himmler and he used his energy to build up the power of the RSHA which he ran, the Reich Security Head Office which embraced the SS's own intelligence service, the SD, the Gestapo and the Kripo or criminal police. He was in charge of mass deportation in Poland, and of the Einsatzkommandos which followed the German Army into the Soviet Union to massacre Jews and political adversaries. Heydrich with Eichmann convened the Wannsee Conference of January 1942 which sanctioned the 'final solution' for European Jewry. This remained Heydrich's responsibility when he was appointed Reichsprotector of Bohemia-Moravia. His car was attacked by Czech resistance fighters and he died of wounds five days later on

4 June 1942. German revenge was terrible including the extermination of the village of Lidice.

Himmler, Heinrich (1900–1945)
Reichsführer–SS, commander of the SS and German police. Himmler was an opportunist and supreme bureaucrat of death, a Nazi party member from 1923 who trailed in Hitler's wake to become briefly one of the most powerful and perhaps in perpetuity one of the most infamous figures in recent history.

Himmler's power base was the SS (which see). He achieved control of the Gestapo and concentration camp system in 1934 and connived at the elimination of the SA as a rival power base in June that year. In 1936 Himmler was made Reich Chief of Police independent of the Ministry of the Interior while the SS raised their first field combat formation (see *Waffen – SS*). All these were steps in the creation of an all embracing apparatus of terror and repression within the borders of the Reich which would travel outward in the wake of German conquests.

Himmler delegated control of this process to his underlings, the most important of whom was Reinhard Heydrich. Rudolf Hoess was in charge of the extermination operation at Auschwitz, Adolf Eichmann oversaw the 'final solution' (or the death) of the Jews of Europe, Muller in charge of the Gestapo, Schellenberg of the SD and Kaltenbrunner (after Heydrich's assassination in 1942) of the RSHA (*Reichssicherheitshauptamt*), the Reich Chief Security Office.

Himmler was never a member of Hitler's inner circle like Goebbels or Bormann and concerned himself with the minutiae of running the SS with its Aryan 'purity', mystic blood lines and ancestor worship rather than the realities of the war or the horrors perpetrated by the empire of which he was the chief executive. He was still ambitious however, dreaming of a separate SS-state of 'Burgundia' carved out of France and the Low Countries, and more practically scheming to take control of the V-weapons programmes, the *Abwehr* (both of which he achieved) and becoming C-in-C of the home-based *Ersatzheer*, the Replacement Army which had been the focus of the July plotters' attention. In the last months of war Himmler was made military commander of Army Group Upper Rhine, then Army Group Vistula where his amateur efforts did nothing to reverse the situation. He retired to a sanatorium where, in the last weeks of war, the great mass murderer entered into negotiations with neutrals to spare the lives of those who remained alive in his concentration camps. When Hitler found out via a neutral radio broadcast, in a convulsive rage he ordered Himmler arrested. Himmler shuffled papers with Dönitz at Flensburg for a few days before attempting to slip through the British lines in disguise. He was recognized and arrested but bit on a phial of cyanide concealed in his teeth. Himmler was buried in an unmarked grave on Lüneburg heath.

Horthy, Admiral Miklos (1868–1957)
Regent of Hungary from 1920 to 1944.

Ironside, General Sir William Edmund (1880–1959)
Chief of the British Imperial General Staff (CIGS) 1939–40, replaced by Sir John Dill in May 1940 after the period of British military disasters.

Ismay, Sir Hastings Lionel (1887–1965)
Deputy Military Secretary to the British war cabinet 1939–40, Chief of Staff to the war cabinet 1940–45. Ismay was right at the head centre of Britain's war effort. From 1952 to 1957 he was the First Secretary-General of NATO.

Jeschonnek, Colonel General Hans (1899–1943)
Chief of Staff of the Luftwaffe from February 1939, Jeschonnek came under increasing blame as the Allied bombing offensive took its toll. He committed suicide in August 1943.

Jodl, Colonel General Alfred (1890–1946)
Chief of OKW's Operations Office throughout the war, Jodl was perhaps the most important military decision-taker after Hitler himself. Injured in the 20 July bomb plot, Jodl signed the instrument of surrender at Reims on 7 May 1945. He was convicted of war crimes in 1946, and executed.

Joyce, William (1906–1946)
An American citizen, Joyce was known to the British as 'Lord Haw Haw', the English language propaganda broadcaster on the German radio. He was executed for treason.

Kaltenbrunner, Ernst (1903–1946)
A general of the SS and head of the RSHA in succession to Heydrich from 1943. Executed for war crimes committed as Head of the Security Police, the Security Service and the Gestapo.

Keitel, Field Marshal Wilhelm (1882–1946)
From February 1938 until May 1945, Keitel was Chief of the High Command of the Armed Forces (OKW). Disparagingly known as 'Lackeitel', the lackey, for his servile submission to Hitler's will, Keitel was at Hitler's side from the days of triumph to the surrender of the Third Reich. He was found guilty of war crimes and hanged on 16 October 1946.

Kesselring, Field Marshal Albert (1885–1960)
A Luftwaffe general, Kesselring in fact is best known as one of the most able of Germany's land commanders. He commanded air fleets in the campaigns over Poland and the Low Countries, and during the Battle of Britain commanded Luftflotte II. At the end of 1941, Kesselring's air fleet was sent from the Soviet Union to the Mediterranean theatre, and he became Commander in Chief South, with his headquarters at Rome. In spite of the disaster in North Africa, Kesselring really showed his mettle following the Allied invasion of Sicily and Italy itself, conducting the slow retreat

187

People

up the peninsula that denied the Allies victory until 1945. At the last gasp in March 1945, Hitler transferred him to the West to replace Rundstedt, but even his abilities in the defence were to no avail. He surrendered the southern portion of the divided German forces on 7 May 1945, to the advancing Americans.

He was sentenced to death in 1947 after a trial in Italy for war crimes, but the sentence was commuted to life imprisonment, and he was released in October 1952 due to ill-health.

Kimmel, Admiral Husband Edward (1882–1968)
Commander in Chief of the US Fleet Base at Pearl Harbor when the Japanese struck on 7 December 1941. Kimmel received much of the blame for the unreadiness and poor response of the US Naval Forces, and his lack of liaison with General Short, the Army Commander. Kimmel was removed from command on 17 December 1941, and took no further part in the war. He was cleared of the charge of dereliction of duty in 1946.

King, Fleet Admiral Ernest Joseph (1878–1956)
King is one of the key strategic figures of the war, yet one of the least known by the public. He was appointed C-in-C of the US Fleet following Pearl Harbor, and from March 1942 he was also Chief of Naval Operations. He was a member of the US Joint Chiefs of Staff Committee and also of the Combined Chiefs of Staff Committee with the British. In the Atlantic, King's primary responsibilities were to keep communications with Great Britain open, and in the Pacific to hold key positions to contain the Japanese and take the offensive as soon as possible. By 1943, the Battle of the Atlantic was substantially won, while the burden of the Pacific fighting was substantially the Navy's. After the US victories at Coral Sea and at Midway, the US Navy never again went on the defensive, taking the war to the home islands of Japan.

Kleist, Field Marshal Paul Ewald von (1881–1954)
Key panzer commander in the German Army. Panzer group
Kleist sliced through the French line at Sedan and struck
into the heart of Northern France. Kleist commanded the
German I Panzer Group in the Balkans, capturing Belgrade
on 12 April 1941. I Panzer Army captured Kiev in September, and Kleist's forces captured Rostov on the Don in
November. In summer 1942, Kleist, now commanding Army
Group A, recaptured Rostov and drove towards Baku.
After Stalingrad, Kleist's Army Group A fought in the long
retreat through the Ukraine to 1944. Hitler relieved his
commanders in the South, Kleist and Manstein, on 30
March 1944, blaming them for the succession of military
setbacks. Kleist was captured by the British, handed over
to the Yugoslavs, who in turn handed him to the Soviets
who imprisoned him for war crimes. He died in prison in
November 1954.

Konev, Marshal Ivan (1897–1973)
The Soviet commander responsible for some of the Russian
army's greatest victories. In July 1943 he stopped the
Germans at Kursk and went on the counter-offensive,
leading the Second and First Ukrainian Fronts. Appointed
Marshal in February 1944, his army accompanied by Zhukov
advanced from the Vistula to the Oder and eventually to
Berlin itself. He was Commander-in-Chief of the Warsaw
Pact Armies 1955–1960.

Kurita, Vice Admiral Takeo (1889–1977)
Commander of the Japanese Navy 1943–44, including
actions at Leyte Gulf.

Laval, Pierre (1883–1945)
French politician, pre-war Foreign Minister. Deputy Head
of State and Foreign Minister in Petain's Vichy regime.
Tried in France at the war's end and shot for treason 15
October 1945.

People

List, Field Marshal Wilhelm (1880–1971)
Commander Fourteenth Army in the attack on Poland, Commander Twelfth Army which led the advance into Belgium 1940, appointed Field Marshal 19 July 1941, see Commander in Chief of German forces in Operation Marita, the invasion of Greece.

Commander, Army Group A, July–October 1942 in the Soviet Union, his failure to break through led to his dismissal. Tried for war crimes at Nuremberg and sentenced to life imprisonment.

MacArthur, General Douglas (1880–1964)
One of the most controversial commanders of the war, and one of its most colourful. Before the war MacArthur was military adviser to the Philippines; he retired from the US Army in 1937. He was recalled to service in July 1941 and appointed Commanding General US Army Forces in the Far East. MacArthur left the Philippines for Australia on 11 March 1942, ordered out by Roosevelt. His words on his arrival were: 'I shall return.' In April, he became Supreme Commander of the huge South-west Pacific Area Command, while Admiral Nimitz was given command of the Pacific Ocean areas. MacArthur backed the tactic of 'island hopping', isolating Japanese garrisons without support and air cover.

MacArthur persuaded Nimitz to attack the Philippines rather than Formosa, and on 20 October 1944 US troops landed on Leyte and MacArthur waded ashore, fulfilling his promise to return.

MacArthur was made Supreme Commander of the Allied Powers in Japan, presiding over the rebirth of the defeated nation. In Korea, he overreached his authority and was recalled in early 1951.

Mannerheim, Marshal Carl von (1867–1951)
Head of the Finnish National Defence Council, leader of resistance to the Soviet invasion of 1939–40, and again, head of the Finnish forces that fought with the Germans from 1941 to 1944. When defeat loomed, Mannerheim used

considerable skill to secure an armistice on favourable terms for Finland.

Manstein, Field Marshal Fritz Erich von (1887–1973)

One of the ablest German field commanders of the war, Manstein was both an excellent staff planner, and an operational commander particularly effective in mobile defensive battles. He commanded Army Group Don from July 1942 and very nearly broke through to Stalingrad in a relief operation. In February 1943 his forces recaptured Kharkov, and he participated in the last great German offensive in Russia at Kursk. After the failure of his last offensive, Manstein led his forces in great defensive battles while under pressure from Hitler not to give up an inch of ground, denying him the ability to manoeuvre. He was personally dismissed by Hitler on 30 March 1944, and spent the rest of the war in obscurity. He was convicted of war crimes in Russia and sentenced to 18 years' imprisonment, commuted to four.

Metaxas, General Joannis (1881–1941)

Dictator of Greece from 1936 to 1941, and successful defender against the Italian attack of October 1940. He died before the German intervention and the overrunning of his country.

Mitscher, Vice Admiral Mark (1887–1947)

US Navy's Carrier Aviation Commander through the Pacific War. From January to October 1944 his vast carrier force was responsible for destroying no fewer than 795 enemy ships and almost 4500 aircraft.

Mölders, Werner (1913–1941)

Luftwaffe fighter ace, with 14 victories in Spain and 101 in World War II. Made General of Fighters at the age of 28, he was killed in an air crash flying to Berlin in November 1941.

People

Molotov, Vyacheslav (1890–   )
Soviet Commissar for Foreign Affairs from 1939. He represented the Soviet Union at the Teheran, Yalta and Potsdam conferences, as the most important politician in the Soviet Union after Stalin himself. Stripped of Communist Party membership in the de-Stalinization of the 1950s, he was rehabilitated in 1984 at the age of 94.

Montgomery of Alamein, Field Marshal Bernard Law (1887–1976)
Outspoken, domineering, yet one of Britain's most effective, certainly the most famous field commander of the Second World War. As a major general, Montgomery commanded the Third Division with the BEF, evacuated from Dunkirk in May 1940. For two years Montgomery served in England. In August 1942 he was appointed to the Eighth Army in Egypt, with General Sir Harold Alexander as his superior.

At the set-piece Battle of Alamein, undertaken after months of careful preparation, Montgomery showed his style, a mixture of attention to detail and caution, tempered by persistence.

Montgomery showed these characteristics in the Sicily invasion, staying with the Eighth Army in the Italian campaign until the end of 1943, when he came home to England to command the 21st Army Group preparing for the Normandy invasion. He was the Deputy Commander of all ground forces to the Supreme Commander, General Dwight D. Eisenhower.

With the landings successfully concluded and Normandy cleared, the two generals clashed as to how best to exploit the victory. Montgomery wanted Eisenhower to permit a single thrust along a northern axis by Anglo-Canadian forces into Germany itself. Eisenhower and Bradley would not divert supplies from Patton and held out for a 'broad front' approach.

During the Ardennes attack, Montgomery was given temporary command of US forces north of the Bulge, but never became commander of ground forces. The plan for

192

Operation Market Garden, even though it was a failure, showed Montgomery was capable of bold and imaginative planning.

After the German surrender, Montgomery became C-in-C of the British Forces of Occupation and British Member of the Allied Control Council. CIGS from June 1946–48. From 1951–58 he was Deputy Supreme Allied Commander in Europe.

Mountbatten of Burma, Earl (Lord Louis Mountbatten) (1900–1979)

Captain of the Fifth Destroyer Flotilla with his flag in HMS *Kelly*, sunk in the Mediterranean 1941. Chief of Combined Operations, Mountbatten was concerned with the early planning for the Normandy invasion. In 1943 he was appointed Supreme Allied Commander South East Asia, responsible for operations against the Japanese in Burma, Thailand, Malaya and Singapore, and to defend Ceylon and the North-west Frontier of India. It was under Mountbatten's overall command the war in this theatre was brought to a successful conclusion, with the complete defeat of the Japanese. From March 1947 to June 1948, Earl Mountbatten of Burma was Viceroy of India, and after independence, Governor-General.

Mussolini, Benito (1883–1945)

Italian Duce, 'leader'. Mussolini was the prototype for Hitler, the demagogic leader of the Fascist party which had seized power in Italy in 1922 from a crumbling democracy. Italy invaded Abyssinia in October 1935, supplied military aid to Franco, and entered the Axis alliance in 1936.

From then on Mussolini was set to become the junior partner. Italy's military weakness became apparent in its actions at Germany's side. Even as France crumbled Italy's invasion was checked. The Italians were held by the Greeks until Germany intervened, routed at sea in the Mediterranean and in North Africa, again until German military power arrived. The last German intervention was in Italy itself, disarming the Italian Army when Mussolini was ousted from power in July 1943.

The Duce was 'rescued' from house arrest by German commandos and installed as leader of the puppet Salo Republic in northern Italy. On 28 April 1945 Mussolini and his mistress Clara Petacci were shot by Italian partisans, their bodies then strung up in a Milan garage.

Nimitz, Admiral Chester W. (1885–1966)

Commander in Chief of US Pacific Fleet. Appointed CINCPAC soon after Pearl Harbor Nimitz had to hold the line of Japanese advance at Hawaii, and then turn the strategic situation round and go on the offensive. The first such action was the Battle of the Coral Sea, May 1942. Knowledge of the Japanese codes enabled Nimitz to deploy the US fleet to successfully engage the Japanese attempting to capture Midway. After Midway, Nimitz's next target was Guadalcanal, the first US seaborne amphibious operation of the war, and scene of intense fighting

By mid 1943, supplied with reinforcements, Nimitz was able to take the offensive and was an advocate of amphibious landings using the Central Pacific islands as the ladder, 'leapfrogging' heavily defended islands where necessary. Nimitz was drawn into the King-MacArthur controversy and not unnaturally favoured King's naval weighted strategy. After the capture of the Marianas it was decided that Nimitz's fleet should assist in the recapture of Luzon and Okinawa, then moving on to Iwo Jima.

Nimitz had been a submarine specialist and submarines made a vital contribution to his war, accounting for two thirds of Japanese merchant tonnage sunk and one third of warships sunk. In all, by the time of Japan's surrender, Nimitz's command had sunk two thirds of Japan's warship tonnage and virtually eliminated it as a fighting force. The Japanese surrender was signed on Nimitz's flagship, the USS *Missouri*, in Tokyo Bay, 2 September 1945.

Novikov, Colonel General Aleksander

Commander in Chief of the Soviet Air Force 1942–46. Responsible for reorganizing air force after disasters of 1941 and planning air assaults at Stalingrad, Kursk, Belorussia and in East Prussia.

Nye, General Archibald (1895–1967)

Vice Chief of British Imperial General Staff (Vice-CIGS) to General Alan Brooke 1941–45.

O'Connor, General Sir Richard (1889–1983)

Appointed commander of British Western Desert Force in Egypt, June 1940. In September Marshal Graziani's Italian forces invaded from Libya. The British, under the overall command of General Archibald Wavell, C-in-C Middle East, began a counterattack which took Tobruk and reached El Agheila by 5 February 1941. O'Connor ably commanded forces on the northern flank and captured vast numbers of Italian troops. O'Connor was made GOC British troops in Egypt, with General Neame commander in Libya, but when Churchill ordered Wavell's forces to Greece, the Italians attacked with German assistance and both British generals were captured, removing their talents at a crucial time. He was held prisoner until Italy's capitulation, repatriated and led 7th Corps in the Normandy landings.

Olbricht, General Friedrich (1886–1944)

Head of the Supply Section of the German Replacement Army, personal deputy to its head, General Fromm. Olbricht was a key member of the military plot against Hitler and a vital figure in any potentially successful outcome as a commander of the Home Army. He prepared the detailed planning for Operation Valkyrie, the seizure of power and takeover on Hitler's death. However, when Hitler survived Stauffenberg's bomb, Olbricht moved too late by which time the Führer's HQ had got through to Berlin with the news that Hitler was alive. Olbricht had arrested Fromm but, as the coup broke down, Fromm had Olbricht and Stauffenberg shot by the light of car headlights in the courtyard of the war ministry.

People

Onishi, Vice Admiral Takijiro (1891–1945)
Japanese naval aviation commander, instigator of Kamikaze suicide attack. Onishi drew up the air attack plans that proved so successful at Pearl Harbor. In October 1944 he was air commander on Luzon and formed the first Kamikaze Special Attack Corps. A die-hard fanatic, Onishi opposed surrender to the very end, committing suicide by ritual disembowelling.

Ozawa, Vice Admiral Jisaburo (1886–1966)
Commander of Japanese Navy's Third Fleet which contained most of the Japanese Navy's carriers from November 1942 onwards, replacing Nagumo. His force played a vital part at the battles of the Philippine Sea and Leyte Gulf. Ozawa was appointed commander of what remained of the combined Fleet in late May 1945 following the failure of Admiral Toyoda to prevent the US capture of Okinawa.

Papagos, General Alexander (1883–1955)
Commander in Chief of the Greek Army in October 1940 who successfully resisted the Italian invasion. Captured by the Germans and held as a prisoner in Dachau from 1943, he was liberated by the Americans in 1945.

Park, Air Marshal Sir Keith (1892–1975)
New Zealand-born RAF air commander, Park was Commander No 11 Fighter Group during the Battle of Britain where his tactics of forward engagement of enemy attacks proved controversial but successful. AOC Malta from 15 July 1942, again Park was in a critical place at the right time and, with reinforcements becoming available, he was able to go on to the offensive, attacking Axis convoys. He provided a component of the air cover for the Torch landings and the invasions of Sicily and Italy. In January 1944 Park was appointed commander of all air forces in the Middle East and a year later became Air C-in-C SEAC, providing air support for the British offensive against Rangoon.

Patch, General Alexander (1889–1945)
US General who commanded US forces in their first land victory over the Japanese at the Battle of Guadalcanal. In March 1944 he became Commander of US Seventh Army which landed in Southern France as part of Operation Dragoon. It advanced rapidly up the Rhone Valley, meeting Patton's Third Army then reaching the Saar by 15 March 1945. With German Army Group G in full retreat Patch crossed the Rhine on 26 March heading south-east from Munich towards the Brenner Pass in a move to cut out the feared 'National Redoubt'. Eisenhower held Patch in the highest regard as a field commander.

Patton, General George S. (1885–1945)
US general and exponent of armoured warfare. Commander of US Third Army during its epic drive from the Normandy bridgehead to the heart of the Reich.

A West Point educated cavalryman, Patton commanded one of the first US tank regiments in France in 1918 and kept alive interest in tanks between the wars in the face of official US Army lack of interest. During the war his verve in battle was matched by a personal flamboyance which was sometimes politically embarrassing.

During the Torch landings in North Africa, November 1942, he acted as Eisenhower's deputy, leading the Western Task Force ashore at Casablanca. He took command of 2nd Corps in March 1943 attacking pugnaciously in Tunisia until relieved by Bradley in April. Patton, now appointed to command the Seventh Army, returned to Morocco to plan the invasion of Sicily.

Patton's army landed near Licata to the west of the island with orders to protect the rear of Montgomery's Eighth Army landing to the east. With the British bogged down, Patton struck out and took Palermo in the north, wheeling round to meet Montgomery's slow advance. Sicily demonstrated his military flair but poor diplomacy and an incident in which he slapped a shell-shocked soldier for 'cowardice' caused him to be relegated from command.

Patton came to Normandy in late July 1944 to take

command of Third Army to the far west of the bridgehead. His arrival was kept secret as his presence in Britain had been used to reinforce the idea of a landing in the Pas de Calais. Patton's Seventh Corps quickly cleared Brittany and there was no hoaxing about Patton's main breakout launched on 1 August which pushed the Germans back to the Seine well east of Paris by 25 August. Pausing scarcely to get permission, Patton crossed the Seine the next day and was on the Meuse a week later, his advance sustained largely by captured fuel, but now halted by lack of supplies. Logistic priority was given to Montgomery advancing at a slower pace to the north while Patton pleaded his advance could pierce the Reich before winter broke and end the war. Within three days Patton was on the move again but the Germans had concentrated reserves in his path, fearing his attack the most. Patton was now further slowed by logistic problems and German counterattacks throughout the autumn.

When the German Ardennes offensive fell on the US First Army Front, Patton was ordered north to its relief and on 26 December 1944, Patton's 4th Armoured Division punched a narrow corridor into besieged Bastogne.

Through February 1945 Patton was assigned by 12 Army Group Commander Gen. Omar Bradley to 'active defence' while First Army prepared a breakout into the Rhineland. In fact, typically, Patton's command battered their way to the Westwall while First Army meanwhile got across the Rhine at Remagen. Patton overtook the advance, driving deep into the Rhineland rolling up the opposition and pugnaciously seizing two more Rhine bridgeheads at Oppenheim and Boppard. Pausing only to let his infantry catch up with armoured spearheads, Patton advanced further and faster than any other Allied commander in the west. On 4 May the Third Army took Linz in Austria and was approaching Pilsen in Czechoslovakia. Eisenhower proposed that Patton take Prague but was vetoed by the Soviets.

Patton was an inspired practitioner of the armoured offensive but was no political soldier, frequently clashing

with Allied commanders. The embarrassment of his out-
spokenness was removed when he was killed in a road
accident in Germany in December 1945.

Paulus, Field Marshal Friedrich von (1890–1957)
Von Paulus was a field marshal for one day, appointed by
Hitler hours before he surrendered his surrounded forces in
Stalingrad. He had served as VI Army's Chief of Staff in
Poland, Belgium and France, then chosen as Halder's
Deputy Chief of the General Staff with a brief to prepare
plans for an invasion of the Soviet Union. In the summer of
1942 he was given the objective of capturing Stalingrad and
by November his forces had captured nine tenths of it but
now his own command was encircled. In December
Manstein launched a relief offensive (*Wintersturm*) but von
Paulus refused to break out, obeying Hitler's commands to
stand and fight to the last. In the end, with his command
reduced to a frozen, starving and ammunitionless remnant
he surrendered on 31 January 1943. Later in the war von
Paulus broadcast over Soviet radio for the Soviet National
Committee for a free Germany. He gave testimony at the
Nuremberg trials and settled in Dresden where he died in
1957.

Pavlov, General Dimitry (?–1941)
Commander of Soviet forces on the western front who
faced the German invasion. Within a week he had lost half
of his armour and his defences had collapsed. He was shot
for incompetence along with his Chief of Staff.

Peirse, Air Marshal Sir Richard (1892–1970)
Vice Chief of the British Air Staff, 1940. C-in-C Bomber
Command 1940–42, Allied Air Commander SEAC,
November 1943–November 1944.

Percival, Lt. Gen Arthur (1887–1966)
GOC Malaya, when the Japanese began their invasion on 8
December 1941. He ordered a retreat into island fortress of
Singapore after defeat in northern Malaya. Percival and the

85,000 men under his command surrendered to General Yamashita 15 February 1942.

Pétain, Marshal Henri Philippe (1856–1951)
Hero of France in the First World War and symbol of shame in the Second. The saviour of Verdun was ambassador to Spain in 1940 when recalled by Reynaud to be Vice Premier. With German armour sweeping into the heart of France, Pétain rejected continuing the fight alongside Britain. He assumed the Presidency on 17 June 1940 and sued for an armistice on 22 June. From the provincial town of Vichy, Pétain was figurehead of an unoccupied France with a nominal army of 100,000 men but no real independence of the conqueror. Pétain offered shattered France a symbol of order, clinging to neutrality with the bargaining counters of the French fleet, the French empire and the prospect of joining the war on the Axis side. The pro-German Pierre Laval was dismissed as Premier in December 1940 but reinstated under German pressure in April 1942. When the Allies invaded French North Africa in November, Vichy's forces were disarmed and the fleet scuttled at Toulon and Pétain became a puppet. He was removed to Germany in August 1944. He was tried after the war and sentenced to death, commuted to life imprisonment.

Petrov, General Ivan (1896–1950)
Defender of Sevastopol, Commander of Soviet Black Sea Front, October 1941–July 1942. Commander North Caucasus Front May–November 1943. Commander of the Fourth Ukrainian Front from August 1944–April 1945.

Phillips, Admiral Sir Thomas (1888–1941)
Commander of Force Z, the Royal Navy task force sent to Malaya by Churchill and promptly sunk by Japanese air attack, 10 December 1941.

Popov, General Markian (1902–   )
Soviet general, a staff officer who won distinction at Leningrad and Stalingrad, commander of the Bryansk Front to the

north of the Kursk salient during the Soviet counterattack of July 1943. Nineteen forty-four Commander of Second Baltic Front.

Portal, Air Chief Marshal Sir Charles (1893–1971)
British Chief of Air Staff, 1940–45. Portal was an important figure in inter-Allied planning and decision-making as well as directing the policy and operations of the RAF. An original advocate of area bombing, he contributed to the combined bomber offensive compromise with the USAAF's daylight precision bombing leading him into conflict with Harris, seeing airpower as a component of combined operations rather than a war winning strategic bludgeon on its own.

Pound, Admiral Sir Dudley (1877–1943)
Britain's First Sea Lord at the outbreak of war, Admiral of the Fleet and Chairman of the British Chiefs of Staff Committee until 1942. He was Britain's most important naval professional in the critical years of the war, and died worn out by work in October 1943. By then he had seen the German surface threat in the Atlantic eliminated, the U-boats contained, and Allied supremacy in the Mediterranean, so nearly lost, regained and could report at the January 1943 Casablanca Conference that victory at sea was in sight.

Raeder, Admiral Erich (1876–1960)
Commander in Chief of the German Navy from 1935 to 1943. After the early successes of the raiders followed by the losses in Norway and the sinking of the *Bismarck*, the German surface fleet was relatively inactive. After the failure of the Battle of the Barents Sea, Hitler dismissed Raeder in January 1943 threatening to scrap the battle fleet. Raeder was sentenced to life imprisonment in Nuremberg, released in 1955.

Ramsay, Admiral Sir Bertram Home (1883–1945)
Flag Officer Dover in 1940, Ramsay organized Operation Dynamo, the evacuation of the BEF from Dunkirk. Naval

force commander for the Algerian landings in North Africa, November 1942, now an expert in amphibious warfare, he planned the seaborne assault on Sicily, commanding the Eastern Task Force at the actual landings. In 1944, he was appointed Naval Commander-in-Chief for Operation Overlord, responsible for the naval aspects – Operation Neptune. He was killed on 2 January 1945, in a plane crash while on his way to a conference at Montgomery's headquarters.

Rashid Ali (1889–1944)
Leader of a coup in Iraq, April 1941, Rashid Ali had pro-Axis sympathies. In May, hostilities broke out between Rashid Ali's forces and the British garrison at RAF Habbanaya. British air power and the intervention of ground forces from Transjordan rapidly defeated the Iraqis.

Reichenau, Field Marshal Walther von (1884–1942)
An able German field commander, and an ardent supporter of Adolf Hitler. Reichenau was Commander of X Army during the invasion of Poland, VI Army in 1940 and took Brussels. He was one of the nine generals promoted to Field Marshal in July 1940. In the invasion of the Soviet Union he was Commander of VI Army. He died of a stroke in January 1942, shortly after taking command of Army Group South after the purge of the Eastern generals in December 1941.

Reynaud, Paul (1879–1966)
Reynaud was Prime Minister, Minister of War, and Foreign Minister of France in the crucial months of March to 16 June 1940. He succeeded Daladier on 21 March, and met Chamberlain on the 28th to issue a declaration in which both England and France pledged not to make peace with Germany. After the fiasco in Scandinavia, Reynaud moved to dismiss Gamelin, but the German attack on France on 10 May held him back.

Three days after the German breakthrough at Sedan, Marshal Pétain was brought into the Cabinet, and Reynaud took over as War Minister from Daladier, replacing Gamelin with General Weygand, who was flown in from Syria. Neither Weygand nor Pétain were resolved to continue the war, and on 13 June Reynaud asked Britain to release him from the pledge not to make a separate peace. On 16 June he finally resigned and Pétain took over.

He was interned by the Vichy regime in September 1940, and 1942 deported to Germany and imprisoned at Oranienburg. He was freed in 1945.

Ribbentrop, Joachim von (1893–1946)
Ribbentrop was German Ambassador to Great Britain from midsummer 1936 until 1938. In February he succeeded Konstantin von Neurath as German Foreign Minister. Ribbentrop negotiated the Munich Agreement of September 1938, and the Soviet-German non-aggression pact of August 1939. His influence and that of his large Foreign Office declined as the war progressed, with an overlapping network of organizations including Himmler's SS bidding for power in the occupied territories.

He was captured by the British in Hamburg and stood trial at Nuremberg. He was condemned to death and hanged on 16 October 1946, as a war criminal.

Ridgway, General Matthew Bunker (1895–   )
US airborne commander. He led the 82nd Airborne Division from 1942, making combat jumps in Sicily and Normandy, until he became Commanding General of 17th Airborne Corps just before the airborne invasion of the Netherlands, going into action at Eindhoven.

Ritchie, General Neil (1897–   )
Ritchie replaced Cunningham in command of the British Eighth Army on 26 November 1941, in the middle of the Tobruk siege and the closing operations of Operation Crusader. Rommel counterattacked on 21 January, and took Tobruk on 21 June 1942. Ritchie was replaced by Auchinleck himself four days later.

People

Rokossovsky, Marshal Konstantin (1896–1968)

One of the most successful and able Soviet commanders of the war. He distinguished himself in the opening phases of Barbarossa and in the defence of Moscow, as Commander of the Southern Section, Siberian Army.

In 1942 he was Commander of the Don Front, and was responsible for the destruction of VI Army at Stalingrad, accepting Paulus' surrender. At Kursk he commanded the Central Front, holding his ground throughout the German offensive. His forces then broke through to the Dnieper, continuing to the Pripet Marshes in the autumn, and after a series of battles, his second Belorussian Front joined with the First Belorussian and First Ukrainian Fronts in the drive on Berlin. In May 1945, Rokossovsky's troops met the British at Wittenburg on the Elbe.

Rommel, Field Marshal Erwin (1891–1944)

In 1940 Rommel was an unknown German army officer. He had been decorated for bravery in Italy in 1917, but as a military professional he had not been considered General Staff potential, and held routine positions, but had had the fortune to have met Hitler. Two years later he was Germany's best known war hero, and his reputation as an outstanding commander has been reinforced by the respect of his wartime adversaries.

He showed his mettle commanding the VII Panzer Division in the Battle of France, leading his tanks from the front all the way to the Channel coast. In February 1941 he was chosen to lead the Afrika Korps sent by Hitler to bolster the collapsing Italians in North Africa. His original orders were defensive only, but eighteen months of attack and counterattack created the Rommel legend, being named a Field Marshal on 22 June 1942, the day after he captured Tobruk. He was ordered out of North Africa before the final Axis collapsed, and in January 1944 was made Commander of Army Group B in France, facing the expected Allied invasion. He disagreed with Rundstedt, overall commander in the West, on defensive strategy, Rommel favouring meeting and destroying the invasion on the beaches.

On 17 July his staff car was caught by an RAF fighter and his skull was fractured. He was in hospital when the 20 July attempt was made on Hitler's life. During the subsequent weeks, Rommel's flirtation with opposition to the Nazi regime became known. He was forced into suicide with a threat hanging over his family, and took his own life on 14 October 1944. He was given a Nazi state funeral, and it was announced that he had died of wounds.

Rundstedt, Field Marshal Gerd von (1875–1953)
German supreme commander in Western Europe, when the Allies invaded 6 June 1944. Rundstedt was recalled from retirement to command Army Group A, which invaded Poland in September 1939. He held the same command in the invasion of France, and it was his panzers which broke through at Sedan. Following this victory, he was promoted to Field Marshal. He commanded Army Group South in the invasion of Russia, driving through the Ukraine and capturing Kiev. In 1942, Rundstedt's forces were defeated at Rostov, and he was removed from his command in the East and transferred to France, being put in charge of all defences from the Pyrenees to the North Cape of Norway. When the Allies finally landed, Rundstedt's forces were in the wrong place. On 1 July 1944, he was replaced by Field Marshal von Kluge, who had no more success in containing the Allied breakout. Rundstedt was reinstated in September, and was in nominal command when the Ardennes offensive broke. He retired on 13 March 1945, and was captured on 1 May by US troops. Because of ill-health, he was never tried before a war crimes tribunal.

Sauckel, Fritz (1894–1946)
German slave labour chief. Plenipotentiary General for the allocation of labour from 1942 until the end of 1944, Sauckel organized the deportation of over five million people to work in German industry. Hanged at Nuremberg, 10 October 1946.

People

Schacht, Dr Hjalmar Horace Greeley (1877–1970)

President of the German *Reichsbank* from 1923 to 1930. Although not a member of the Nazi Party, Schacht supported Hitler and was reappointed President of the *Reichsbank* from 1933. From 1934–37 he was Minister of Economics, but feuded with Herman Göring, Chief of the Four Year Plan. Schacht oversaw German economic recovery in the thirties, generating the funds for rearmament, although he resigned in January 1939 over what he regarded as excessive military expenditure. He was imprisoned after the 20 July bomb plot, and was one of the three defendants to be acquitted at the Nuremberg Trials.

Schellenberg, SS General Walther (1910–1952)

Schellenberg had a busy and exotic career from joining the SD in 1934, carrying out the orders of Heydrich and Himmler in his role as an SS secret serviceman. In 1944 Schellenberg became head of all German secret services after the arrest of Admiral Canaris and the proscription of the *Abwehr*. He acted as a go-between for Himmler and neutral representatives towards the end of the war, including the head of the World Jewish Congress and the Swedish diplomat Count Bernadotte. He was tried and sentenced in 1949 to six years' imprisonment, but released in 1951 on ill-health grounds.

Schirach, Baldur von (1907–1974)

Reich Youth Leader from 1933, Schirach had been head of the Hitler Youth from 1931. In 1940 he was appointed *Gauleiter* of Vienna, where he was responsible for the roundup and deportation of Viennese Jews. He was sentenced to 20 years at Nuremberg, being finally released from Spandau in 1966.

Schörner, Field Marshal Ferdinand (1892–1973)

Known as 'last ditch' Schörner, in July 1944 he was appointed commander of Army Group North on the Eastern Front. In January 1945 he was moved to command Army Group Centre in Czechoslovakia, still believing in final victory. In the last ten days of the war, he was appointed Commander-in-Chief and was one of the recipients of Hitler's will on the Führer's death.

Seyss-Inquart, Artur von (1892–1946)
Austrian Nazi, made Governor (*Reichsstatthalter*) following the Anschluss of 1938. In May 1940 he became Reichs Commissioner for the Netherlands, an office he conducted with exceptional brutality. He was found guilty and hanged at Nuremberg.

Sikorski, General Wladyslaw (1881–1943)
A former War Minister of Poland during the 1920s, Sikorski was in Paris when his country collapsed. He became premier of the Polish government in exile and built up an army of 100,000 men. After the fall of France, the provisional Polish government escaped to London, and in June 1941 Sikorski reached an agreement with Stalin that invalidated the Soviet-German partition of 1939. He also provided an amnesty for Polish prisoners in the Soviet Union. In 1943 Sikorski presented Churchill with evidence of the Katyn Massacre of more than 4000 members of the Polish Officer Corps. The Soviets broke diplomatic relations with Sikorski's government in April 1943. He died in an aircraft crash at Gibraltar on 4 July 1943, and was succeeded by Stanislaw Mikolajczyk. The political influence of the London Poles subsequently went into steep decline.

Skorzeny, Lieutenant Colonel Otto (1908–1975)
Once known as 'the most dangerous man in Europe', Skorzeny was an officer of the SS who made a speciality of daring and secret operations. He snatched Mussolini from the plateau of the Gran Sasso in September 1943 and spirited him to Germany. His next mission was to kidnap the Hungarian Regent Horthy's son, in an operation codenamed 'Mickey Mouse'.

In December 1944 he organized Operation Greif, which infiltrated Germans in American uniforms behind Allied

207

lines during the Battle of the Bulge. He was tried and acquitted at Nuremberg, and settled in Spain.

Slessor, Air Marshal Sir John (1897–   )
Slessor was AOC of Coastal Command during the critical period of the Battle of the Atlantic, 1943. In January 1944 he became C-in-C of RAF forces in the Mediterranean and Deputy Commander in Chief of Allied air forces in the theatre. From 1950–52, he was Chief of Air Staff.

Slim, General Sir William Joseph (1891–1970)
Slim arrived in Burma in March 1942 as a lieutenant general, just when the Japanese were beginning their advance. He presided over a 900-mile fighting retreat from Rangoon to the Indian frontier. Slim took command of the newly formed 15th Indian Corps, preparing it for jungle warfare. In October 1943 he was made commander of the newly established British Fourteenth Army, organized to mount an offensive in Burma. The campaign opened in December 1943 with an intensive struggle to retake the Arakan. The Japanese counterattacked and took Kohima and cut the road to Imphal, but Slim's army held them and defeated the lengthy siege at Imphal. Slim now went on the offensive, crossed the Chindwin River and pushed the Japanese out of Burma, taking Mandalay in late March 1945 and reaching Rangoon on 3 May.

Smigly-Rydz, Marshal Eduard (1886–1943)
Commander-in-Chief of the Polish armed forces, when the Germans invaded.

Somerville, Admiral Sir James (1882–1949)
Somerville commanded Force H in the Mediterranean from 1940 to 1942, with his flag at Gibraltar. He was in charge of the operations against the French fleet at Oran and Mers-el-Kebir, and his force was active in the pursuit and sinking of the *Bismarck*. He also fought through vital convoys to Malta.

After Pearl Harbor, Somerville was selected to command

the newly formed Eastern Fleet in the Indian Ocean, which
he led until 1944. From there he was head of the British
Naval Delegation in Washington until the end of the war.

Sorge, Richard (1895–1944)

Soviet spy, based in Japan, Sorge passed vital strategic
Axis secrets to Soviet Intelligence from 1933 to 1941. He
informed his controllers in May 1941 of the impending
German attack on the Soviet Union, as well as the fact that
Japan was unlikely to intervene militarily against Russia.
Sorge was arrested on 16 October 1941, and hanged 7
November 1944.

Spaatz, General Carl (1891–1974)

'Tooey' Spaatz, commanded US Air Forces in Europe and
the Pacific. He was in London during the Battle of Britain
as an official observer. From July 1942 he was commander
Eighth Air Force, based in Britain as the strategic long arm
of US air power against Germany. He favoured daylight
precision bombing, against the RAF doctrine of night area
bombing. In February 1943 he took command of the North-
west African Air Forces. In March he became Deputy
Commander of Mediterranean Allied Air Forces, returning
to Britain in January 1944 as Commanding General US
Strategic Air Forces in Europe, including the Eighth Air
Force in England and the Fifteenth Air Force based in
Italy. In March 1945 he set up headquarters on Guam to
command the US Strategic Air Forces Pacific, the Eighth
and Twentieth Air Forces, directing the bombing of
Japanese cities, including the atomic bomb operations
against Hiroshima and Nagasaki, an appropriate finale for
the United States' most senior executive of strategic air
power.

Speer, Albert (1905–1982)

Armaments Minister of the Third Reich from 1942. Speer
came to Hitler's notice first as the architect of the Nuremberg Rallies. When Fritz Todt was killed in 1942, Speer was
appointed Minister for Armaments and Munitions, taking

charge of total war production in 1943. Despite the flail of Allied bombing he was able, through a policy of rationalization and dispersal and ruthless use of slave labour, to actually increase production. It was the destruction of the transportation network which overwhelmed his efforts rather than direct attacks on centres of production. Tried at Nuremberg for the use of slave labour, he was sentenced to 20 years, which he served in Spandau, being released on 1 October 1966. In his memoirs he fully acknowledged his past guilt.

Sperrle, Field Marshal Hugo (1885–1953)
Luftwaffe air commander. Sperrle commanded the Condor Legion during the Spanish Civil War, until 1937. He commanded Air Luftflotte 3 during the Battle of Britain.

Spruance, Vice Admiral Raymond (1886–1969)
One of the US Navy's most successful commanders in the Pacific War. Spruance sprang to fame at the Battle of Midway when he assumed tactical command following the loss of Vice Admiral Fletcher's flagship, the *Yorktown*. His execution of air strikes on the Japanese fleet disabled four carriers and six other ships.

After Midway, Spruance became Chief of Staff to Admiral Nimitz and played a vital role in planning operations in the Central Pacific. In August 1943 he returned to active command as Commander of the Fifth Fleet, commanding the bombardment of Tarawa in November of that year. Two months later, Spruance was attacking Kwajalein in the Marshall Islands, and in February 1944 Spruance was promoted Full Admiral. In March 1944, Spruance assaulted the Carolines, and Mitscher's Task Force under Spruance's command participated in the Hollandia invasion in New Guinea.

Spruance commanded the force invading Iwo Jima in February 1945, and Okinawa in April 1945. He succeeded Nimitz as Commander of the Pacific Fleet. A class of US destroyers is named after him.

Stauffenberg, Colonel Claus von (1907–1944)
The instrument of the 20 July 1944 bomb plot to assassinate Hitler. Stauffenberg was a brilliant career soldier, scion of a noble Prussian family, who had served with great bravery in Poland, France and North Africa, where he was severely wounded. When he left hospital, he was appointed to the Reserve Army Headquarters, and as Chief of Staff to Olbricht, was drawn into the conspiracy to eliminate Hitler. As the only member of the conspirators to attend Hitler's conferences, he volunteered to carry the fatal bomb, which he did on three occasions, to Berchtesgaden and to Rastenburg, and finally to Rastenburg again on 20 July. The bomb blew up, but Hitler was saved from the main blast by a heavy table. Stauffenberg flew back to Berlin but the coup was stalled and already foundering. Along with Olbricht and others, he was shot in the courtyard of the War Ministry on the orders of General Friedrich Fromm.

Stilwell, General Joseph Warren (1883–1946)
Chief of Staff to General Chiang Kai-Shek from 1942 to 1944, and Commander of Chinese and US Forces in Burma.

Stirling, David (1915–   )
British officer who, in 1941, founded the Special Air Service.

Streicher, Julius (1885–1946)
Virulent anti-semite, editor of *Der Stürmer,* the anti-Jewish newspaper, until 1943. Tried and executed at Nuremberg.

Stroop, Jürgen (1901–1951)
SS officer responsible for suppressing the Warsaw ghetto uprising of 1943, he was hanged in Warsaw, 1951.

Strydonk de Burkel, Victor van (1876–1961)
Belgian general who commanded Free Belgian Forces in England from 1940. He led the Belgian Military Mission to General Eisenhower's headquarters from September 1944.

People

Student, General Kurt (1890–1978)

Commander of the German Parachute Forces. In 1940, Student commanded the élite Parachute Troops (*Fallschirmjäger*), who seized the Belgian fortress of Eben Emael, and the river crossings which let German armour into the heart of the Low Countries. He planned and led Operation Mercury, the airborne descent on the island of Crete, but losses were extremely heavy and never again was the German parachute arm able to mount an operation on such a scale.

Luftwaffe field formations, however, continued to grow into a full scale parachute army of ten divisions. Commanding this force, and later Army Group H (I Parachute and XV Armies), in the West, Student was in command in Holland and led the counterattack against the Allied airborne descent at Arnhem.

Stülpnagel, General Karl Heinrich von (1886–1944)

Stülpnagel was Military Governor of occupied France, and a member of the military resistance to Hitler. When Stauffenberg's bomb exploded at Rastenburg, Stülpnagel began to arrest Gestapo and SS officials in Paris. However, when Kluge, Commander-in-Chief in the West, learnt the Führer was still alive, he refused to help the coup. Stülpnagel unsuccessfully attempted suicide. He was arrested and suffering from severe self-inflicted head wounds, was put on trial and slowly strangled by piano wire from a meat hook in August 1944.

Sugiyma, General Hajime (1880–1945)

Japanese Army Chief of Staff, 1938–1944.

Tedder, Air Marshal Sir Arthur (1890–1967)

Tedder was appointed AOC Middle East in 1941, and during the Western Desert campaigns he evolved successful techniques of air and ground force cooperation. He began a partnership with Eisenhower in 1943 when he was appointed AOC Mediterranean, and responsible for coordinating land and air operations in the invasion of Sicily and Italy. He returned to Britain in 1944, again as Eisenhower's deputy, in the run-up to the D-Day landings. In planning the preparatory bombing of communications (the Transportation Plan), he was able to get the cooperation of the strategic bombing specialists, Harris and Spaatz. Isolating the Normandy battlefield from the rest of France by air power was perhaps his greatest contribution to final victory in the West, but his diplomacy and skill as Eisenhower's deputy commander was as important. He signed the instrument of surrender of the German forces in the West in May 1945, on Eisenhower's behalf.

Terauchi, Field Marshal Hisaichi (1879–1945)
Supreme commander of the Japanese Southern Army, he commanded the invasions which so rapidly evicted US, Dutch and British power from his operational theatre.

Terboven, Josef (1898–1945)
Reichs Commissioner for occupied Norway.

Timoshenko, Marshal Semyon (1895–1970)
A commander in the First Cavalry Army during the Civil War, his friendship there then with Stalin probably saved him from the political purges of the 1930s. He was the victorious commander in the 1940 Winter War, made a marshal that year and appointed Defence Minister. In June 1941, Timoshenko was temporarily made Commander-in-Chief of the Soviet armies following the German invasion, but two weeks later Stalin claimed this position for himself. In September 1941 he was transferred to the South-western Front, but could not hold the Germans breaking through to Stalingrad and to the Crimea. In May 1942 he mounted a major counter-offensive at Kharkov, but ran smack into a German offensive of their own. Timoshenko was soundly defeated and transferred to the quieter North-western Front, never returning to the preeminence he had gained in the early stages of the war.

People

Tito, (Josip Broz) Marshal (1892–1981)

Tito was General Secretary of the proscribed Yugoslav Communist Party before the war. Soon after the German invasion, Tito organized a resistance movement and rapidly went on the offensive in Serbia, establishing large-scale liberated areas. Tito clashed with the Cetniks, a Serbian nationalist movement, and the Yugoslav government in exile under King Peter. From 1943 the British began supporting Tito and supplying him with material and advisers, parachuted in, switching their support from Mihajlovic, leader of the Cetniks, having realized after urgent intelligence reports that he was more anti-Communist than anti-Axis.

When the Italians collapsed in September 1943, Tito was able to seize large tracts of territory and Italian weapons to arm his army of a quarter of a million men. Tito's forces tied up large numbers of Axis troops engaged in 'counter-bandit' operations, and with Allied air support and the approach of the Red Army, Tito captured Belgrade on 20 October 1944. Tito himself took part in a coalition government, but the Communists won the first elections with a large majority and the monarchy was abolished, King Peter being condemned as a collaborator.

Tizard, Sir Henry (1885–1959)

Tizard was key scientific administrator in Britain during the run-up to the war, pushing the development of radar.

In spite of his antipathy to Lindemann, Churchill's own scientific adviser, Tizard was active throughout the war, leading a mission to the United States to initiate Anglo-US scientific cooperation. He was a strong opponent of area bombing, believing this to be less effective than precision strikes against critical targets such as U-boat pens.

Tojo, General Hideki (1884–1948)

Japanese premier who initiated the Pacific War, and directed it until July 1944. In July 1940, Tojo was named War Minister in Prince Konoye's cabinet, and was a voice against compromise with the United States. Tojo was

214

granted near-dictatorial powers on 16 October 1941, and began to lead his country into war. He forced the French Vichy Government to allow the occupation of all of French Indo-China, while negotiating with the US up to the eve of the attack on Pearl Harbor. By February 1944, Tojo was both premier, War Minister and Army Chief of Staff, but the war was by now completely un-winnable. He resigned on 18 July 1944, the day that Saipan fell, to be succeeded by General Koiso.

Tojo unsuccessfully attempted suicide after Japan surrendered, and was one of the seven Japanese to be hanged by the Allies.

Tolbukhin, Marshal Fyodor (1884–1949)
Commander of the Fifty-seventh Army at the Battle of Stalingrad, commander of the Soviet South Front from April to October 1943, commander of the Fourth Ukrainian Front, October 1943–May 1944, from May 1944 to June 1945, Tolbukhin was commander of the Third Ukrainian Front. In these commands, Tolbukhin led the offensives which recaptured the Crimea, cleared the Balkans, and liberated Belgrade with the help of Tito's partisans in October 1944. In spring 1945, he led the offensive which cleared Hungary and reached Austria.

Tovey, Admiral Sir John (1885–1971)
Commander-in-Chief of the Royal Navy Home Fleet, 1940–43, Tovey's greatest achievement was the destruction of the *Bismarck* in May 1941.

Promoted Admiral of the Fleet in 1943, he ended the war as Commander-in-Chief of the Nore (Naval Command for Eastern England), and was closely associated with naval planning for Operation Overlord.

Vasilevsky, Marshal Alexander M. (1895–1977)
Chief of the Soviet General Staff for most of the war. When the German invasion broke, Vasilevsky was Chief of the Operations Directorate, becoming Stavka's head in January 1942. He planned the massive counter-stroke at

215

Stalingrad in November 1942, and at Kursk in July 1943 he supervised the fortifying of the Salient, and overruled suggestions that the Red Army should take the offensive first, waiting for the German attack to be repulsed. From 1944 he coordinated the advance of the second and third fronts in East Prussia and Belorussia and organized the final advance on Berlin, taking over personal command in March 1945 at the front. In August 1945 he led Soviet forces in the short period of hostilities against Japan.

Vatutin, General Nicholi F. (1901–1944)

Vatutin commanded the South-west Front in the Stalingrad offensive. In the Battle of Kursk, July 1943, he halted Manstein's advance, counterattacking to take Kharkov. Commanding the First Ukrainian Front, his forces took Kiev in January 1944. On 29 February his car was ambushed by Ukrainian nationalists and Vatutin was fatally wounded.

Vlasov, General Andrei (1900–1946)

Soviet general who became a Nazi collaborator.

Voroshilov, Marshal Kliment (1881–1969)

Voroshilov was a veteran of the First Cavalry Army, whose civil war associations with Stalin saved him from the purges of the 1930s. He was appointed commissar for defence in 1934, and dismissed in May 1940 after the set backs in Finland. On 3 July 1941 with Stalin, Molotov, Beria and Malenkov he joined the State Defence Committee. Voroshilov was also given command of the North-west Front but was unable to stop German forces reaching Leningrad. He was replaced by Zhukov and assigned to staff positions until the end of the war, playing a diplomatic role at the Teheran Conference. He was Soviet president 1953–60.

Wainwright, Major General Jonathan (1883–1953)

US general who conducted the last stand in the Philippines, January–May 1942. He led the retreat through Bataan, and the defence of the fortified island of Corregidor from 8 April to 4 May. Wainwright survived the Bataan death march, to be held at a POW Camp in Manchuria. He stood with the British General Percival who had surrendered Singapore next to MacArthur on the deck of the USS *Missouri*, when the Japanese unconditionally signed the surrender document on 2 September 1945.

Warlimont, General Walther (1894–   )
Deputy Chief of OKW Operation staff, from September 1939 to September 1944.

Wavell, Field Marshal Sir Archibald (1883–1950)
A career soldier since graduating from Sandhurst, in 1901. Wavell was an able commander who faced critical situations in the early years of the war and held the line, only to be removed from command once the crisis reached its peak. He found himself in frequent conflict with Churchill. On the outbreak of war, Wavell was C-in-C of the Middle East and North Africa, a vast territory covering the Eastern Mediterranean and much of East Africa. Wavell's Western desert force managed to repulse the Italian invasion of September 1940 although heavily outnumbered and had cleared Egypt by January 1941, retaken Tobruk and cleared all of Cyrenaica with a huge bag of prisoners by 6 February. Operations meanwhile in East Africa had led to the Italian surrender of Addis Ababa on 6 April. The diversion of forces to Greece however proved a disaster, and once Rommel appeared in Africa with German forces the skeleton army left in Cyrenaica was overwhelmed till by 11 April, Rommel was on the Egyptian border. In July 1941 Wavell and Auchinleck swapped roles, Wavell becoming C-in-C India, but another crisis was about to break. Wavell was named head of ABDA Command (American-British-Dutch-Australian) with his head-quarters at Java, but could do little to stem the Japanese tide. ABDA was disbanded in February 1942. In December 1942 Wavell mounted an unsuccessful offensive into Burma, and in June 1943, Churchill, who had lost confidence in Wavell's military ability, appointed him Viceroy of India.

217

People

Weygand, General Maxime (1867–1965)

Weygand was commander of the French forces in the Levant, when recalled by Reynaud on 19 May 1940 with the French front collapsing. Despite his advanced age (73), he seemed much more decisive than Gamelin whom he had replaced as Allied Commander in Chief. He was too late to save the French First Army and the BEF in the north, but attempted to create a new front south of the Somme called the Weygand Line. When this was broken, he withdrew his forces south but refused to contemplate fighting on from North Africa and joined with Pétain in seeking an armistice.

Wingate, Major General Orde (1903–1944)

An exponent of irregular warfare, Wingate showed his style leading Gideon Force in Italian East Africa, 1940. He organized Long Range Penetration Groups or the 'Chindits' in Burma in February 1943. Conducting guerilla operations behind the Japanese lines, their first operations had limited success but in February 1944 Wingate organized a second 'Chindit' operation, this time with six brigades airdropped deep into Burma. Wingate died before the outcome could become clear in an air crash in India, 24 March 1944.

Witzleben, Field Marshal Erwin von (1881–1944)

Military conspirator against Hitler. Witzleben was to have been Commander in Chief of the German Armed Forces had the 20 July bomb plot succeeded. He was executed 8 August 1944.

Wolff, Karl Friedrich Otto (1900–1984)

Waffen SS general, military governor of northern Italy from 1943. In March 1945, Wolff had secret negotiations with Allen Dulles of the Office of Strategic Services (OSS) in Switzerland for the surrender of the German army in Italy. On 23 April Wolff and Vietinghoff, the German general in command, unilaterally ended resistance. On 29 April they signed a surrender and on 2 May it came into effect, six days before VE Day.

Yamamoto, Admiral Isiroku (1884–1943)
Japan's outstanding naval commander. Yamamoto was responsible for building the Japanese Imperial Navy pre-war into a world class fighting machine. Aware of the grave dangers of taking on the enormous power of the US, he planned a pre-emptive strike against Pearl Harbor to eliminate the US Pacific fleet. The attack of 7 December 1941 failed to eliminate the US carriers. Yamamoto planned the Midway operation to eliminate US naval power in a decisive battle. Midway was a disaster for the Japanese, but Yamamoto continued to play further counter-strikes. Yamamoto's aircraft was ambushed by US aircraft and he was shot down and killed on 18 April 1943.

ROYALTY

Bernhard, Prince of Netherlands (1911–   )
Bernhard renounced his German citizenship in 1937, when he married the Dutch heiress to the throne, Princess Juliana. He escaped to Britain in 1940, training as a pilot in the RAF. He was promoted Lieutenant-General in the Dutch Army, and Rear-Admiral in the Dutch Navy, serving from November 1940 as liaison officer between British and Free Dutch Forces. In September 1944 he was appointed Commander-in-Chief of the Netherlands Forces of the Interior, directing partisan activities.

Boris III, King of Bulgaria (1894–1943)
King of Bulgaria since October 1918, he approved of a fascist coup in 1934, and met Hitler at Berchtesgaden in November 1940. In March 1941, Boris joined the Axis and declared war on Britain and on the USA on 12 December 1941. He died in mysterious circumstances on 28 August 1943.

Carol II, King of Rumania (1893–1957)
Carol ruled Rumania from June 1930 with near dictatorial powers. He declared for the Axis after the fall of France,

but Hitler forced him to cede territory to the Soviet Union. In August 1940, he ceded Transylvania to Hungary, and further territory to Bulgaria, incurring increasing hostility. On 5 September 1941, he abdicated in favour of his son, Michael, and went into exile in Spain and South America.

Farouk, King of Egypt (1920–1965)

Bound by treaty to Great Britain, Farouk however sympathized with the Axis with pro-Nazi sympathizers in his government. With Rommel at the gates of Cairo, the British forced Farouk to dismiss his pro-German Prime Minister. Egypt declared war on Germany February 1945.

George II, King of the Hellenes (1890–1947)

King of Greece since 1922, George was deposed in 1923, spending eleven years in exile. When General Metaxas died in January 1941, Alexander Korizis assumed the premiership. George fled to Crete on the German invasion and thence to Cairo, where his first government in exile was established. In a 1946 plebiscite, the Greek people voted in favour of a restoration, and King George returned.

George VI, King of Great Britain and Northern Ireland (1895–1952)

King George succeeded to the throne in 1936 following the abdication of his older brother, Edward VIII. In May 1940 he refused suggestions that the Royal Family should seek safety in Canada, remaining in London through the Blitz when Buckingham Palace itself was bombed. The King and Queen Elizabeth made frequent morale boosting trips around the embattled country, and to the British armed forces. In June 1943 he visited British and Commonwealth forces in North Africa and Malta, and in June 1944 he visited the Normandy beachhead.

Haakon VII, (1872–1957)

King of Norway from 1905, Haakon just escaped German capture in Oslo, April 1940, remaining in Norway until the final British withdrawal. He was the head of the Norwegian government in exile, broadcasting to Norway, encouraging resistance.

Haile Selassie, Emperor of Abyssinia (1891–1976)
Haile Selassie was driven into exile by the Italian invaders, 1936. At the beginning of Britain's East Africa campaign, he moved to the Sudan, and by January 1941 was back on Ethiopian soil. Independence from Britain came in 1942, and in 1945 Ethiopia became a charter member of the UN, and he signed the Peace Treaty as a co-belligerent.

Hirohito, Emperor (1901–   )
Emperor of Japan since 1926. Commander in Chief of the armed forces. Considered as divine, Hirohito presided over the Imperial Council although manipulated by Japan's military rulers. He acquiesced in the attacks of December 1941 and in subsequent aggressions. Hirohito urged acceptance of surrender after Hiroshima. Postwar he was forced to renounce his divinity but permitted to retain the title of emperor.

Michael, King of Rumania (1921–   )
Michael became king when Carol II abdicated, September 1940. For four years Michael accepted the government of Marshal Antonescu and the Rumanian fascists, the Iron Guard. On 23 August, Michael, with the aid of a section of the military, staged a coup, arresting Antonescu and his Cabinet. On 12 September, an armistice was signed with the Soviet Union and Rumania declared war on Germany. He abdicated 30 December 1947, when Rumania became a People's Republic.

Paul, Prince of Yugoslavia (1893–1976)
Paul became Regent of Yugoslavia when his cousin, King Alexander, was assassinated in 1934, serving as Regent for King Peter II.

On 27 March 1941 he was deposed in an anti-Nazi coup, having signed a secret pact with the Axis two days earlier. Paul fled first to Greece and then, in 1943, to South Africa.

221

People

Peter II, King of Yugoslavia (1923–1970)

Peter came to power at the age of eighteen, on 27 March 1941, when a coup overthrew the pro-Axis government of his uncle, the Regent, Prince Paul. Germany and Italy invaded 6 April, and by the 16th, resistance had collapsed. Peter and his Cabinet set up a government in exile in London, the King attempting to coordinate the guerrilla operations of the royalist Cetniks.

When the Allies switched support to Tito's Communist partisans, Peter bowed to the inevitable and signed an agreement with Tito on 1 November 1944. Yugoslavia was declared a republic on 29 November 1945, and Peter, the last King of Yugoslavia, remained in exile.

Victor Emmanuel III, King of Italy (1869–1947)

King of Italy from 1900, Victor Emmanuel linked his monarchy with Mussolini's fascism. After years of acquiescence, the King became drawn into a plan to depose Mussolini – and on 25 July 1943, the Duce was arrested, the King appointing Badoglio Prime Minister. When the Germans took over, Badoglio and the King fled to Brindisi in southern Italy, and for a while was seen by the Allies as an alternative to establishing an Allied military government for Italy. With his associations with the fascist regime he passed over powers to his son Umberto, when Rome was liberated 5 June 1944. Two years later, in May 1946, he finally abdicated in favour of Umberto, spending the last months of his life in exile in Egypt.

Umberto II, King of Italy (1904–1983)

Son of Victor Emmanuel III, Umberto founded the Italian forces which attacked France in 1940. Made Regent in June 1944, he became King Umberto II in May 1946, on his father's abdication. In June, the Italian people voted to abolish the monarchy, and Umberto went into exile.

SECTION 3

Weapons

Armoured Fighting Vehicles

Tanks dominated the land fighting of the Second World War, effectively restoring the mobility which artillery and the machine gun had removed from the battlefield in the First. Not just tanks (defined as a tracked armoured vehicle with a high velocity gun in a rotating turret) but a whole range of specialized armoured fighting vehicles were produced in profusion by the combatants including assault guns (typically a tank chassis mounting a fixed forward firing weapon), armoured personnel carriers, half tracks, armoured cars, armoured engineer vehicles, flame throwers, armoured recovery vehicles, self propelled artillery, tank destroyers and so on. Britain, France, Germany, the Soviet Union, Italy, the United States and Japan all built tanks of their own either before or during the war while Czechoslovakia, Poland, Canada, Australia, Hungary, Belgium, Sweden and the Netherlands also built tanks or armoured fighting vehicles to their own designs. In fact Czech Pz38(t)s and Pz35(t)s made up an important part of German tank strength in 1940–41.

Britain had pioneered the 'tank' in the First World War and in the 1920s had conducted some of the first large scale experiments in independent armoured warfare. But being first in the field brings penalties and by 1939 British tank design and tactical thinking had technically and imaginatively stagnated. The British were unable to make up their minds whether the next war would be a repeat of trench attrition or a swirling war of mobility. They went for compromise, 'cruiser' tanks for mobile exploitation and infantry or 'I' tanks for ponderous frontal breakthroughs. The result was a multiplicity of experimental types at the expense of numbers and the bulk of what few tanks the British Army had, were left behind at Dunkirk in 1940. In the desert campaigns of 1941–42, the new cruiser types may have been fast but they were mechanically unreliable. The Matilda II infantry tank may have been heavily armoured but it was pitifully slow and undergunned.

Subsequent British armour designs never quite got the right mix of mobility, fire power and protection. The Cromwell was fast but suffered from severe design defects. The Churchill may have been a good all round design but it was too slow and ponderous in the infantry tank mould. The Valentine, produced in greater numbers than any other British tank from 1941–44, was not as effective as its German opposition. Where Britain did excel was in specialized armour which proved so effective on D-Day and beyond and British and Commonwealth armoured divisions made good use of US vehicles from 1941 onwards, the Stuart and Honey light tanks, the Lee and Grant tanks with their sponson mounted 75 mm guns and the all important M4 Sherman. The British modified this vehicle with the 17 pdr high velocity anti tank gun as the Sherman 'Firefly.' The British also used quantities of Staghound and Boarhound US armoured cars, White scout cars and half tracks.

BRITAIN

Tanks

Tanks, light, Mks VI, VIA, VIB and VIC.

This series of light tanks first came into service in 1936, armed with machine guns only. The Mark VIB was used by the BEF in France 1939–1940, where it formed a high numerical proportion of the British Army's total tank strength. Later Marks were used in the early stages of the campaign in Libya. By now they were totally outclassed and moved to training roles.

Max Armour:	14 mm
Armament:	1 Vickers .303, 1 Vickers 0.5-in mg
Crew:	3
Speed:	35 mph

Tank, light, Mks VII, Tetrarch

First British light tank with a gun bigger than a rifle calibre machine gun, the Mark VII mounted a two-pdr. Only a limited number were produced, used in the Madagascar campaign, and some were supplied to the Soviet Union. About half a dozen Tetrarchs were sent to Normandy with the 6th Airborne Division in Hamilcar gliders.

Max Armour:	16 mm
Armament:	1 × 2-pdr, 1 mg
Crew:	3
Speed:	40 mph

Tank, Cruiser, Mk I

Placed in production in 1937, the cruiser Mark I was already obsolete when they were used by the First Armoured Division in France, 1940. Some also served in the Middle East up to the end of 1941.

Max Armour:	14 mm
Armament:	1 × 2-pdr, 3 Vickers mg
Crew:	6
Speed:	25 mph

Tank, Cruiser, Mk II and IIA

A development of the Mark I, the Mark II or A10 was intended to be an infantry version with thicker armour. Small numbers of cruiser Mark II's served in France and the Western Desert up to the end of 1941.

Max Armour:	30 mm
Armament:	1 × 2-pdr, 1 Vickers mg
Crew:	4
Speed:	16 mph

Tank, Cruiser, Mk III

This tank design was distinguished by the large wheel 'Christie' type suspension giving it very high speed (up to

227

50 mph on roads). A small number served in France in 1940.

Max Armour: 30 mm
Armament: 1 × 2-pdr, 1 Vickers mg
Crew: 4
Speed: 30 mph

Tank, Cruiser, Mk IV

Very similar to the cruiser Mark III from which it was developed, the Mark IV had increased armour thickness. Tanks of this type went to France with the BEF and were in action during the early battles in Libya to mid-1941, where their speed was an asset in the desert campaign.

Max Armour: 30 mm
Armament: 1 × 2-pdr, 1 Vickers mg
Crew: 4
Speed: 30 mph

Tank, Cruiser, Mk V, Covenanter

The Covenanter was never used in battle. It was a development of the earlier cruiser line and in spite of nearly 2000 being produced they were only used for training in the United Kingdom and turn up frequently in propaganda shots of the period 1940 to 1942.

Max Armour: 40 mm
Armament: 1 × 2-pdr, 1 Besa mg
Crew: 4
Speed: 31 mph

Tank, Cruiser, Mk VI, Crusader

Crusaders were first used in action in the Western Desert, June 1941, continuing to fight up to the end of the North African campaign. One hundred and five of the 6-pdr armed Crusader fought at Alamein, 1942 and Crusader Mark III's were used in Tunisia. The Crusader was faster than the

German opposition but nowhere near the equivalent in fighting ability.

Max Armour:	30 mm
Armament:	1 × 2-pdr, 1 Vickers mg
Crew:	4
Speed:	30 mph

Tank, Cruiser, Mk VII, Cavalier

The first British cruiser tank designed under wartime conditions, the prototype Cavalier was completed in January 1942. Only a few hundred were produced and they were not used in battle as the faster Cromwell, derived from the Cavalier, became available in quantity by 1944.

Max Armour:	76 mm
Armament:	1 × 6-pdr, 1 or 2 Besa mg
Crew:	5
Speed:	24 mph

Tank, Cruiser, Centaur

Using the same basic hull and turret as the interim Cavalier, the only Centaurs to see action were those armed with 95mm howitzers in the close support role on D-Day and the days following.

Max Armour:	76 mm
Armament:	1 × 95 mm Howitzer, 1 or 2 Besa mg
Crew:	5
Speed:	27 mph

Tank, Cruiser, Cromwell

The Cromwell was one of the fastest tanks of the war, capable of a speed of up to 40 mph on roads. However this, perhaps the most effective British design to see major combat, was flawed and cannot be judged the equivalent of its German contemporaries. For example the driver's hatch was inoperative with the turret in a certain position and if the tank was hit, crew could not escape. The armoured reconnaissance regiments of all British armoured divisions in the North west Europe campaign were equipped with Cromwell, and it formed the major part of the tank strength of the Armoured Brigade of the 7th Armoured Division in Normandy.

Max Armour:	76 mm
Armament:	1 × 75 mm, 2 Besa mg
Crew:	5
Speed:	40 mph

Tank, Cruiser, Comet

At the end of the war British industry at last produced a tank, the equivalent of its German counterparts such as the Panther. The Comet was armed with a new 77 mm gun while the hull and turret were improved derivations of the Cromwell. The Comet was not used in action until after the Rhine crossing in early 1945, and in its weeks of war left it proved very successful.

Max Armour:	101 mm
Armament:	1 × 77 mm, 2 Besa mg
Crew:	5
Speed:	29 mph

Tank, Infantry, Mk I

British tanks were officially divided into two main types, faster cruiser tanks, and 'Infantry' tanks designed to accompany infantry on the battlefield World War I style. The Mark I fulfilled this prescription by being heavily armoured and slow but its armament was just a single machine gun. Mark I's formed the bulk of the equipment of the First Army Tank Brigade in France, 1939–40. They gave a good account of themselves before being abandoned at the Dunkirk evacuation.

Max Armour:	16 mm
Armanent:	1 × Vickers mg
Crew:	2
Speed:	8 mph

Tank, Infantry, Mk II, Matilda

Slow and heavily armoured, nevertheless the Matilda gave a good account of itself, whether in the British counterattack at Arras, June 1940, or in the Western Desert, until 1941, when the German 88 mm gun was introduced, capable of piercing even the Matilda's heavy armour.

Matildas were supplied to the Soviet Union and were also used by the Australians in the Pacific where, equipped with flame-throwers, they were known as Matilda Frogs and used up to the end of the war.

Max Armour:	77 mm
Armament:	1 × 2-pdr, 1 Besa mg
Crew:	4
Speed:	15 mph

Tank, Infantry, Mk III, Valentine

Manufactured between 1940 and spring 1944, more than 8000 Valentines were produced in eleven main Marks, and it was one of the most important British tanks of the war.

Designed as an infantry tank, it in fact equipped the newly equipped British armoured divisions from 1941 onwards, in spite of its slow speed. It was also delivered to the army tank brigades in its design function of infantry support. Its combat debut was in the Western Desert, 1941, with the Eighth Army. Valentines took part in the subsequent North African fighting, in Tunisia, in the Pacific and in North-west Europe. Valentines also served with the Red Army on the Eastern Front.

Max Armour:	65 mm
Armament:	1 × 6-pdr (Mk VIII)
Crew:	3
Speed:	15 mph

Tank, Infantry, Mk IV, Churchill

A slow and heavily armoured infantry tank, Churchills were first used in action in the Dieppe raid of August 1942. The

231

Weapons

Churchill operated in Tunisia, and in Italy up to the end of the war. Several brigades fought in North-west Europe where their heavy armour proved useful, especially in head-on assault operations, but their gunpower was by no means the equivalent of their German counterparts.

Max Armour:	152 mm
Armament:	1 × 75 mm (Churchill IV)
Crew:	5
Speed:	15 mph

Armoured Cars

Armoured Car, Humber, Mks I–IV

Humber armoured cars entered service with the British and Commonwealth forces from 1941 onwards, and served in all significant theatres of war.

Mk I:

Max Armour:	15 mm
Armament:	1 × Besa 15 mm Cannon
Crew:	3
Speed:	45 mph

Mk IV:

Max Armour:	15 mm
Armament:	1 × 37 mm Cannon
Crew:	3
Speed:	45 mph

Armoured Car, Daimler, Mk I

The Daimler armoured car was of advanced engineering conception, having no chassis, the wheels and automotive components being attached directly to the armoured hull. Towards the end of the war the so-called Littlejohn adaptor was fitted to the 2-pdr gun, affording a higher muzzle velocity and greater penetrative power for the projectile. Daimler armoured cars entered service in 1941 and saw action in Italy, North-west Europe, North Africa and the Far East.

Max Armour: 16 mm
Armament: 1 × 2-pdr
Crew: 3
Speed: 50 mph

Armoured Car, AEC, Mks I–III

A total of 629 AEC armoured cars was built, and they saw action in the North African theatre from 1942, in North west Europe, and some were supplied to Tito's partisans in 1944.

Max Armour: 30 mm
Armament: 1 × 2-pdr, 1 Besa mg
Crew: 3
Speed: 36 mph

Scout Car, Daimler, Mk I

A small two-seat armoured vehicle for liaison and reconnaissance duties in forward areas. Types used by the British forces included the Alvis Dingo, and the BSA Scout Car Mk I, subsequently manufactured by the Daimler company.

Max Armour: 30 mm
Armament: 1 × Bren mg
Crew: 2
Speed: 55 mph

Improvised Armoured Vehicles

With the threat of invasion hanging over Britain from June 1940, many and varied types of improvised light armoured vehicles were created based on civilian cars or lorries. Home Guard units produced their own armoured vehicles, some armoured with boiler plate or concrete. The 'Beaverette' was an attempt at standardization produced originally at the instigation of Lord Beaverbrook, after whom it was named, for the defence of aircraft factories. It was armoured with a mixture of mild steel and oak planks.

233

Weapons

Specialized Armour

The British in particular excelled at developing a range of specialized armoured vehicles, from mine-clearing flail tanks via bulldozers, bridge layers, to specialized armoured assault vehicles such as the AVRE (Assault Vehicle Royal Engineers).

The British Army was also a pioneer in grouping specialist armour under unified command. The 79th Armoured Division, under its very innovatory and energetic commander, Major General Sir Percy Hobart, was given responsibility for the development of all the special equipment to be used in breaking the Atlantic War in April 1943. On D-Day it proved an outstanding success, and by the time of the running crossing, March 1945, it was the largest division in the British Army, with more than 1500 tanks alone.

Assault Vehicle, Royal Engineers

One of the lessons of the Dieppe raid of August 1942 was the need for a special engineer vehicle to assault the concrete and obstacles of Fortress Europe. The AVRE was developed through 1943 by the 79th Armoured Division, converted from Churchill tank hulls. Its main armament was a short range demolition mortar called the 'Flying Dustbin'. All sorts of other special weapons were developed for the AVRE, and they proved their value from their first time in action in the Normandy landings, right from the beginning of the assault, laying carpets on the beaches, breaching sea walls, cross-spanning anti-tank ditches with box girder bridges, and blasting away concrete fortifications.

Self-Propelled Guns and Carriers

In spite of several pre-war experiments, no self-propelled guns were in use by the British Army in 1939, and it was not until two years later that development work began on a proper self-propelled field gun, after an urgent need for such a weapon was shown up on the desert battlefields. 25-pdr weapons were mounted on Valentine tank chassis as

234

the Bishop from July 1942, and the Sexton on Sherman chassis and saw extensive service in Italy and in north-west Europe. The Archer was a combination of the excellent 17-pdr gun and a Valentine chassis.

Carrier, Universal

This vehicle, strongly associated with British and Commonwealth forces in all the theatres of war from 1939 to 1945, was based on the earlier Cavalry and 'Bren' carriers of pre-war vintage, and the Universal type is often wrongly called a Bren Gun carrier.

Max Armour:	12 mm
Armament:	1 × Bren mg
Crew:	4/5
Speed:	32 mph

GERMANY

The word 'panzer' simply means armour in German, applied as much to a warship as a fighting vehicle – in the context of World War II however, the word 'panzer' has become a synonym for German armoured forces. When the war began with the assault on Poland, the panzer divisions were equipped in fact with largely obsolete weapons. The panzer *Kampfwagen* (PzKw) I, which formed the bulk of the equipment numerically, was a light training vehicle armed with only two machine guns. The PzKw III had just a 37 mm gun, and the bigger PzKw IV was armed with a short-barrelled 7.5 cm gun for infantry support. These vehicles, the Mks III and IV, formed less than a quarter of the total tank force that fell on France in May 1940, which included large numbers of PzKw I and PzKw II light reconnaissance tanks, and captured Czech vehicles.

Three thousand, three hundred and thirty-two tanks were assembled for Operation Barbarossa, the assault on the Soviet Union. Like the blitzkriegs in the West, the success of the German tank arm was stunning, facing, on paper at least, some 20,000 Red Army armoured fighting vehicles.

235

However, when the first encounters were made with the T-34 and heavier KV1, the going was far more difficult. After the failure before Moscow in the winter of 1941, and the German assumption of a defensive, if only just for the winter, the technical balance became the deciding factor in tank warfare – training, dash, and brilliant tactics were no longer enough and gave way to factors such as muzzle velocity and angle of armour. Protection and gun power would now be more important than speed and mobility. The appearance of the T-34 led to a drastic change in German policy. Initially, in 1942, the tide was held by up-gunning the original Mk IIIs and Mk IVs, and doubling their armour thickness. The PzKw IV, the Tiger, which first appeared in the summer of 1942, reflected the new emphasis on armour and hitting power at the expense of mobility. Here was a heavyweight weapon of defence rather than a vast and mobile weapon of attack. In mid-1943, the PzKw V appeared, the Panther, perhaps the best all-round tank of World War II. It had sloped armour like the T–34, a long 75 mm gun able to take on most of the opposition, and a road speed of 34 mph. After early teething troubles, the Panther proved to be one of the most formidable tanks encountered by the Allies.

The Tiger II, known as the King Tiger, was an even more formidable machine but produced only in small numbers. It had an 88 mm gun, weighed 69 tons, but was still remarkably mobile, capable of 26 mph on roads. King Tigers spearheaded the Ardennes offensive of December 1944.

Even the King Tiger was made to look puny by the prototype tank ironically called *Maus*, two of which were built at the end of the war. *Maus* weighed 188 tons, three times as heavy as the King Tiger, and was armed with a 150 mm gun with a Panther 75 mm gun as a side armament. Such monsters would have been tactical dinosaurs on the battlefield, and in April 1944 work on giant tank projects was slowed down in favour of getting as many proven designs into the front line as possible. But in the ruins of the Krupp factory at the end of the war, Allied Intelligence Officers found studies for the most fantastic super-heavy tank of all – a gigantic 1500-ton vehicle with an 800 mm gun as main armament, and two 15 cm guns in side turrets. Four submarine engines were to power this monster.

Assault Guns and Tank Destroyers

German industry produced a variety of specialized tracked assault guns, tank destroyers, and self-propelled artillery pieces often mounted on obsolete or captured tank chassis. The *Sturmgeschutz III* (StuG III) was a purpose-built design for an assault gun to accompany infantry into battle, armed with a short 75 mm gun firing high explosive, but early experience showed that there was room for a dual purpose vehicle capable of dealing with tanks. In early 1942, the StuG III 7.5 cm L/43 appeared, with a long-barrelled tank gun, which had all the fighting performance of a tank bar the rotating turret in a vehicle that was far cheaper and easier to make. Again in reaction to the appearance of the T–34, anti-tank guns were mounted on various types of self-propelled mountings from captured French or Czech chassis to reworked obsolete German tanks. These vehicles, called *Jagdpanzer* (hunting tanks), included the *Jagdpanzer IV* introduced in late 1943, and the *Panzerjäger Ferdinand* (or *Elefant*) with a 8.8 cm gun, which had its disastrous combat debut at Kursk. The best vehicle of all was the *Jagdpanther*, an 88 mm anti-tank gun on a Panther chassis, but these vehicles did not serve with the panzer divisions but with army anti-tank units. Similarly the *Jagdtiger*, armed with a very large 12.8 cm gun, saw service with army heavy tank hunter battalions, the *Hetzer*, a 75 mm gun based on the PzKw 38 (t) which equipped infantry divisions, the *Nashorn* (Rhinoceros), and 88 cm anti-tank gun on a PzKw IV chassis, which also went to heavy tank hunter battalions.

The main self-propelled artillery in the panzer divisions were the 10.5 cm light field Howitzer called *Wespe*, and a 15 cm heavy Howitzer mounted on a PzKw IV chassis called *Hummel* (Bumblebee). The heaviest gun in this class to be mounted was the 150 mm infantry Howitzer placed on a PzKw IV chassis, known as the *Brummbär* (Grizzly Bear) of which over 300 were built.

German Tank Production 1939–1945

PzKw I	c. 3000
PzKw II	c. 3580
PzKw III	c. 5644
PzKw IV	c. 9000
PzKw V	
(Panther)	4814
	1350
PzKw VI (Tiger)	c. 27872

In addition, c. 12,000 assault guns were manufactured, including conversions from obsolete tank chassis.

PzKw I:

Max Armour:	13 mm
Armament:	2 × mg
Crew:	2
Speed:	25 mph

PzKw II:

Max Armour:	14.5 mm
Armament:	20 mm
Crew:	3
Speed:	25 mph

PzKw IIIF:

Max Armour:	30 mm
Armament:	50 mm
Crew:	5
Speed:	25 mph

PzKw IVD:

Max Armour:	30 mm
Armament:	75 mm
Crew:	5
Speed:	27 mph

PzKw V Panther:

Max Armour:	110 mm
Armament:	75 mm
Crew:	4
Speed:	34 mph

PzKw VI Tiger I:

Max Armour:	110 mm
Armament:	88 mm
Crew:	5
Speed:	23 mph

PzKw VI Tiger II:

Max Armour:	150 mm
Armament:	88 mm
Crew:	5
Speed:	25 mph

StuG III:

Max Armour:	50 mm
Armament:	75 mm
Crew:	4
Speed:	25 mph

JagdPz V (Jagdpanther):

Max Armour:	80 mm
Armament:	75 mm
Crew:	4
Speed:	25 mph

Weapons

FRANCE

When the Germans struck in the West in May 1940, France had about 3000 modern tanks, of which some 800 were medium or heavy. There were two types of armoured formations, the so-called *Division Cuirassée* (DCR) and the *Division Légère Mecanique* (DLM). There were three DLMs in May 1940, mobile and well-balanced formations containing the best of the modern Franch tanks, the Somua S.35. There were three DCRs, largely equipped with H–35s and one more forming, in total, some 1500 tanks of all sizes contained in these independent tank formations. The balance of armour was contained in the tank battalions organic to French armies, distributed along the frontier and behind the Maginot Line defences, with the so-called 'Interval' troops.

Char de Cavalerie, Somua S. 35

The Somua S. 35 was one of the best tanks of its class on the outbreak of war. Each of the French DLMs had one regiment of S. 35s in its tank brigade, together with a regiment of Hotchkiss H-39s. The Somua's armament of one 47 mm gun was as good or better than that of the majority of German tanks in 1940.

Max Armour:	55 mm
Armament:	47 mm, 1 × 7.5 mm mg
Crew:	3
Speed:	25 mph

UNITED STATES

Despite its small size, the pre-war US Army was an active experimenter in tank technology. Soon after Dunkirk, a British buying mission arrived in the US and bought the M3 off the shelf. The M3, known as the Grant and the Lee in British service, had its 75 mm gun mounted in a side sponson because at that stage US industry could not build a turret capable of housing a high velocity 75 mm weapon.

240

The M3s reached the British Army in North Africa in early 1942, and saw their first major action in the Battle of Gazala in May, where their 75 mm gun power outranged the PzKw IIIs and PzKw IVs. M3s also served with the US Army in North Africa, in the Far East with the Australians, and in small numbers with the Soviet Army.

The most important US tank of the war, however, was the M4 Sherman which combined the M3's chassis and suspension with a rotating turret mounting a 75 mm gun. The Sherman was the most significant tank of the Western Allies during the war, but its original 75 mm gun armament became progressively outdated by German opposition. From 1944 a version equipped with a high velocity 76 mm gun appeared, and in British service about 600 M4s were modified by installing 17-pdr anti-tank weapons. These were known as Sherman VC 'Fireflies', and were particularly effective in the campaigns in North-west Europe.

Medium Tank, M3

Max Armour:	80 mm
Armament:	1 × 75 mm, 1 × 37 mm
Crew:	6
Speed:	25 mph

Sherman V

Max Armour:	81 mm
Armament:	75 mm
Crew:	5
Speed:	21 mph

Sherman VC 'Firefly'

Max Armour:	81 mm
Armament:	17-pdr
Crew:	5
Speed:	25 mph

SOVIET UNION

It was in the great armoured battles on the Eastern Front that the German Army was ground down to final defeat. The quality and the direction of Soviet armour was therefore of vital importance to the outcome of World War II. The first T–34s appeared soon after the German invasion of July 1941, but their combination of fighting power was wasted by commanders and crews, who could not yet find the formula to stop the German onrush. In the first months of the invasion, obsolete Soviet armour was massacred in droves. Where a T–34 or the heavier KV–1 was encountered however, it was a different story, and from late 1941 onwards a huge new tank plant called 'Tankograd' evacuated from Kharkov was turning out heavy tanks by the thousand and a new T–34 production centre had been set up in the Urals. During 1943 Soviet tank production reached 10,000, of which approximately 6000 were T–34s, and the new T–34/85 with an 85 mm gun was beginning to appear. Faced with the threat of Soviet armour, in 1943 OKH (High Command of the German Army) suggested that all German tank production programmes except the Tiger and Panther should be suspended to concentrate production on these two. General Guderian noted, however, that by stopping production of the Mk IV, Germany would be limited to the production of only 25 Tigers a month. As the German tank pioneer said: 'this would certainly have led to the defeat of the German Army in the very near future . . . the Russians would have won the war even without the help of their Western Allies . . . no power on earth could have stopped them.'

The Soviet Union produced a line of successful heavy tanks from the KV–1 to the Josef Stalin III, plus self-propelled guns and tank destroyers which paralleled their German counterparts in effectiveness.

T–34/76

Max Armour:	65 mm
Armament:	76.2 mm, 1 × 7.62 mm machine gun
Crew:	4
Speed:	33 mph

T–34/85

Max Armour:	90 mm
Armament:	85 mm, 1 × 7.62 mm
Crew:	5
Speed:	33 mph

KV–1

Max Armour:	110 mm
Armament:	76.2 mm, 3 × mg
Crew:	5
Speed:	22 mph

BT–7

Max Armour:	22 mm
Armament:	45 mm, 1 × mg
Crew:	3
Speed:	45 mph

Infantry Weapons

The basic infantry weapon of the Second World War was the same as that of the First – the bolt action rifle, the single shot weapon with a five round magazine and an effective range up to six hundred yards. Typical were the German Mauser K98, the British SMLE Lee-Enfield, the US M1 Garand and the Japanese Arisaka. What was different was the automatic rifle or light machine-gun which gave the infantry platoon lightweight mobile firepower, unlike the dug in water cooled weapons of 1914–18. The British Bren was typical, firing .303 in ammunition at a cyclic rate of fire of 450 rounds per minute (the magazine held thirty rounds) yet weighed only 23 pounds, (see table for comparable weapons). Particularly effective was the German MG 42, the replacement for the prewar light machine-gun, the MG 34 (known in popular parlance as the 'Spandau') characterized by reliability in the field and general serviceability.

'Submachine-guns' had been introduced at the end of the First World War but, churned out and distributed en masse, in the second they gave infantry in the attack and in the defence lightweight massed firepower. The British bought large stocks of US Thompson guns in the first years of the war before developing their own crude but reliable 'Sten' submachine-gun. The Soviets manufactured enormous quantities of the famous PPSh series while the so-called German 'Schmeisser' or MP 38 was in fact too sophisticated and well made for its own good. In the last months of the war Hitler ordered mass production of a German copy of the British Sten, far cheaper and simpler to make but just as effective.

Principal German, British and US Small Arms of the War

	Nationality	Weapon	Calibre	Weight	Approx Maximum range	Effective range	Cyclic rate of fire rpm
Pistols	German	Luger P 08	9 mm (0.354 in)	2lb	up to 30 yards	–	–
	German	Walther P 38		2lb 5oz	up to 30 yards	–	–
	British	Webley 0.380 no 2	0.38 in	1lb 11½oz	up to 30 yards	–	–
	American	Colt M1911A1	0.45 in	2lb 11oz	up to 30 yards	–	–
Rifles	German	Rifle 98		9.05lb	2,200 yards	600 yards	–
		S/L rifle G 41W	7.92 mm (0.311 in)	10lb 14oz	2,200 yards	600 yards	–
		FG 42 Auto rifle		9.75 lb	1,500 yards	300–600 yards	–
	British	SMLE Rifle No 1	0.303 in	8lb 10½oz	2,000 yards	600 yards	–
	American	Garand	0.30 in	9lb 7oz	2,000 yards	600 yards	–
		Carbine M 1	0.30 in	5lb 3oz	2,000 yards	300 yards	–
Sub-Machine Guns	German	Schmeisser MP40	9 mm	9lb	200 yards	30 yards	450–540
	German	Schmeisser MP44	7.92 mm	10lb	200 yards	30 yards	800
	British	Sten Mk III	9 mm	6.5lb	200 yards	30 yards	500–550
	American	M3	45 in	6lb	200 yards	30 yards	450

Principal German, British and US Small Arms of the War (cont)

	Nationality	Weapon	Calibre	Weight	Approx Maximum range	Effective range	Cyclic rate of fire rpm
Machine Guns	German	MG 34	7.92 mm	26lb	2,750 yards	800 yards	800–900
		MG 42		24lb	2,750 yards	800 yards	1,200
	British	Bren		23lb	2,000 yards	800 yards	450–550
		Vickers MkVI	0.303 in	30lb (no tripod)	3,500–4,000 yards	800–1,200 yards	500
	American	Browning Auto Rifle M1918		17lb	2,000 yards	600 yards	500
		Johnson LMG (used by US Marines)	0.30 in	15lb	2,000 yards	600 yards	450–750
		Browning MMG		33lb	3,500–4,000 yards	800–1,200 yards	400–520

Artillery and Rockets

The diversity of artillery pieces deployed by the combatants in the Second World War was enormous. The Germans alone employed over 200 distinct types of weapon discounting many experimental types while Britain and the US fielded more than a hundred different types. These ranged in size from light infantry support weapons to colossal outsize weapons and long range railway guns. In between came general purpose field artillery, anti-tank weapons, anti-aircraft artillery, heavy artillery and self-propelled artillery mounted on wheeled or tracked chassis.

Out of diversity the Germans brought forth some formidably effective weapons. Most famous perhaps was the '88', developed through the '30s as an anti-aircraft weapon but used with devastating effects as an anti-tank gun, its large high velocity projectiles being able to defeat the heaviest armour.

The British began the war with a comparatively puny anti-tank gun, the 2-pounder. The next weapon was the far more effective 57 mm 6-pdr but this only just kept pace with German armour developments and could not defeat a Tiger tank for example. Best British weapon of the war was the 25-pdr gun/howitzer.

The Soviet Army made very good use of artillery – the principal weapon was the 76 mm field gun which fired a 14 pound shell up to 15,260 yards. The Soviets developed mass fronts of anti-tank weapons, which proved the rock on which many German attacks such as those at Kursk broke. The Germans copied the technique with so called 'Pak-fronts' (PAK = *Panzer Abwehr Kanone*) in turn in 1943 to counter mass Soviet armour assaults. Up to ten guns were put under unified command able to concentrate devastating fire on a single target.

Technical developments during the war included the 'squeeze gun' which extracted higher muzzle velocity from lightweight weapons, the 'hollow charge' which reversed the principles of the jet engine to defeat armour by blasting a jet of hot gas through it and the recoilless gun or RCL which allowed large calibre weapons to be mounted on lightweight mountings. German paratroops in Crete for example used experimental light-weight 75 mm RCL weapons.

The development of rockets closely followed that of artillery. First as anti-tank weapons, the British PIAT, the US Bazooka and German *Faustpatrone* were tube-launched rocket projectiles with hollow charge warheads allowing infantry to defeat tanks at short range. The British deployed crude anti-aircraft rockets (Z-batteries) in 1940 which were effective in scaring off low level intruders if nothing else. The Germans developed a series of potentially very significant guided anti-aircraft rockets toward the end of the war, the *Enzian*, the *Rheintochter* and *Wasserfall* but none were used operationally, resources being transferred to the V-weapons programme. The Germans also developed radio guided rocket boosted bombs for air launch and a small number were used operationally. The RAF developed unguided air launched rockets used with devastating effect in the Normandy campaign and beyond in anti-armour operations.

The Soviet Army made very effective use of unguided bombardment rockets called 'Katyusha', launched in massive softening up barrages from the back of trucks. The Germans had a more sophisticated weapon called the *Nebelwerfer* whose distinctive screaming noise was particularly damaging to morale.

The German V-weapons programme was again designed to attack morale but on a grand strategic scale. The *Vergeltungswaffe I*, revenge weapon 1, was not a rocket but a small ramjet-powered robot aircraft. The programme was run by the Luftwaffe and was seen as a way of striking back at British cities if not attacking critical military targets. In fact, in spite of the psychological impact of the 'buzz-bombs', they were largely contained by conventional anti-aircraft defences, fighter aircraft and gunfire. Much more sinister was the V–2 which was a true rocket, developed by the German Army and totally immune to interception. More than 13,000 V-1s and 5000 V-2s had been fired by the war's end, the main targets of the V-2 offensive being London and the Belgian port of Antwerp. Five thousand eight hundred and twenty-three V-1s and 1054 V-2s fell on Britain killing nearly 900 civilians and seriously injuring 35,000 more.

Aircraft

GREAT BRITAIN

Aircraft of the RAF

Hurricane, Hawker

Numerically the most important RAF fighter during the Battle of Britain, the prototype Hawker Hurricane beat the Spitfire into the air by six months, flying first on 6 November 1935. It was the RAF's first aircraft capable of flying more than 300 mph, powered by a Rolls Royce Merlin and armed with eight rifle calibre Browning machine guns. By 7 August 1940, the RAF had on strength over 2300 Hurricanes in 32 squadrons, compared with 19 squadrons of Spitfires. In the Battle of Britain they shot down more enemy aircraft than did any other of Britain's defences, air and ground combined.

Although obsolete in overall design, the Hurricane served on in several Marks; the IIC carried two 500 lb bombs, and the Mark IID had twin 40 mm cannon operating successfully as an anti-tank aircraft in the Western Desert. The Soviet Union received almost 3000 Hurricanes out of the total 12,780 British built and 1451 Canadian built aircraft.

Spitfire, Supermarine

At the outset of the Battle of Britain, the RAF had some 1400 in 19 squadrons. It is a tribute to the original design that when production ended in 1947, the total of all Spitfires produced for the RAF was over 20,000. This elegant and evocative aircraft had within it the potential for absorbing enormous increases in power and performance through a succession of marks of Rolls Royce Merlin and Griffon engines. The Spitfire I and Ia which fought the Battle of Britain had a 1030 hp Merlin and an armament of eight .303 inch machine guns. Compared with its principal opponent, the Messerschmitt Bf 109, the Spitfire was only a fraction faster, less powerfully armed but had the edge in manoeuvrability.

By the beginning of 1942, the new Fw–190 and later marks of Bf 109 outclassed the Spitfire V. There was still plenty of stretch in the original design, however, and a Spitfire IX with a 1720 hp engine had a top speed of 404 mph at 21,000 ft. The Spitfire Mk 21 was the first Griffin-engined variant selected for mass production, but only 122 had been built by the end of the war.

Various marks of Spitfire were modified for high altitude reconnaissance, their armament removed and cameras mounted in the fuselage. Another significant conversion was the Seafire, fitted with folding wings and development broadly following the lines of their land-based counterparts.

Typhoon, Hawker

From the same design stable as the Hurricane, the Typhoon was originally designed as a new generation fighter able to best the Fw-190 at speeds up to 400 mph. However, design problems plagued the programme and almost led to complete cancellation of the aircraft – it was discovered that the fighter had excellent performance at low altitude, and from being a defensive fighter, the Typhoon became an outstanding instrument of ground attack. In the run-up to D-Day, Typhoons ranged over northern France, attacking critical communications targets. In the fighting following the Allied landing, rocket-armed Typhoons were devastating in their effect on German armour, adopting a technique called 'cab rank' in which they maintained standing patrols over the battlefield, being called in to make pinpoint attacks by a forward air controller. Some 3300 Typhoons were produced.

Mosquito, de Havilland

First flown in November 1940, the Mosquito was a private venture prototype which made extensive use of wood in the airframe. Powered by two Rolls Royce Merlins, it was extremely fast and operationally just as flexible. As an unarmed bomber, it could outrun most opposition, and fitted with such electronic devices as Oboe and carrying incendiaries, the Mosquitos served with the RAF's Pathfinder Force.

The aircraft was readily adaptable as a fighter, armed with cannon and machine guns in the nose, serving as a night-fighter, for making ground attack or shipping strike missions over north-western Europe, in the Mediterranean, and in the Pacific.

Altogether, 7781 Mosquitos were delivered in 42 different marks, of which the most numerous was the Mk VI fighter bomber.

Wellington, Vickers

Bomber Command's most significant aircraft on the out-break of war, the Wellington was powered by twin radial engines and built on the 'geodetic' structure devised by Barnes Wallis, the aircraft's designer. Altogether 11,461 Wellingtons were delivered, which included a number of maritime reconnaissance and ASW variants, the roles in which the Wellington ended the war.

Stirling, Short

First of the RAF's four-engined 'heavies', the Stirling was built with a wingspan to fit the then standard RAF hangar and its service ceiling was a mere 17,000 ft. The Stirling flew on its first raid in February 1941, took part in the attack on the *Scharnhorst* at Brest, July 1941, and the thousand plane raid on Cologne in 1942, but by 1943 was out of the operational front line, reverting to transport and glider towing roles.

Halifax, Handley-Page

The prototype Halifax flew the week before the invasion of Poland, and was in action first on the night of 11–12 March

1941. With the Lancaster, the Halifax formed the backbone of Bomber Command's night offensive in Europe, dropping 227,610 tons of bombs in 75,532 sorties. Altogether 6176 Halifaxes were built for the RAF. Not one survives in any museum today.

Lancaster, Avro

The most significant and certainly the most famous RAF bomber of the war, the Lancaster evolved from a twin-engined prototype called the Manchester, which had been fitted with unreliable Rolls Royce Vulture engines. Fitting four Merlins saved the programme and resulted in a superb combat machine – a 'bomb truck' capable of carrying 14,000 lbs of high explosive to Berlin. Lancasters were modified to carry the Barnes Wallis bouncing bombs that were used to attack the Ruhr dams, and single weapons such as Tallboy and 12,000lb Blockbuster earthquake bombs.

Seven thousand, three hundred and seventy-seven Lancasters were made in several marks; they made 156,000 sorties over Europe and dropped 6,801,645 tons of bombs.

Sunderland, Short

Long range flying-boat, operational with Coastal Command from 1938 through the war. With its heavy defensive armament, the Sunderland earned the nickname 'Flying Porcupine' by Luftwaffe pilots. Attacked by eight Ju-88s over the Bay of Biscay, a single Sunderland skimmed the waves to protect its vulnerable underside, shot down three of the German aircraft and drove off the rest.

(Note: The RAF made extensive use of US aircraft, including the Douglas A20 (Boston), the B-17 (Fortress One), the P-40 (Warhawk and Kittyhawk), the consolidated B-24 Liberator, and small numbers of Brewster Buffalos, P-38 Lightnings, and P-51s (known in the RAF as the 'Invader').)

Weapons

Fleet Air Arm Aircraft

Fairey Barracuda

The FAA's first monoplane torpedo bomber, the prototype Barracuda first flew in late 1940. Barracudas made the successful attack on the *Tirpitz* in Alten Fjiord, north Norway in April 1944 and went into action against Japanese targets for the first time, in Sumatra the same month. Total production was 2500 aircraft.

Fairey Swordfish

The legendary 'Stringbag' first flew in 1934 and was obsolete by the time the war began but its superb low speed handling ideal for carrier operations kept it in service through the war and action in some of the Royal Navy's most dramatic engagements.

It was Swordfish from the carriers *Eagle* and *Illustrious* which crippled the Italian fleet at Taranto on 11 November 1940 and a Swordfish strike which slowed down the *Bismarck*. Only five of the 18 FAA pilots who tried to bar the Channel to the German battleships *Scharnhorst, Gneisenau* and *Prinz Eugen* on 12 February 1942 survived the heroic action, all six swordfish aircraft being shot down.

Later marks of Swordfish carried ASV radar and under-wing rockets proving a formidable anti-submarine weapon.

Fairey Fulmar

Designed as an eight gun, two-seat fleet air defence fighter, the Fulmar first flew in early 1940 and gave the FAA a modern fighter aircraft at a critical time. As the Supermarine Seafire became operational, Fulmars were progressively turned over to the night fighter or second line roles. Maximum speed with the Merlin VIII engine was 280 mph and range 800 miles.

Supermarine Seafire

The Seafire was a 'navalized' Spitfire equipped for carrier operations with folding wings and arrester hook. Several versions were built paralleling the land based equivalent, with Merlin and Griffon engines. The type first entered service with No. 807 squadron in mid-1942, and the later models were retired from the front line in 1952.

UNITED STATES

United States Army Air Force (USAAF)

B–17, Boeing, Flying Fortress

Early marks of B–17 did not live up to the 'Fortress' tag, proving under-armed and vulnerable, carrying a relatively small bomb load. The 'E' model, with increased defensive armament, was the first Fortress to arrive in England. The USAAF's daylight raids of 1943 over Regensburg and Schweinfurt showed how vulnerable unescorted B–17s were in daylight, in spite of their heavy defensive armament. The B–17G of which 8680 were built made the first US raid on Berlin in March 1944, by which time the P-51 Mustang long range escort fighter had made its appearance. The 'G' model had a top speed of 287 mph and could carry three tons of bombs a distance of 2000 miles. It was armed with thirteen .50 calibre machine guns.

B–24, Consolidated, Liberator

Stablemate of the B–17 in the USAAF's bomb wings, the B–24 was also developed through various models, and featured heavy defensive armament. The Liberator is best remembered for the low level attack against the Ploesti oil refineries in mid-1943.

B–25, North American, Mitchell

Twin-engined medium bomber. It was Mitchell's launch from a US aircraft carrier which made the Doolittle raid on Tokyo in April 1942. The B–25J was a special ground

255

attack model, able to carry both bombs and a heavy nose armament.

B–26, Marauder, Martin

Rushed into production in 1940, early models of the B–26 gained a bad reputation from pilots because of their very high landing speed. A larger wing accommodated an increase in weight and gave better handling characteristics, and the B–26 showed its combat potential as a tactical support aircraft with the Ninth Air Force. It ended the war with the lowest loss rate per 1000 sorties of any US light bomber.

B–29, Superfortress, Boeing

The US Army Air Corps produced a requirement for a 'hemisphere defence weapon' in February 1940, before Hitler became master of Europe. The new aircraft had to have transatlantic range with a 2000 lb bomb load and a speed of 400 mph, with heavy defensive armament and armour. Hap Arnold approved a production contract before Boeing had got even as far as a wooden mock-up. But the company delivered, and the prototype XB–29 flew in September 1942 with orders behind it totalling over 1500.

With Britain still a base for operations over Europe, it was decided to use the long range high-altitude B–29s exclusively against Japan, at first from bases in China and then from airfields on Pacific islands bringing the whole of Japan in range. The first B–29 mission was 5 June 1944, against Bangkok. Nine days later the first target in Japan was attacked, the steel production centre of Yawata. In November 1944 high level daylight raids began, without much success, but on 9 March 1945, a low level night attack was made on Tokyo with incendiary bombs, leaving some 80,000 dead. B–29s carried out the final act of the Second World War, dropping the two atom bombs on Hiroshima and Nagasaki. B–29s flew 34,790 sorties during the war, dropping just under 170,000 tons of bombs. Four hundred and fourteen B–29s were lost, while their defensive power was credited with destroying 1128 Japanese aircraft. Production ended in May 1946, with a total at 3960.

P–38, Lockheed Lightning

Powered by supercharged in-line engines, the Lightning was distinguished by its twin boom tailplane; armament was 1 20 mm cannon and four 0.50 inch machine guns in the nose.

P–39, Bell Airacobra

The Airacobra was distinctive in having the in-line Allison engine, located behind the cockpit, driving the propeller to a shaft passing under the pilot. This arrangement left room for a 37 mm cannon firing the propeller boss. The Airacobra was undistinguished as a fighter, but an excellent ground support aircraft. The Soviet Air Force received roughly half the production, and used them successfully in this role.

P–40, Curtiss

The P–40 was in production in various marks until late 1944, with a total of 12,302 aircraft being accepted for service. It was not a fighter design in the same class as its wartime contemporaries, but proved sturdy and adaptable. P–40s in various marques saw service with the USAAF as the Warhawk, with the British as the Tomahawk and Kittyhawk, and with Dominion Air Forces, with the Soviet Air Force, and with the American Volunteer Group in China.

P–47, Thunderbolt, Republic

This massive single-seat fighter was the heaviest fighter in the world when it first flew in 1941, but in spite of its weight it attained speeds about 400 mph. The barrel fuselage contained the trunking for the complex exhaust-driven turbo supercharger, which boosted the twin-row radials output to well above 2000 hp.

In Europe, Thunderbolts served initially as bomber escorts, but when the P–51 arrived they switched to ground

257

attack with an armament of eight 0.5 inch machine guns and a bomb load of 2000 lbs. A total of 15,683 Thunderbolts were built, 5222 were lost in action, Thunderbolt pilots in Europe claimed 3752 German aircraft in the air and destroyed 3315 on the ground. Eight hundred and thirty Thunderbolts were supplied to the RAF from September 1944, and were used exclusively in Burma.

P–51, North American Mustang

One of the most significant aircraft of the war, the P–51 lightweight fighter was able to escort USAAF bombers all the way from Britain to Berlin and back. It was the combination of the Merlin engine, built by Packard in the US, with the advanced airframe design, which gave the Mustang its high top speed, long range with auxiliary fuel tanks, and excellent performance at altitude. The fastest Mustang was the lightweight P–51H which had a 1380hp Packard Merlin, and a top speed of 487 mph. In the European theatre, P–51s flew more than 200,000 sorties, shot down 4950 enemy aircraft, and destroyed 4131 on the ground. In RAF service, Mustangs destroyed 323 V–1 flying bombs over the UK.

US Naval Aircraft

Douglas SBD Dauntless

For two crucial years after entering service in 1941, the Douglas Dauntless fulfilled the US Navy's dive bomber and scout aircraft requirements almost entirely, providing the strike power used with such effect at Midway, Coral Sea and the Solomon Islands campaign.

A total of 5936 were built before production ended in July 1944.

Top speed was 255 mph and range over a thousand miles.

Grumman Wildcat

The F4F Wildcat was first ordered by the US Navy in 1939. Over 8000 were built and these diminutive fighters were used operationally on a wide scale by the US Navy in the Pacific, participating in the battles of the Coral Sea, Midway and Guadalcanal. The stubby, barrel-fuselaged aircraft was designed round the strictures of carrier operations and, although inferior to the Zero in some respects, it proved particularly rugged in combat and operations, capable of operating from rough forward airstrips. The British Fleet Air Arm operated the type as the Martlet from 1941 to the end of the war.

Grumman Hellcat

Perhaps the most significant naval aircraft of the war, the F6F Hellcat succeeded the Wildcat in production and gave US Navy and Fleet Air Arm pilots the edge over Japanese opposition. The first Hellcat action was in August 1943 during an attack on Marcus Island and by the end of the war 75% of air to air combat kills had been achieved by Hellcat pilots. The Hellcat was thus of prime importance in winning air superiority in the last years of the Pacific War.

Curtiss Helldiver

The SB2C Helldiver was designed as a divebomber to replace the SBD Dauntless but, because of production delays, did not enter service until 1943. The type was subject to constant development but was never an unqualified success as a combat aircraft.

Grumman Avenger

The TBF Avenger was a comparatively large carrier aircraft with a crew of three, designed as a torpedo bomber to replace the elderly Douglas TBD Devastators which were slaughtered at the Battle of Midway.

The Avenger first flew in 1941 and a handful were operational during the Battle of Midway. From December 1943 the type was manufactured by General Motors, a total

259

of 9830 being built altogether. The type also served with the Fleet Air Arm and the RNZAF.

Maximum speed was 278 mph and range over a thousand miles.

Luftwaffe Aircraft

Junkers Ju 87 Stuka

Sturkzkampflugzeug (Stuka) means 'dive bomber' in German and the word applied to several aircraft types but overwhelmingly to this crank-winged, fixed undercarriage machine which epitomized the Luftwaffe's early days of Blitzkrieg success. First flown in 1935, the type was tested in combat in Spain and the B-model proved highly successful in the campaigns of 1939–40, cowing the opposition by delivering precise strike power to clear a path for the panzers in close support missions. But in the Battle of Britain in the face of determined fighter defence, the type's weaknesses were shown up. In the Mediterranean and Balkans however it was a different story and the Royal Navy lost many ships to Stuka attack.

The D model entered production in 1941 and production rose sharply in 1942 as it was realized there was no replacement for this, by now outmoded design. The Ju 87G model was armed with twin 37 mm cannon for tank busting missions on the Eastern Front.

Ju 87s fought to the end of the war flying night harassment missions.

The 1940-vintage Ju 87B-1 had a top speed of 238 mph and could carry over 1000 lb of bombs over 370 miles.

Messerschmitt Bf 109

The Bf (for *Bayerische Flugzeugwerke*) 109 was built in larger quantities than any other World War fighter aircraft and remained a principal weapon in developed versions ten years after its first flight. Messerschmitt's nimble single seat fighter flew in 1935, was battle tested in Spain and in the Bf

109E the Luftwaffe had the outstanding fighter of 1939–40, better certainly than the Spitfire I fitted with a fixed pitch airscrew. The British fighter could have the edge above 20,000 feet but the fuel-injected Messerschmitt had the advantage in a dive. Over southern England however the type's short range showed up with only 20 minutes' combat time and London as the limit of their tactical radius. Tying the fighters to the close escort of bombers further limited their effectiveness, where the fact it could be out-turned by the Spitfire and Hurricane (but not outrun or outgunned) was a serious disadvantage.

Just as the Spitfire's basic design proved capable of enormous stretch so was the Bf 109. The G-model was the most important sub-type, fighting on all the fronts where German forces were engaged, in defence of the Reich against Allied bombers and with the Finnish, Rumanian, Italian, Slovak and Hungarian 'satellite' air forces.

In the closing weeks of the war there were still some 800 Bf 109s serviceable with the Luftwaffe, mostly G and the last of the line K sub-types.

The Bf 109E–1 of 1940 vintage was powered by a DB601 engine delivering over 1000 hp. Top speed was 340 mph at 13,120 feet and armament two machine guns and three cannon, slower firing but delivering a greater weight of fire than the eight-machine gun armed Spitfire and Hurricane.

Messerschmitt Bf 110

Designed as a long range escort fighter or 'Zerstörer' (destroyer), the Bf 110 squadrons were the Luftwaffe's elite before the Battle of Britain but they were given a severe mauling by the much more agile RAF single seaters. The type was put into production again in 1942 in the G-model series as a heavy day fighter and ground attack aircraft but the Bf 110's prime role to the end of the war was as a night fighter, a prominent aerial array bristling from its nose. When used in emergency against USAAF bomber formations in daylight, they were not a success. The last Bf 110G was completed in March 1945, the end of a 6050 run.

261

Weapons

Junkers Ju 88

The Ju 88 was one of the most versatile aircraft of the war. In fact it was designed as a high speed bomber and first flew at the end of 1936. The Ju 88 was powered by two 12-cylinder in-line engines but cowled with annular radiators giving the appearance of radial engines and the characteristic 'beetle-eye' nose was made up of optically flat panels to give the bomb aimer/nose gunner the best forward visibility.

Early model Ju 88As served with the *Kampfgruppen* (Luftwaffe bomber squadrons) during the day and night bombing attacks on Britain 1940–41 where it fared better than the Heinkel 111, its high diving speed allowing it to outrun even a Spitfire.

The Ju 88C model, in various sub types, used the same basic airframe except with a solid gun-armed nose and was used as a heavy long range fighter, for ground attack and, equipped with radar, as a night fighter – which was to be the type's principal role until the end of the war. By spring 1944 the night fighter arm provided some 15% of the Luftwaffe's total strength with the Ju 88C-6 its principal aircraft.

The D-series were reconnaissance aircraft, the G-series improved night fighters, the H-series long range shipping strike aircraft, the P-series anti-tank cannon-armed and the S-series high speed, high altitude bombers while some 250 Ju 88 airframes in a variety of types were used in the abortive 'Misteln' (Mistletoe) composite flying bomb programme.

Dornier Do 217

The Do 217 was a lineal descendant of the pre-war Do 17 'flying pencil' but in fact was an entirely new aircraft. Classified originally as a 'heavy bomber', the machine had a relatively light bomb load. From 1942 the type was built as a night fighter with nose radar and heavy cannon armament (Do 217J). Some also equipped Italian night fighter units.

262

Focke-Wulf Fw 190

A radial engined fighter was out of step with the times when the prototype Fw 190 first flew in May 1939, but the Fw 190A–2, the first true production model, immediately established an ascendancy over the RAF's Spitfire V when combat was first joined in 1941. The Fw 190 was an outstanding air superiority fighter but also very effective in the ground attack and fighter bomber roles. The short nose BMW radial engined A-series was developed through a multitude of sub-types. The long nose B model was a high altitude version with in-line engine cowled in an annular radiator. The same formula was applied to the D-series, the most successful version of the Focke-Wulf fighter to get into the front line in quantity. The short nose Fw 190G-series was an extended range, purpose-built fighter bomber.

Junkers Ju 52/3m

The ungainly Junkers Ju 52 trimotor with its slab sided, corrugated construction was one of the key aircraft of the war, accounting for much of the German armed forces' success in victory and much of its resilience in defence. In the time of victory it was the means whereby fuel and logistic support was kept flowing for the panzer spearheads and forward based fighter aircraft. The parachutists it carried were crucial in the campaigns in Norway and the Netherlands but during the assault on Crete, the Ju 52 fleets were decimated – 271 being lost. Operations flying supplies to the Afrika Korps proved equally dangerous at low altitude and without fighter escort.

On the Eastern fronts Ju 52s supplied the pockets at Demyansk and Stalingrad where 266 Ju 52s were lost. As their organization broke down and numbers dwindled, Ju 52s continued to fly desperate supply missions to isolated 'pockets' until the end of the war.

Total production of Ju 52s from 1939 to mid-1944 when production ended was 3225 machines.

Weapons

Heinkel He 111

The He 111 medium bomber, the 'terror weapon' of 1940, was compelled to soldier on way past its design span because German industry failed to come up with a replacement. The He 111 was comparatively short ranged and had an undaunting bomb load, compared with say a Lancaster, but it proved very adaptable to a range of missions. In the Battle of Britain it was the Luftwaffe's principal bomber and, lacking in effective defensive armament, it suffered at the hands of Fighter Command. On the Eastern Front He III units, after the initial attack, were increasingly relegated to supply missions. Others, armed with torpedoes, made attacks on the Arctic convoys, including the ill-fated PQ 17.

In the summer of 1944 He 111Hs were used in Operation *Rumpelkammer*, (Lumber Room) launching V-1 flying bombs in mid-air against Britain, losing 77 aircraft in the launching of 1200 missiles.

Total production exceeded 7300 aircraft.

Other Luftwaffe Aircraft

Arado Ar 196: Single-engined two seat shipborne floatplane.

Arado 234 Blitz: Four-jet bomber, operational in closing months of war. Flew some reconnaissance missions over Britain.

Blohm and Voss Bv 138: Triple-engined flying boat. Operational in Atlantic, North Sea, Arctic, Baltic, Mediterranean and Black Sea.

Fiesler Fi 156 Storch: High wing, short landing and take off battlefield reconnaissance and liaison aircraft.

Focke Wulf Fw 200 Condor: Converted airliner, long range maritime recce and strike aircraft. Successful in Atlantic until driven off by catapult armed merchant ships and escort carriers.

Heinkel He 177: Heavy bomber of advanced design. Technical over-ambition plagued its service career, and thus the Luftwaffe was never able to mount a sustained large scale strategic offensive.

Heinkel He 219 Uhu (Owl): Purpose designed and highly effective night fighter. It was armed with upward firing guns to rake a bomber's' vulnerable belly.

Henschel Hs 123: Biplane dive bomber and assault aircraft. Used in Spain, in early Blitzkrieg campaigns and on Eastern Front.

Henschel Hs 129: Heavily armoured, twin-engined ground attack and anti-armour aircraft. Operational in Tunisia and on Eastern Front.

Messerschmitt Me 163: Diminutive rocket-powered interceptor with phenomenal rate of climb.

Messerschmitt Me 210: Unsuccessful attempt to supplant Bf 110 'Zerstörer' (destroyer). Cancelled by Luftwaffe and replaced by redesigned Me 410.

Messerschmitt Me 262: Twin turbojet fighter. Ordered into action as a bomber on Hitler's command which drastically reduced its effectiveness.

German Aircraft Production 1939–45

From records of Dept. 6 (Quartermaster General), Luftwaffe Command.

Japanese Naval Aircraft

Mitsubishi A6M Zero-sen

The most famous Japanese aircraft of the war, the 'Zero' earned its name from the fact it was put into production in 1940 or the Japanese year 5700.

The type '00' was dubbed 'Zeke' by the Allied reporting codename committee and the later clipped wing version 'Hamp'. Allied pilots however called their formidable opponent the 'Zero' and the name stuck.

Although it had appeared in combat over China, and its abilities in a dogfight had been reported by American Volunteer Group pilots, the Zero's outstanding combat qualities and feats of long distance flying came as a great

Weapons

German Aircraft Production 1939–45

From records of Dept. 6 (Quartermaster General), Luftwaffe Command.

Ar	196	435	(Seaplanes)
Ar	234	214	(Bombers)
Bv	138	276	(Seaplanes)
Bv	222	4	,,
Do	17	506	(Bombers)
Do	217	1,730	,,
Do	215	101	,,
Do	18	71	(Seaplanes)
Do	24	135	,,
Do	335	11	(Fighters)
Fi	156	2,549	(Liaison)
Fw	190	20,001	(Fighters)
Fw	200	263	(Maritime strike/recce)
Fw	189	846	(Reconnaissance)
Go	244	43	(Transport)
He	111	5,656	(Bombers, Transport)
He	115	128	(Seaplanes)
He	177	1,446	(Bombers)
He	219	268	(Night-fighters)
Hs	126	510	(Recce)
Hs	129	841	(Ground-attack)
Ju	52	2,804	(Transport)
Ju	87	4,881	(Dive-bombers)
Ju	88	15,000	(Bombers, Recce, Night-fighters)
Ju	188	1,036	(Bombers)
Ju	290	41	(Transport, long range reconnaissance)
Ju	352	31	(Transport)
Ju	388	103	(Bombers)
Bf	109	30,480	(Fighters)
Bf	110	5,762	(Escort Fighters, Night-fighters)
Me	262	1,294	(Jet-Fighters, Fighter-Bombers)
Me	323	201	(Transport)
Me	410	1,013	(High-speed Bombers)
Ta	154	8	(Fighters)
Ta	152	67	(Fighters)
	Total	98,755	

shock to the Allies in 1941–2. The type was developed through various versions and still provided the bulk of Navy fighter strength at the end of the war, ground-based and what little remained afloat, while many were expended in Kamikaze attacks.

Max speed (A6M5) was 354 mph and range 976 miles.

Mitsubishi G4M

Land-based, twin-engined torpedo bomber, codenamed 'Betty' by the Allies. Admiral Yamamoto was shot down flying in a G4M and the type had a reputation for exploding if attacked, lacking armour protection and self sealing fuel tanks. Large numbers were lost during the 'Great Marianas Turkey Shoot' of mid-1944 and the survivors were expended as carriers of the Ohka rocket-powered suicide aircraft.

Aichi D3A 2

Codenamed 'Val', the D3A2 was the Japanese Navy's first low wing all metal dive bomber and was the principal weapon in the carrier-based air attacks of late 1941 and 1942. It could carry a bomb load of over 800 lbs 970 miles. Top speed was 266 mph.

The D3A was supplanted in service by the Yokasuka D4Y Susei (Comet) codenamed 'Judy' by the Allies but by the time this aircraft entered service, most of Japan's carriers had been sunk. They were flown from land bases and finally expended as Kamikaze aircraft.

Kawanishi N1K1 Shiden

The Japanese Navy's principal land-based fighter and fighter bomber in the latter half of the Pacific war, the Shiden (known to the Allies as 'George') was developed from an earlier floatplane fighter design. In spite of some technical shortcomings, experienced Shiden pilots gave a good account of themselves against their chief opponent, the F6F Hellcat.

Weapons

Nakajima B5N

Codenamed 'Kate', the B5N carrier-borne torpedo bomber took a major part in the Pearl Harbor attack. It was powered by a single 1020 hp radial engine, had a speed of 224 mph and a range of 600 miles.

Nakajima B6N Tenzan

Developed as a B5N replacement, the Tenzan (Heavenly Cloud) was codenamed 'Jill' by the Allies and entered service in 1942. Like so many other types, remaining B6Ns were expended in Kamikaze attacks.

Japanese Army Aircraft

Kawasaki Ki 45-Kai

Twin-engined fighter and shipping strike aircraft. Codenamed 'Nick' by the Allies, the cannon armed Model-C night fighter accounted for a number of USAAF bomber aircraft over the South-west Pacific and Japan itself.

Kawasaki Ki-61 Hien

When first encountered in combat, the aircraft codenamed 'Tony' by the Allies was thought to be a Japanese built version of the German Bf 109 but was in fact an entirely original design for the JAAF. More than 2800 of this fast and combatworthy fighter were produced, supplanted at the end by a radial engined version, the Ki 100.

Speed of the Ki 61 was 368 mph and range 1180 miles.

Mitsubishi Raiden

The J2M Raiden (Thunderbolt), known to the Allies as 'Jack', was a single-engined land-based fighter powered by a radial engine which served with the Army Air Force in small numbers from late 1942 onwards.

268

Mitsubishi Ki-21

Most important Japanese Army bomber aircraft, in production up to 1944. Codenamed 'Sally' by the Allies, the type served in every theatre where the Japanese Army was engaged. Top speed was just over 300 mph and range 1350 miles.

Mitsubishi Ki 67 Hiryu

The Hiryu (Dragon) was a twin-engined bomber of which some 700 were built for service with the Army Air Force. A development was the Ki 109 interceptor armed with a 75 mm cannon, a small number of which were used without much success against USAAF Superfortress bombers attacking Japan. Others were expended on suicide missions packed with 1600 kg of explosive.

Nakajima Ki 43 Hayabusa

Built in large numbers (5900 aircraft by the end of the war) the Hayabusa was codenamed 'Oscar' by the Allies and equipped fighter squadrons of the Army Air Force from late 1941 onwards. It was largely outclassed by the Allied fighters it encountered but was exceptionally manoeuvrable. Most of the JAAF's aces established the bulk of their scores flying this aircraft.

Nakajima Ki 84

Exceptionally fast and combat worthy single seat fighter, in production for the JAAF from 1943 onwards. The 'Frank' was also capable of carrying 500 kg of bombs for ground attack missions.

Top speed was 388 mph, range over a thousand miles and armament of the last models, twin 20 mm plus twin 30 mm cannon.

Weapons

Soviet Aircraft

Polikarpov I-16

When this diminutive barrel-fuselaged, single-seat fighter first flew in 1933, it represented a very advanced machine. When the Soviet Union was invaded in 1941, the I-16 was outclassed but remained the Red Air Force's most numerous fighter aircraft. Large numbers were destroyed on the ground, but in the hands of skilled pilots some managed to get the better of the invaders. Max speed was 233 mph and range 249 miles.

Petlyakov Pe-2

Deployed widely from 1941 onwards as a bomber and ground attack aircraft, the twin-engined Pe-2 also served successfully as a long-range fighter and reconnaissance aircraft and was one of the best all-round Soviet aircraft of the war. Speed was 335 mph and range 750 miles.

Yakovlev Yak 1/3/7/9

The Yak 1 single seat fighter first flew in 1939 and showed that the Soviet aircraft industry was in step with the rest of the world. The Yak 3 was a lineal development, powered by a 1650 hp Klimov in-line engine and, in performance at least, the match of the Bf 109G and Fw 190A. The further refined Yak 9 which first appeared during the Stalingrad fighting was an even more formidable opponent for the Luftwaffe and more than 17,000 of this version alone were built. The Yak 9B was a fighter bomber variant, the -9D a long range fighter and the -9PVO a night fighter, the -R, reconnaissance and the -9DK anti armour variants. More than 37,000 of the Yak series of fighters were built in total.

Lavochkin La-5 and La-7

After the in-line Lagg 3, Semyon Lavochkin used a radial engine on his next design, the La-5 which again made extensive use of wood construction. The La-7 was a developed version with a more powerful engine and by the end of the war, was the Soviet air force's most important fighter type next to the Yak-3. Maximum speed of the La-7 was over 400 mph and armament twin 20 mm cannon.

Ilyushin DB-3

Twin engined medium bomber of undistinguished performance which served throughout the war. On 8 August 1941 DB-3s attacked Berlin in reprisal for a German raid on Moscow. The type was also used successfully as a torpedo bomber in the Baltic.

Ilyushin Iz-2 Shturmovik

One of the key aircraft of the war, destined to be built in larger numbers than any other type (some 42,330 including the Iz-10 development) of wartime aircraft.

Designed as a ground attack and anti-tank aircraft, the prototype first flew in December 1939 and production aircraft were just reaching front line squadrons when the invasion began. The Iz-2 had twin cannon armament and could carry a large bombload including rocket boosted armour piercing bombs. Cockpit and engine were themselves extensively protected by armour plate and the swarms of Shturmoviks operating at low level breaking up German armoured formations proved very difficult to swat down.

Top speed was 280 mph and bombload 1300 lb.

Lavoshkin LaGG 3

Known for its design team's initials, Lavochkin, Gorbunov and Gudkov, the LaGG 3 single-seat fighter employed a novel method of wooden construction but was underpowered and lacking in manoeuvrability; nevertheless it served throughout the war, particularly as an escort for II-1 Shturmovik formations.

Science and Technology at War

The story of science and the Second World War is of how effectively the brilliance and invention of the individual was realized in the field. Allied victory in the scientific war was dictated by superior organization at this stage, providing speedy answers to the most simple and the most complex of problems. To every advance the enemy made counter-measures had to be devised, tested, and mass-produced and this called for the greatest flexibility and constant operational liaison to turn a problem on the battlefield into a solution in soldiers' hands. For each new weapon, teams of operators had to be quickly trained, and their knowledge – together with the unfamiliar new weapons – had to be passed on to millions. New theatres of war brought new challenges, whether it was malaria in New Guinea, or wrecked harbours in France – and a rapid answer had to be found in every case.

The war years themselves produced massive challenges to which massive research programmes were one answer; but the basic discoveries, often the work of an individual starved of resources, which allowed the development of an atom bomb, radar, the jet engine and the rocket, had been made before 1939. German scientists, drawing on the lessons of 1914–18 when Germany's war-machine had been run on a siege economy, had invested much effort in material science. Germany not only had a healthy synthetic rubber industry but a plastics and hydrogenated petrol programme based on coal. The same was true in metallurgy. When I.G.Farben scientists first produced magnesium alloys for aircraft construction and engine castings they created a technological gap which British and American scientists launched crash programmes to close.

Before the war, however, Great Britain alone had taken

272

the trouble to organize cadres of scientists to be ready to assist the services. This is ironic when one considers how much the political climate of appeasement in Britain and France during German re-armament was born of a popular fear of the scientific unknown. The prospects of strategic bombing, the distortedly high estimates of deaths 'per bomb tonnage' and the vision of aeroplanes raining lethal gas on London or Paris sapped the will to prepare for war in the West. And there had been a revolution in communications too. It had already altered the face of politics; now the rival propagandists had, in mass broadcasting and the cinema, the instruments to reach their populations instantly. Marconi's idealistic hope that radio might go some way to averting the 'evils of war' was turned on its head in World War II.

Just as the major areas of research had been opened before the war, the war itself ended with a series of 'might have beens' heralding the age of the nuclear umbrella. Basic research on nerve gases had been implemented in the course of German insecticidal research before the war. By 1945, 'Tabun', 'Sarin' and 'Soman' had been stockpiled by the Germans in vast quantities. Toxic gases had been used operationally by the Japanese in China; botulinum toxin, the deadliest agent of biological warfare, was under test in the United States in 1943. Long-range rocket bombardment of London and Antwerp was carried out by the Germans in an attempt to reverse the tide of the war. The German A-9 rocket and the *Laffarenz-projekt*, on the drawing board in 1945, were the ideas from which the ICBM and the Polaris submarine were developed; above all, the atom bomb had been dropped on two Japanese cities.

The developments in mathematical science, computing systems and instrumentation could ensure new accuracies and prediction of effects. Thus the delivery systems existed; the weapons of total destruction existed. The story of science and the Second World War, underwriting Allied victory, is not only the story of an arms race; it tells of how new weapons were used, and also why some new weapons were never used at all.

Even before 1936, Great Britain was aware that scientific

research was a most integral part of national defence, faced as the country was with the prospect of a massive hostile bombing force negating the two historic British defensive advantages – the Channel and the Royal Navy. In March 1935 the Tizard committee on air defence discovered that the only instrumental aid for providing warning of the approach of hostile aircraft was the telescope. If there was any hope at all, it lay in Admiralty research into the possibilities of locating hostile ships and aircraft by their heat radiation, or the Air Defence Experimental Establishment's work on sound location. In the pre-Munich period, British air defence had rested on biplane fighters and immovable concrete sound-mirrors with a ten-mile range – and they were placed facing France, not Germany. By July 1939, however, an operative system of radio location was in existence.

By 1936, it had been realized in several countries that an aircraft reflects radio waves. Radar was in operation in Britain first, because the brilliance of the individual scientist was backed up by foresight and faith at the committee stage; the Treasury's release of funds through the initial efforts of A. P. Rowe and H. E. Wimperis at the Air Ministry, and through the Tizard Committee, led to the construction of a coastal radar chain with an ability to measure range and plot the position of hostile aircraft approaching Britain – to a range of 100 miles and more.

British industry was becoming geared to the new technology, the infant television service of the BBC had created a mass production base for cathode ray tubes for example. A pool of specialist operators had been established, and Fighter Command group headquarters and fighter stations linked early warning by high-frequency radio-telephony to the eight-gun 350 mph monoplane designs of Camm and Mitchell – the Hurricane and the Spitfire.

The operative lessons of radar research had a wider relevance. A. P. Rowe's Telecommunications Research Establishment at Bawdsey developed a system of operational liaison between scientists and services which allowed prototype testing in action and post-design, in which parties of scientists were sent to squadrons actually using the new radar equipment to find out just how well (or indeed badly) it worked. Operational research – the subjection of military operations to quantitative analysis – largely began in the British Air Ministry, though it was later brought to a high pitch of perfection by the Americans. It came into being through the need to improve the technique of interception by radar direction, a problem which the Germans failed to resolve satisfactorily until comparatively late in the war. The demands made by such militarized technology on manpower justified the compilation of that central register of qualified men and devised by Professor Hill and Dr Goodeve in 1938. Two months before the war it contained the names of 5000 scientists in 'reserved' occupations, thus separating the 'boffins' and operators – each to his allotted task. This made good sense, in direct contrast to the woeful German experience of 1939 when academics were indiscriminately drafted to handle rifles in the infantry.

Scientific organization in the United States between the wars was not so pressured by the immediate prospects of national defence. In 1939 America was the world's largest industrial producer. If its plant was not tuned to munitions production, the slack in the economy and the ample labour supply, both legacies of the Depression, made America both militarily and industrially a 'sleeping giant'. By the time the war ended American technology had established its ability to overcome any problem of logistics and terrain – from the spot-welding of 'Liberty ships' to the mass production of DDT and penicillin: above all it had proved its ability to develop, test and implement new devices, new answers to new problems. Take as examples the whole range of amphibious vehicles designed for the Pacific campaign, or the long-range bomber escort which arrived in quantity to rescue a deteriorating military situation in daylight raids on Germany for which existing technology had until then proved inadequate.

The American scientific effort depended on the immediate assimilation of as much British material as possible and the avoidance of the mistakes of departmentalism and

275

misdeployment of resources. In the summer of 1940, the British government approved the despatch of a scientific mission to the United States led by Sir Henry Tizard. The great research facilities and manufacturing power of the US overruled any security considerations. Due to this mission, 16 months before they entered the war, the Americans were in possession of the most important findings of British research to date: the Kerrison anti-aircraft gun predictor, solid-propellant rockets, the proximity fuse, asdic, RDX explosive, shipborne radar and especially the cavity magnetron.

This last device allowed the second revolution in radar. Its transformation from an early-warning screen to an airborne, seaborne, high- or low-level instrument of acute long-range perception depended on the generation of shorter radio wavelengths. Two devices seemed to have potential: the 'Klystron' developed by the Varian brothers at Stanford University, California, and an American invention of 1921 – the magnetron itself. Two British scientists, Professor J.T. Randall and Dr H.A.H. Boot, applied a simple resonator principle to this last device, producing by February 1940 a wavelength of 9 cm at a power of 400 watts. The valve had made centimetric radar possible. Reducing redundant information echoing from the landscape, it closed a blind spot which prevented low-flying aircraft from escaping detection, and proved of vital importance in the Battle of the Atlantic and the strategic bombing of Germany.

The revelation of the cavity magnetron allowed American radar research to make a quantum jump forward. Karl T. Compton, chief of the Radar Division National Defense Research Committee, had long foreseen the importance of microwaves. He appreciated the prediction of Sir Charles Wright that the side which developed power on the shortest wavelength would win the coming war. The Americans significantly put the project into a civilian laboratory, establishing a short-wave research laboratory at the Massachusetts Institute of Technology. American military research relied heavily on the resources of the universities and of industry. This was largely because the Office of Scientific

Research and Development, established in 1940 under Vannevar Bush, felt itself to be pressed for time. The OSRD reported directly to President Roosevelt and received funds from Congress by direct appropriation, administering them either by negotiating contracts with private or industrial laboratories.

The National Defense Research Committee's work was split into 19 divisions, each responsible for a particular area, such as radar or rocketry. The Committee for Medical Research was responsible – among other things – for the manufacture of penicillin and plasma. There were, however, organizational gulfs within the American scientific effort which went some way to impairing its efficiency. The military establishments, particularly the Army Service Forces under Lieutenant-General Sommervell, placed the army's semi-independent technical services under a single close control, but they never approached the degree of operational liaison current in Great Britain.

Sommervell's sprawling empire included quartermaster, ordnance, signal engineer, medical, chemical warfare and transportation departments. Each department conducted research and development and placed contracts for procurements, functions which overlapped yet remained isolated from the sub-committees of the NDRC. And the sub-committees were themselves compartmentalized, relying on sheer weight of resources to produce results. The products of American science therefore – the Manhattan Project aside, unique in its scale, organization and funding – tended to have a distinct technological bias, characterized by the capacity for series development and volume production.

The Americans excelled in such simple war-winning innovations as the amphibious truck, the DUKW, which allowed rapid turnaround at an invasion beachhead, the bazooka, and the armoured bulldozer which cleared airstrips under fire in the Pacific island-hopping campaign.

The German scientific effort during the Second World War was the one that has subsequently most excited popular imagination. Certainly, the spectacle of long-range rocket

bombardment, jet and rocket aircraft, Mach 10 wind tunnels, helicopters, assault rifles, infra-red devices, true 'submarines' running on hydrogen peroxide, influence warheads
and nerve gases made it possible to imagine the most
ingenious and deadly arsenal which science could put at
man's disposal. Why, therefore, was the German scientific
effort constantly baffled and rendered ineffective by the
Allies? The ability of the Third Reich actually to produce
new weapons capable of deciding the issues of war was not
only greatly overestimated by its enemies (a misapprehen-
sion not without significance for the scientists who worked
on America's atom bomb), but remains so by those who
look only at the products of science – and forget the
significance of their implementation. Germany's programme
of technological development was a programme characterized not by organization but by chaos.

The post-war investigation by the Allies showed that at
the outbreak of war, the German leaders believed they
could achieve final victory with the weapons they already
had. In the crucial years of 1939–43, basic research on radar
had been halted on Hitler's orders. German scientists had
rejected centimetric radar as impractical until an H_2S set
with its magnetron core was recovered from a crashed RAF
Halifax outside Rotterdam.

No scientist was asked to advise effectively on the U-
Boat war until the end of 1943, and the advantage held by
the Allies was by then so great there was no chance of
reversing it. The most significant area of research, the
Army's A-4 rocket project, capable of delivering a ton of
high explosive at a 200-mile range, was advanced in preference to the development of the guided anti-aircraft missiles
capable of blasting the four-engined Allied bombers out of
the sky.

The *Enzian* and *Wasserfall* AA rocket programmes could,
with coherent direction, have interdicted German airspace
to the very bombers pounding all *Vergeltungswaffen* (the
'revenge weapons' V-1, V-2 and V-3) installations. This last
was a huge multi-barrel gun based in northern France
designed to fire rocket assisted shells at London. It was

never operational. But coherent direction was lacking. Partisans of rival schemes fluttered about Hitler's court until a project was rejected or approved, given a highest priority stamp, millions of cubic tons of ferro-concrete allocated (this always found particular favour with the Führer) and labour mobilized. The absolute power of the *Führerprinzip* worked in two ways. A dubious project such as the Coender 'high-pressure pump gun' (the V3) was given a priority far beyond its proven ability, whereas a potentially vital development such as the Me 262 jet fighter was diverted by Hitler himself to a highly unsuitable bomber role, against the pleadings of Luftwaffe experts. During the war there was not one single German agency, let alone one individual, which controlled the vast number of overlapping projects. Only the intervention of a powerful political initiative could ensure the durability of a research programme. The increasing infiltration by the SS into the Army's rocket project and its transfer from Peenemünde to Blizna in Poland shows how completely the political monoliths inside the Third Reich intervened in weapons programmes without imposing the coherence that a 'totalitarian system' may presuppose.

In these ways the undesirable brilliance of individual German scientists was grotesquely framed in the Aryan vision of science which denounced Einstein's relativity theory as being 'Jewish', and saw gruesome medical experiments on concentration camp prisoners as legitimate. The division of scientific effort between the universities, industry, the Wehrmacht and the SS was never reconciled. Reflecting the National Socialist emphasis on practical technology rather than pure science with its Jewish tinge, it was the engineer who could command attention and funds and who was amply rewarded and cosseted by the state – such men as Ferdinand Porsche, designer of the Volkswagen and Tiger tank, Wernher von Braun, the 'interplanetary travel enthusiast' and guiding light of the German rocket programme, or Kurt Tank, designer of the Fw 190 fighter. This emphasis on the engineer coupled with the Nazi distrust of the natural scientist had, long before 1939, already prejudiced their efforts in the field of nuclear technology.

There was never a 'race' for the ultimate deterrent, the atom bomb; the Germans never got near it. Apart from the efforts of the Allied sabotage offensive, the manufacture of heavy water at the Rjukan plant in Norway had never taken place in anything approaching industrial quantities. Germany's uranium production came to a dead halt with the bombing of the Degussa plant in 1943. However, German atomic science was already foredoomed by the usual disadvantages of poor organization and inadequate recognition by the Reich leadership. Another contributory factor to their slow development in this field was the absence of those physicists driven into exile by Nazi racial and ideological policies, such men as Einstein, Pontecorvo and Gullicini. Again, the Germans had insufficient technical equipment, machine tools, telemetry and computers for so vast a project. And finally, in contrast to the rocket lobby who had managed to overcome Hitler's initial indifference by their sheer enthusiasm and got their 'V-weapons' – if not a means to land on the moon – the atomic scientists themselves did little to overcome the authorites' incomprehension of the importance of such research and technical development. Only Göring at the Air Ministry, an agency which proved consistently fecund in its research programmes, saw its potential – but too late. The last V-2, the ideal delivery system for atomic warfare, had already been launched, while a German nuclear reactor, let alone a bomb, had never been tested.

The American atom bomb was, however, not destined for Germany. A highly complex technological war waged by America, Britain and Russia had already defeated the Third Reich. The lesson of that war, in the terms of operational experience, was that finely balanced scientific ingenuity needed political and military scope to use it; it had to ensure the right weapon was in the right place at the right time. But however subtle the 'secret war' may have been, it was often a simple technological factor that swung the outcome of a battle. The elegance of the Allied anti-submarine effort in the Atlantic for example, using high-frequency direction finding, airborne radar and ahead-throwing weapons might have been negated had Schnorkel-equipped U-Boats appeared earlier. Similarly, the RAF night-bombing offensive had by 1944 exhausted all the technical subtleties in its armoury. Oboe and Gee, its navigational aids, H_2S and 'Window', the anti-radar device which showered metal foil into the beams of the German electronic defences, had been rendered largely ineffective by German electronic counter-intelligence and new night-fighter tactics. However, the appearance of the P-51 Mustang long range escort fighter equipped with droptanks in the day-time skies over Germany gave the USAAF bombing effort an absolute advantage. Similarly, the great battle on Germany's Eastern Front was materially turned in 1942 by the appearance of the Russian T-34 tank, with its sloped armour, 77 mm gun, and high standard of durability.

It made obsolete the bulk of Germany's tank and anti-tank arsenal at a stroke. Chronologically, at least, jets, rockets, perhaps even the bomb itself were an afterthought in the story of science and the Second World War, the prototypes heralding an unfought new age of warfare. Where the scientists, technologists, doctors and engineers held the key to victory was in providing devices as simple yet as subtle as a tank that could swim up a beach, an engine filter that might resist the dust of the desert and a spray that would kill malarial mosquitoes. The fact that the German scientific war effort failed to produce the mundane but effective weapons in preference to the spectacular is a factor that largely contributed to the Allied victory in the Second World War. And just as important, war experience had made it apparent that science itself had a vital role to play not only on the battlefield, but in maintaining the social fabric of both war and peace.

Chronology of Weapons and Technology

1935

26 February Watson-Watt demonstrates 'radio location' using Heyford bomber and Daventry radio transmitter
9 March Existence of Luftwaffe publicly admitted
28 July Prototype B–17 Flying Fortress first flight
September Prototype Messerschmitt Bf 109 first flight
6 November Hawker Hurricane prototype first flight

1936

5 March Prototype Supermarine Spitfire first flight

1937

April German rocket scientists arrive at Peenemünde
12 April Frank Whittle test runs turbojet engine
September Heinkel runs Pabst von Ohain's turbojet engine

1938

1939

30 March Soviet LaGG-3 fighter first flight
1 April Mitsubishi A6M Zero first flight
May Prototype Short Stirling first flight
1 June Focke-Wulf Fw 190 first flight
15 June Heinkel He 176 rocket fighter test flight
17 September Luftwaffe sow airborne magnetic mines
October Prototype Handley Page Halifax first flight
November Luftwaffe forms long range anti-shipping Atlantic strike force equipped with Fw 200 Condors
23 November British recover German magnetic mine intact
29 December B-24 Liberator first flight

1940

13 May Sikorsky VS-300 helicopter makes free flight
29 June British magnetron successfully tested generating centimetric wavelengths
20 October North American P-51 Mustang prototype first flight
14 November Aircraft of Luftwaffe KG100 equipped with X-Gerat lead air strike on Coventry
16 December Test flight of Henschel Hs 293 radio controlled bomb

1941

March First RN escort ships equipped with Type 274 centimetric radar
2 April Heinkel He 280 turbojet powered fighter makes its first flight
18 April Me 262 turbojet powered fighter prototype first flight
9 May U110 captured with Enigma machine intact
15 May Gloster E28/39 British jet powered fighter prototype makes first flight
August High Frequency Direction Finding installed on RN escort ships
21 December Fairey Swordfish equipped with ASV (Air to Surface Vessel) radar sinks U-Boat in darkness

1942

8 March First use of RAF 'Gee'-equipped Pathfinder aircraft
27/28 March Bruneval raid captures German 'Wurzburg' air defence radar
13 June First attempted V-2 launch at Peenemünde
July U-Boats equipped with 'Metox' radar warning apparatus
18 July Prototype Me 262 jet fighter first flight
29 September B-29 Superfortress first flight
3 October First successful V-2 launch at Peenemünde
24 December First successful ground launch of V-1 flying bomb

Weapons

1943

30/31 January RAF bombers equipped with H_2S ground mapping radar first operational

5 March Prototype Gloster Meteor jet fighter first flight

April German Navy 'Hydra' U-Boat code broken

March First successful air contact of U-Boat using centimetric radar

March H_2S, 'Rotterdamgerät' (so called Rotterdam device after the location from where it was retrieved), falls into German hands when bomber crashes

17 May No 617 Sqdn Lancasters attack Ruhr dams with 'bouncing' bombs

24 July RAF firestorm raid on Hamburg. First use of 'Window' radar jamming.

17–18 August RAF attacks Peenemünde

9 September Fritz-X radio controlled bomb sinks Italian battleship *Roma*

20 September Prototype De Havilland Vampire first flight

October RAF use 'Corona' to jam German night fighter communications

30 October US Navy receives first operational helicopter

31 October US Navy F4U Corsair makes airborne intercept by radar

December 'Colossus' computer operational at British codebreaking HQ at Bletchley Park

1944

8 January Prototype Lockheed P-80 US jet fighter first flight

January German night fighters introduce 'Naxos,' H_2S homing device

March USAAF bombers make daylight attacks on Berlin with P-51 fighter escort

13 June First V-1s fall on Britain

15 June B-29 Superfortress raids begin on Japan

16 August Me 163 rocket-powered interceptors used against US bombers

8 September First V-2 falls on Britain
25 October First Kamikaze attacks on US warships

1945

13–15 February Allied bombing of Dresden
27 March Last V-2 to fall on Britain
April Last Luftwaffe sortie over Britain
7 May RAF Coastal Command sinks 196th and last U-Boat
7 July First flight of J8M1 Shushui Japanese Me 163 copy
6 August 'Little Boy', first atomic bomb, exploded over Hiroshima
9 August 'Fat Man' exploded over Nagasaki

SECTION 4

Organizations and Armed Forces of World War II

A–Z Directory

ABDA Command

After Pearl Harbor, a joint Anglo-American-Dutch-Australian Command was set up with British General Archibald Wavell as its head, in command of all forces in Burma, Malaya, the Philippines and the Dutch East Indies. Neither Wavell's degree of authority nor the scant forces available to ABDA were able to check the Japanese advance and the command was dissolved on 25 February 1942, two months after it was founded.

Abwehr

The intelligence department of the German Armed Forces, in fact the largest office of OKW. Its head from 1938 was Admiral Canaris and after his implication in the anti-Hitler plot, the Abwehr was largely absorbed by the RSHA.

The Abwehr was organized in three branches with outposts around the Reich and so called 'KO's' (*Kriegsorganisationen*) operating clandestinely in foreign countries.

Abwehr Main Branch 1 oversaw espionage activities, with seven specialist groups concentrating on military, technical, political and economic intelligence. Branch II was concerned with sabotage and Branch III with counterespionage.

Advanced Air Striking Force

The component of the RAF, fighter, bomber and Army co-operation aircraft, that went to France with the BEF in 1939.

Air Raid Precautions (ARP)

British air raid organization under the auspices of the Home Office.

American Volunteer Group

AVG pilots first went into action in December 1941, flying P-40 fighters for the Chinese against the Japanese invaders. Their 'Flying Tigers' original commander General Claire Chennault took over command of the USAAF China Air Task Force in which many AVG pilots continued to serve.

Bomber Command see Royal Air Force

British Army

Between the Munich crisis of 1938 and the outbreak of war, the British Army was hastily expanded and re-equipped but was still tiny compared to its continental equivalents. In 1939 the British Army could field four divisions in France, a division and a brigade in India, two brigades in Malaya and the equivalent of six infantry divisions and an armoured division in the Middle East. Total numbers at the end of 1939 were 897,000 rising to 1,650,000 by June 1940 with more than 10 divisions participating in the disastrous campaign in France.

While after Dunkirk the British Army built up its strength and prepared for an invasion of Britain itself, in the Western Desert the Italians were brought to grips and soundly beaten. The diversion to Greece and the arrival of the Germans in North Africa prolonged the desert campaign into years of hard fighting and meanwhile a new series of defeats and retreats had begun in the Far East. While invasion of Great Britain itself had been averted, it looked by the autumn of 1941 as if Britain could do no more than stay in the Russo-German war on its fringes.

It took the intervention of US power to turn the tide of

the war, and nowhere could the British Army have succeeded in its subsequent victories without US assistance in
manpower and material.

By the time of Operation Overlord, the strength of the
British Army had risen to 2.7 million men. By June 1945
the figure was 2,920,000 with the bulk of British strength in
Montgomery's Twenty-first Army Group that had fought
their way into the heart of northern Germany. The British
Army's total losses were 144,079 killed, 239,575 wounded
and 152,076 POWs. The losses of 1939–45 were however
far less severe than those of 1914–18 when 702,410 were
killed.

British Expeditionary Force, BEF

The first units of the BEF reached France in 1939, the
spearhead of a well-equipped and well-trained army. By
the time of the German attack of May 1940, 10 divisions
were in France, one detached to French command on the
Saar Front. After the disastrous intervention in Belgium,
338,000 men got out at Dunkirk and many thousands more
eventually returned home from ports on the French Atlantic
coast.

Coastal Command: see RAF

Combined Chiefs of Staff

Anglo-US military command committee set up after US
entry into war, based in Washington and meeting at major
wartime conferences (see chart).

Combined Operations

The kernel of Combined Operations Command was set up
in the British War Ministry in June 1940 with a brief to
develop 'Commando' units to raid occupied Europe. After
the first pinprick raid, 'Section MO9' became expanded

into Combined Operations HQ headed by Admiral Sir Roger Keyes who held the post until October 1941 when he was succeeded by Lord Louis Mountbatten. Commando operations grew in scale and scope in the Mediterranean and in the Western Desert and a large scale raid on the French port of St Nazaire was mounted, Operation Chariot. On 18–19 August 1942 came Operation Jubilee when British Commandos covered the flanks of the Canadian attack on Dieppe, beaten off with heavy casualties.

From the end of 1942 onwards Combined Operations grew in importance, spear-heading amphibious invasions by conventional forces in Sicily, Italy, Burma, Madagascar and culminating in the invasion of Normandy.

ENSA

Entertainments National Service Association. An offshoot of NAAFI formed in September 1939 to provide entertainment for British forces at home and abroad, disbanded in mid-1945. Popularly known by the troops as 'Every Night Something Awful'.

ETOUSA

European Theatre of Operations US Army. Established on 8 June 1943, succeeding USAFBI ('US Forces in the British Isles'). When SHAEF (Supreme Headquarters Allied Expeditionary Force) was established in February 1944, it became a logistic operation rather than an operational military command for the Overlord build up.

Fascist Party

Founded by Benito Mussolini and the ruling political party in Italy from 1922 and 'the March on Rome'; lasted to 1943 and the Allied landings in Sicily. The Militia was called the *Milizia Voluntare Sicurezza Nazionale*, and the youth movement the *Avanguardia*. When Mussolini adopted an anti-Jewish posture under German influence in 1938, Jews in the fascist movement were expelled.

FFI

Forces Françaises de l'Intérieur, established on 1 February 1944 in principle to unify the various armed groups of the French resistance.

Fleet Air Arm

Britain's naval air force. The Fleet Air Arm was under RAF control from 1924 but returned to Royal Navy authority in 1939. At the outbreak of war the Royal Navy had nine aircraft carriers, five of which were destined to be lost in action.

French Army

By May 1940 the fully mobilized French Army consisted of 119 divisions, of which 100 were disposed on the north-east frontier. French tactical doctrine was largely outdated, emphasizing continuous defence and relying on the supposed strength of the Maginot Line of fixed fortifications with armour parcelled out in so-called 'interval' formations to plug gaps in defence rather than form an operational mass of manoeuvre. The technical quality of French armour and artillery was meanwhile high.

After the debacle of May-June 1940 the armistice army was officially established in November, 100,000 strong but without heavy equipment and any real fighting power. General de Gaulle's Free French forces to begin with were even less combat worthy but a notable exception was General Leclerc's two brigades which fought in the Western Desert.

From 1943 onwards Free French forces expanded, largely equipped by the Americans. An expeditionary force of four divisions fought in Italy and the First Army under General Jean de Lattre de Tassigny, 12 divisions strong, participated in the liberation of their homeland and General Leclerc's Second Armoured Division took Paris on 25 August 1944. The First French Army ended the fighting in the Vosges mountains and in south-west Germany.

French Air Force

Known as the *Armée de l'Air*, in May 1940 the French Air Force had around 700 modern fighter aircraft, the principal machines being the Morane-Saulnier MS 406 and Dewoitine Dw 520, and a considerable bomber force. The northern zone of Air Operations facing the critical invasion front was commanded by General François d'Astier de la Vigerie.

From the opening attack on 10 May, the Luftwaffe achieved decisive air superiority on their breakthrough front allowing the ground attack Stukas to roam at will. The British meanwhile were unwilling to commit their last fighter reserves to be consumed in the developing debacle. By the end, the French has lost some 700 aircraft in defence of their country.

Free French squadrons formed within the RAF and in the Soviet Union, the so-called 'Normandie-Niemen Squadron'.

French Navy

One of the world's great navy's of 1939 but destined for an ignominious war, the French Navy counted seven battleships, 19 cruisers and 79 submarines and one elderly aircraft carrier – the *Béarn*, with two new superbattleships, the *Jean Bart* and *Richelieu*, nearing completion. Under the armistice terms the French Navy was to return to port and be disarmed but the British quickly took steps to ensure they did not simply become a new Axis fleet. Mers-El Kebir was bombarded by the British in 1940, Dakar unsuccessfuly attacked on 23 September 1940 and other French ships forcibly taken over in Alexandria and in British ports.

Under the command of Admiral François Darlan, appointed Vichy Navy Minister in 1940, the French Navy was reluctant to follow de Gaulle's Free French rallying cry and provided a major part of the Vichy resistance to the Anglo-US Torch landings in North Africa. Nevertheless when the Germans moved on Toulon, the French Mediterranean naval base, on 27 November 1942 the fleet including three battleships, seven cruisers and 32 destroyers was scuttled, fulfilling Darlan's promise given to Admiral Sir Dudley Pound at Bordeaux, 18 June 1940, that the French Fleet would never fall into German hands.

German Army

Adolf Hitler and the Nazi party had captured the German state in 1933 but had to enthrall the German Army to consolidate their absolute power. The Army's acceptance of his presidency and the swearing of an oath of allegiance to his person in August, 1934, marked the first stage of the process. Through the years leading up to the invasion of Poland, the Army was brought in line by a mixture of threat, to turn Röhm's Nazi militia, the *Sturmabteilung*, into a people's army for example, by personal humiliation of the old-guard figureheads such as Field Marshal Blomberg and General Fritsch and by the promise of massive rearmament if not the foreign adventures which in fact the military conservatives resisted. After the western democracies stood back over the Rhineland and Czechoslovakia the road to war was clear and any military resistance to Hitler quiescent, even more so after the campaigns of 1939–40, the audaciousness of which had first appalled the generals, the success of which had bound them even closer to Hitler. Not until 1943 did a handful of regular officers of the old Army stir in revolt and when they acted in July 1944 it was a fiasco, depriving the Army of what was left of its independence.

The leadership of the German Army, OKH, the *Oberkommando des Heeres*, was stripped of its valued authority in December 1941 after the failure before Moscow. Its Commander in Chief Field Marshal von Brauchitsch was removed and replaced by Hitler himself as army commander. In the succeeding months a host of sacked field marshals and generals followed, destroying the respect that had surrounded the old general staff. From now on, Hitler's will and Hitler's wrath would be sovereign and the Army would feebly comply in his miserable military misdirection of the war.

For the invasion of Poland in September 1939 the German Army mustered around 60 divisions including eight mechanized and six panzer divisions armed in the main with comparatively light vehicles. In May 1940 the Army had mobilized five million men, half of them deployed in the west in 135 divisions of which 10 were armoured. For Barbarossa the German Army assembled three million men in 160 divisions, and some 1500 tanks. Facing the Overlord invasion in the West in June 1944 were 58 divisions of which 10 were armoured, and many of the rest understrength.

The organization of the German Army followed the standard pattern. The highest field command was the Army Group, composed of two or more armies, each in turn composed of two or more army corps. A corps was made up of two or more divisions, a division being the largest possible self-contained formation with a balanced composition of arms. An infantry division of 1939 had 17,700 men distributed among three infantry regiments each of three battalions with supporting heavy weapons, anti-tank, engineer and signal units. A panzer division of 1939 mustered 11,800 men, equipped with 328 tanks and 101 armoured cars with motorcycle troops, motorized infantry and supporting artillery.

The German Navy

The *Kriegsmarine*, the German Navy, came near to producing a decisive result in the course of the war with the U-Boat offensive waged in the Atlantic. But after the crisis of spring 1943, the U-Boat threat was contained and the convoy link to Britain secured allowing US power (and with it British) to intervene decisively on the continent of Europe in June 1944.

The German Navy went to war unprepared and under-armed. The 'Z-plan' building programme foresaw no fewer than 13 battleships, 12 battlecruisers, 8 aircraft carriers and 162 ocean going U-Boats but not until 1947 and Hitler had promised his admirals 'no war with Britain until 1944'. There were only 16 ocean-going U-Boats in the Atlantic on 1 September 1939 and after the scuttling of the *Graf Spee*, German naval commanders talked of seeking 'death with dignity' at the hands of the numerically far superior Royal Navy.

The German surface fleet after some initial success were all effectively contained by 1942 although the threat of such a 'fleet in being' drew off RAF Bomber Command and the menace of the *Tirpitz*, bottled up in a Norwegian fjord, led to the destruction of PQ 17 at the hands of submarines and shore-based aircraft. In fact after the battle of the Barents Sea on 31 December 1942, Hitler was convinced of the surface fleet's uselessness and ordered it scrapped. Admiral Raeder, the German naval commander, resigned to be replaced by Admiral Dönitz, commander of the U-Boat arm and Germany's last Führer in the closing week of war in Europe.

It was Dönitz's U-Boats which came so close to a decisive victory. In mid-March 1943 the submarine wolf packs sank 20 ships for the loss of one of their own but a combination of improved tactics, numbers and technology swung the Battle of the Atlantic in the critical spring of 1943 in the Allies' favour. From now on, all the U-Boat arm could do was scramble to catch up technologically, which they did with the Schnorkel boats but too late. The U-Boat's war was eventually lost but not before 14 million tons of Allied shipping had been sent to the bottom. Of the 1162 U-Boats built, 785 were destroyed, 156 were surrendered and the rest scuttled.

One of the German Navy's last surface operations was the evacuation of large numbers of soldiers and civilians cut off in the Courland pocket on the Baltic and east Prussia.

From mid-1944 the cruiser *Prinz Eugen* and two pocket battleships operated in the Baltic in support of the surrounded land forces while from January to May 1945 two million Germans were shipped westwards on merchant ships and warships. In the last few weeks of the war, what remained of the German surface fleet was sunk in harbour by bombing, only the *Prinz Eugen*, the *Nürnberg* and the *Leipzig* remaining afloat.

German Air Force

Luftwaffe

The existence of the Luftwaffe was revealed in March 1935, but German airpower had been clandestinely reborn in the late 1920s, with Soviet assistance. The prototypes of the aircraft which would spearhead the German offensives of 1939 and 1941, were in existence by 1936 and were tested in battle over Spain. Here the Luftwaffe were able to develop their ground support techniques, but in spite of such actions as the razing of Guernica, strategic bombing over long ranges was not its speciality. After the death of General Wever in 1936, the Luftwaffe neglected long range four-engined bombers.

The basic unit was the *Gruppe* of 30 aircraft, holding three *Staffeln* (equivalent to a squadron). Three *Gruppen* were formed into a *Geschwader*. The strength of a *Luftflotte* or air fleet varied during the war between 200 and 1200 aircraft. For the attack on Poland, the Luftwaffe deployed more than 600 bombers and over 200 fighters and 219 dive bombers, plus 474 other aircraft. In the first two days, the Germans won air superiority by smashing the Polish Air Force on the ground and severing its communications. With the skies cleared, the Luftwaffe could function in the air to ground role, and it was here that the JU87 Stukas first won their fearsome reputation.

The attack on Norway showed the first use of paratroops, while for the assault on France and the Low Countries the Luftwaffe gathered around 4500 front line aircraft, including

475 transports and 45 gliders for laying an airborne carpet into the heart of Holland. As in Poland, air and ground cooperation swept away the opposition.

The defence of the Dunkirk evacuation, in range of the RAF based in southern England, gave a taste, however, of what was to come. The Battle of Britain, August-October 1940, was the first German defeat of the war.

In June 1941 the Luftwaffe deployed three air fleets for the invasion of the Soviet Union. The Balkans had been cleared and the Mediterranean island of Crete seized by airborne attack, but at the expense of vast losses in transport aircraft and in paratroopers. The assault on Russia was in the first phases as successful as the attack in the West had been, vast numbers of obsolete Soviet aircraft being destroyed on the ground or in the air. As the distances increased, however, and the Soviet Air Force found new strength, the Luftwaffe was forced increasingly on the defensive. By mid-1943 operational strength was around 4000 aircraft, Germany was being hammered night and day by the Allied bombing offensive, and the demands of the Eastern Front finally wore it down. Too late the Germans realized their mistake in not attacking strategic Soviet industries, and when remaining bombers were hastily put together to mount an offensive in February 1944, by then every aircraft was needed to stem the tide of Soviet armour.

In spite of its high level of technical innovation, the Luftwaffe was at the end of the war virtually grounded through lack of aviation fuel, a handful of operational jets being towed onto airfield by oxen. By the time Göring was relieved of his command on 23 April 1945, the Luftwaffe in the West had ceased to exist. The last remnants, some 1500 aircraft of all types, remained in northern Austria and Czechoslovakia, there to operate barely 50 sorties a day against the Soviet forces until final surrender on 8 May.

The Luftwaffe lost 70,000 aircrew killed in action, 25,000 wounded, 100,000 aircraft destroyed, missing or damaged beyond repair. The Soviets claimed the Luftwaffe lost a total of 77,000 aircraft on the Eastern Front.

Italian Armed Forces

When Mussolini brought Fascist Italy into the war in June 1940, the Italian Army showed how unprepared it was by being checked in southern France by a few divisions of French Alpine troops, even though their country was already in extremis. The invasion of Greece proved an equal fiasco and the Italians had to be bailed out by the far more efficient Germans. In North Africa the grandiose march on Cairo was checked and the tiny British Western Desert Force conquered Cyrenaica and Italian East Africa again with comparative ease. The Italian infantry that fought with Rommel, however, could be tough opponents although let down by poor equipment and indifferent morale.

With Germany still winning Italian forces trailed in Hitler's wake but the Italian Eighth Army, the 'expeditionary legion' sent to fight Bolshevism, went down to defeat in Stalingrad with the rest.

From the armistice of September 1943, Italian forces in the Balkans and in the Aegean melted away to be replaced by Germans. The Navy had been either sunk in harbour or used up on convoys to North Africa and its remnants surrendered at Malta in September 1943.

Italian midget submarines and frogmen proved tougher opponents – they disabled two British battleships in Alexandria harbour while some Italian submarines operated in the Atlantic to a limited extent, traversing the Strait of Gibraltar without loss.

The Italian Air Force, the *Regia Aeronautica*, also suffered from technical backwardness after a period of being in the technical forefront in the early 1930s. The standard fighter in 1940 was the biplane Fiat CR42, some of which appeared over Britain in September 1940. Standard bombers were the trimotor SM 79 and twin engined Fiat Br 20. Later Italian aircraft such as the Macchi C-202 Folgore and Reggiane Re-2001 designed round German supplied in-line engines arrived too late to matter, although some of these later aircraft served with the 'Co-Belligerent Air Force' on the Allied side post 1943.

Japanese Armed Forces

The Japanese soldier, derided in 1941 as a 'yellow monkey' was one of the toughest opponents of the war. The Japanese Army showed its initiative and resourcefulness in the victories of 1941–42, and its ferocity in defence thereafter. It also showed its callous indifference to death and suffering both to its own soldiers and to its cruelly misused prisoners of war.

The Japanese Army expanded rapidly from 1937 with the intensification of the war in China. By 1941 it mustered 1.7 million men in 51 active divisions. Through the war years, the Japanese Army grew to a peak of 5 million men organized in 140 divisions. As in the US, Japan's land based air arm was a component of the Army with an Inspector General of Army Aviation subordinate to the Imperial General Headquarters in Tokyo.

Throughout the war years the 700,000 strong 'Kwantung Army' garrisoned Manchuria. It fought a series of border clashes with the Soviet forces in 1938–39 and again in the last weeks of war in August 1945, but otherwise was militarily useless. Likewise the million strong 'China Expeditionary Force', although capable of mounting offensives as in 1944, was cut off from the defence of the homeland.

The Japanese Imperial Navy was the third largest in the world and in certain respects the most modern although some Japanese warship design innovations were less successful than others. Japan had been a pioneer of naval aviation (under British tutelage) from 1922 and in December 1941, the Japanese Imperial Navy had 10 aircraft carriers, old and new, ideal instruments for power projection over a vast area of ocean. There was an equal mix of elderly and modern battleships including the enormous *Yamato* and *Musahi*, each with nine 18-inch guns.

Japanese submarine strength was high but they were used in fleet actions rather than in a U-Boat style independent offensive while anti-submarine warfare and naval electronics were comparatively primitive, allowing US Navy submarine operations to devastate the Japanese merchant marine.

Japanese naval aviation was their primary arbiter of power in the Pacific war and remained so as the threat of surface ships and submarines declined. As their carriers were sunk one by one, land-based naval aircraft still proved effective, culminating in the final desperate Kamikaze attacks of 1944–45. The Japanese Navy however had already run out of trained pilots capable of winning even local air superiority. They had not been rotated home to train new pilots but rather expended in ferocious battles. The 'Great Marianas Turkey Shoot' showed how inexperienced the new generation had become.

National Socialist German Worker's Party
National Sozialistische Deutsche Arbeitpartei (NSDAP)

The sole political party permitted in Germany from 14 July 1933, the Nazis very rapidly bound the German state and its institutions to their own political machine. On Chancellor Hindenburg's death in August 1934 Adolf Hitler became Führer and Reich chancellor with the Army bound to him by personal oath. A rival power centre had already been removed by the destruction of the *Sturmabteilung* (the SA) leadership in the so called 'night of the long knives' 30 June 1934. The fusing of party and state meant that every aspect of German life in war and peace was imbued with Nazism – from the party emblem on the postman's uniform, to the institutionalizing of anti-semitism and then genocide.

Nazi Germany was characterized by an apparently highly centralized political structure, flowing from the absolute rule of the Führer, Adolf Hitler. But in fact many separate organizations, agencies and command structures grafted themselves onto the Nazi monolith with overlapping responsibilities and divisions of power. The structure of the police and 'security' services is typical with the SS functioning as an empire within an empire, responsible for enforcing Nazi rule within Germany and the occupied countries but itself split into a web of overlapping organizations. Paramilitary organizations flourished and all aspects of 'civilian' life were drilled and regulated. The *Reichsarbeitdienst* or labour service was obligatory for Germans for six months following the age of 20, which itself would be the culmination of ten years in the *Jungvolk*, the Adolf Hitler Schools and the Hitler Youth. After that would come military service and voluntary service with one or other of the party organizations – the SA, the SS, or the naval, flying and motoring branches of the same, (the Marine SA, the NSKK and NSFK).

Here is a glossary of the major organizations that proliferated under the Nazi regime.

Abwehr: Intelligence operation of OKW, supreme command of the German Armed Forces. Absorbed by SS from early 1944.

Abwehrpolizei: Frontier police controlled by Gestapo.

Allgemeine SS: The general body of the SS, consisting of full time, part time and honorary members, as distinct from the armed or *Waffen SS*.

Auslandorganisation: The Nazi Party organization concerned with supervision of Germans abroad. Ranked as a *Gau* in own right.

Bezirk: A district administratuve unit.

Chef der Sicherheitspolizei und des SD: Chief of the Security Service – Reinhard Heydrich until 1942, then Ernst Kaltenbrunner in 1943–45.

DAG, DAW, DET: Economic 'enterprises', armaments and quarrying etc using concentration camp and slave labour. The *Deutsche Wirtschaft Betreibe* was a holding company set up to cover all such economic undertakings.

Einsatzgruppe: Task force of Sipo and SD for 'special missions in occupied territories'. Four such *Gruppen* followed the German Army into the Soviet Union to organize the liquidation of Soviet Jews. Three hundred thousand had been murdered by the end of 1941.

Ersatzheer: The Replacement Army centre for plotters against Hitler to July 1944. Taken over by Himmler.

Feuerschutzpolizei: Fire and air raid police. A branch of the Orpo.

Führer: Leader. 'Der Führer' used only for the person of Adolf Hitler.

303

Gau: Main administrative division of the NSDAP. Germany divided into 42 *Gau* with a *Gauleiter* as highest party official.

Geheime Feldpolizei: Secret field police. Army executive branch of *Abwehr* but taken over by Sipo and SD, post-1942.

Geheime Staatspolizei: The Gestapo. Originated in Prussia 2 April 1933 with an HQ set up at 8 Prinz Albrechtstrasse, Berlin which became notorious as a prison and interrogation centre for any opponents of the Nazi regime. In 1939 the Gestapo became a department (*Amt*) of the RSHA, the Reichs Security Head Office run by Reinhard Heydrich. In the areas of German conquest, the Gestapo operated as the organ of terror using the notorious 'night and fog' tactics of disappearance and torture. The Gestapo's head was *Obergruppenführer* Heinrich Muller, throughout the war.

Geheim Staatspolizeiamt (Gestapo): The national HQ of the secret state police absorbed by the RHSA, in 1939.

Gemeindpolizei: Municipal police.

Gendarmerie: Rural police.

Generalgouvernement: The Government General, that part of occupied Poland not directly incorporated into the Reich.

Grenzpolizei: Border police, controlled by Gestapo.

Höhere SS und Polizeiführer (HSSPF): Higher SS and police commander, in effect Himmler's personal representative in each military district and occupied territory.

Jagdverbande: SS sabotage and clandestine operations unit headed by Otto Skorzeny.

Kreis: A district or county. Principal subdivision of a *Gau*.

Kreisleiter: Party official in charge of a *Kreis*.

Lebensborn: SS maternity homes where Himmler planned a superrace would be nurtured.

Leibstandarte SS Adolf Hitler: The Führer's bodyguard. First SS military formation formed in 1933. Division of the *Waffen SS*, 1941.

Kriminalpolizei (Kripo): The criminal police which formed the *Sicherheitspolizei* (Sipo) along with the Gestapo.

Amt V of the RSHA from 1939. Its head was *SS-Gruppenführer*, Artur Nebe.

NSFK: National Socialist Flying Corps.

NSKK: National Socialist Motoring Corps.

Oberkommando des Heeres, OKH: High Command of German Army.

Oberkommando der Wehrmacht: High Command of German Armed Forces.

Oberste SA-Führer: Supreme Commander of the SA (Hitler from 1940), Ernst Röhm, the SA's chief of staff, was assassinated 1934.

Ordnungspolizei: Order police, umbrella title for ordinary uniformed police comprising *Schutzpolizei*, fire police and gendarmerie.

Organisation Todt: Construction agency established under Fritz Todt 1933, built autobahns, Westwall etc. Todt was killed in 1942, succeeded by Albert Speer as Armaments and Construction minister.

Reichsführer SS und Chef der Deutschen Polizei: Reichs SS leader and Chief of the German Police. Heinrich Himmler's title from June 1936.

Reichsführung SS: High Command of the SS.

Reichs Sicherheitshauptamt, RHSA: Reichs Security Head Office formed in 1939 combined the *Sicherheitspolizei* (the Sipo which in turn embraced the Gestapo and Kripo) and the SS's own security service the *Sicherheitsdienst* or SD.

Schutzpolizei: 'Protection police', the regular municipal and rural constabulary who formed the main part of the *Ordnungspolizei*.

Sicherheitsdienst, SD: The SD was the SS's own security service first formed in 1932 under Reinhard Heydrich, and intended to be the party's single intelligence organization.

SS: The 'Schutz Staffel' or protection squads were first organized in 1925 for the protection of Nazi meetings after the SA or *Sturmabteilung* were proscribed. Under Himmler's leadership the SS became a state within a state responsible for crushing resistance within and without Germany to Nazi domination by the apparatus of terror.

The Reich *Sicherheitshauptamt* or RSHA created in 1939 combined the SS's own security service the SD with the anti-political and anti-criminal police, the Gestapo and Kripo.

By 1940 the SS numbered nearly a quarter of a million men and was broadly divided into the *Allgemeine* or general SS made up of voluntary, parttime and honorary members, the SS *Verfügungstruppe* or armed SS, the *SS-Totenkopfverbande*, the 'deaths head formations' which guarded concentration camps, the SD and the *Rasse und Siedlungshauptamt* or race and resettlement department responsible for the colonization of conquered territories.

The SS had its own recruitment, training operations, own rank system and organizational divisions. A *Sturm* was the equivalent of a company and a *Standarte* the equivalent of a regiment. (see *Waffen-SS* below)

Streifendienst: Hitler Youth patrol operation.

Sturmabteilung, SA: The original 'brown shirt' Nazi militia formed in 1921.

Technische Nothilfe, Teno: Technical emergency corps, auxiliary force of the Orpo formed for civil defence work and salvage.

Verfügungstruppe: Original militarized units of the SS, renamed *Waffen-SS* in late 1940.

Volkssturm: German 'Home Guard' formed from 25 September 1944, made up in the main of old men of 60+ and boys of 16 or younger and organized on a *Gau* basis with Himmler in charge as chief of the Replacement Army.

Waffen–SS: Fully militarized SS units dating from the creation of Hitler's guard unit in March 1933, the 'Leibstandarte SS Adolf Hitler.' The *Deutschland* and *Germania* regiments were formed in 1936 and *Der Führer* in 1938 from Austrian volunteers. After the Polish campaign, the three regiments were brought together into the so-called *Verfügungsdivision* to be at Hitler's personal disposal with two more, the *Totenkopf* and *Polizei*, raised from concentration camp guards and the police. The '*Verfugungstruppe*' were renamed *Waffen-SS* at the end of 1940.

By the time of Barbarossa, the *Waffen-SS* had grown to a force of 150,000 representing the 'racial elite' of Germany carefully selected from volunteers only. After Stalingrad however all that changed – from the end of 1942, it was able to draw on the Wehrmacht intake for recruits and thenceforth the Hitler Youth and 'Volksdeutsche', volunteers from the satellite or occupied nations. By 1943, of 38 *Waffen-SS* formations, only 15 were of German or *Volksdeutsch* origin. By 1944 its ranks included Scandinavian, Dutch, Walloon, Fleming, French, Latvian, Lithuanian, Ukrainian, Albanian, Croat, Rumanian, Bulgarian, Slovene, Russian, even Indian personnel.

By December 1944, the *Waffen-SS* had approximately 600,000 men under arms, one Army HQ, 12 Corps headquarters and over 30 divisions. The *Waffen-SS* were immensely tough combat soldiers but their toughness extended to barbarism towards POWs and civilians. In the west the SS murdered British POWs in 1940, again in June 1944 after D-Day and the Ardennes when 71 American POWs were machine-gunned. The SS Division *Das Reich* committed the atrocity at Oradour-sur-Glane in central France while in the Balkans and the East partisans and POWs were treated with brutal savagery.

OSS

Office of Strategic Services – US wartime intelligence and special operations organization. The OSS was formally constituted on 13 July 1942 to replace the prewar Coordinator of Information (COI) with Col. William 'Wild Bill' Donovan as its Director. The OSS was tasked with the gathering of foreign intelligence and the undertaking of special operations under the control of the US Joint Chiefs, while internal faction fighting excluded it from South America and from General MacArthur's South-west Pacific Command.

Donovan had worked with the British SOE since 1941 and used it as a model. OSS teams operated in the Mediterranean, in Burma and in the run up to D-Day in occupied

Europe. In Switzerland OSS station-head Allen Dulles ran a successful spy ring and played a vital part in the secret negotiations of a separate German armistice in northern Italy. The OSS was officially shut down on 1 October 1945.

Royal Air Force

The RAF was established as an independent service in the last year of the First World War, 1 April 1918, merging the Royal Flying Corps and Royal Naval Air Service. Between the wars the RAF was largely engaged in colonial policing and building up a deterrent bombing force, but with aircraft only having the range to strike a little beyond Paris. Serious rearmament did not begin until the mid-30s. Separate functional commands, such as fighter and bomber, were created in 1936, and in 1939 control of the Fleet Air Arm was divested to the Admiralty.

Overall direction of the RAF was vested in the Air Council of the Air Ministry. The Air Council's principals were the Secretary of State for Air and the Chief of the Air Staff – Sir Archibald Sinclair and Sir Charles Portal respectively, from 1940 to 1945.

On the outbreak of the war the strength of the RAF was 1911 aircraft, with 20,033 aircrew and 153,925 ground personnel. In May 1945 the RAF's front line strength was 9,000 aircraft, 144,488 RAF aircrew, 41,107 Dominion aircrew, 831,541 RAF ground personnel and 33,976 Dominion ground personnel. RAF Fighter Command was formed on 14 July 1936, with its HQ at Bentley Priory just north of London, and its first commander was Air Marshal Sir Hugh Dowding.

Fighter Command suffered severe losses in its squadrons in France and Dowding refused to commit any more as the defence crumbled. With the Luftwaffe now established on the Channel coast, the Battle of Britain was fought from 10 July to 31 October 1940. The first phase of the battle opened with the Germans attacking coastal convoys to bring up RAF fighters into battle. In August the Luftwaffe launched a series of attacks against radar stations and

Fighter Command airfields – the RAF adopted the tactic of first engaging the Luftwaffe escort, and then sending in other fighters to knock down the bombers. On 31 August the British lost 37 fighters to the Germans' 60, in dogfights above the bombers – the Luftwaffe believed meanwhile that it had begun to win. However, following an RAF raid on Berlin, on 5 September, Hitler ordered the attacks on fighter airfields switched to London itself, and Göring took over personal command. The huge attacks on London by as many as 625 bombers were designed to get RAF Fighter Command into the air and destroyed. On 15 September all the British reserves were committed, but the German fighters could not escort a second wave of bombers before the RAF had landed, refuelled and was ready once again. After months of attack, the RAF could still field 300 fighters after a time, and that Sunday afternoon battle resulted in a British claim of 185 Germans shot down (the actual number was 56).

Having so nearly broken the RAF with the attacks on their airfields, the Luftwaffe's effectiveness and morale went into decline, and although daylight attacks on British cities continued until the end of September, losses ran at such a high rate that attacks were switched to night bombing, which continued to the end of the year.

During the course of the Battle of Britain, the RAF lost 790 fighter aircraft, the Luftwaffe 1389 aircraft of all types. To meet the night blitz, Fighter Command developed air-craft equipped with Airborne Intercept (AI) Radar such as the Beaufighter and later the Mosquito. After mid-1941, Fighter Command made offensive sweeps over France and the Low Countries and fought a large scale air battle over Dieppe in August 1942. With the formation of the Allied Expeditionary Air Force on 15 November 1943, Fighter Command as such reverted to a defensive role under the title Air Defence of Great Britain (ADGB). It reverted to its earlier title in mid-October 1944. The Command's last significant campaign was the defence against the V-1 flying bombs, from August 1944 to the end of the war. One thousand eight hundred and forty-seven were claimed destroyed by aircraft of Fighter Command out of some 5000 which flew over the British Isles.

The RAF's biggest effort in terms of number of aircraft, personnel, and loss of life was made in the strategic bombing offensive over Germany. At the outbreak of war there were 33 squadrons or 480 aircraft in Bomber Command. After the failure of daylight raids on German naval targets, the Command switched to night bombing and under the direction of Sir Arthur Harris, AOC-in-C from February 1942 until the end of the war, it built up into a great offensive bludgeon, making the first thousand-bomber raid on Cologne, 31 May 1942, attacking Hamburg, targets in the Ruhr, and Berlin itself.

Of the total of 70,253 officers, NCOs and airmen of the RAF killed or missing on operations between 3 September 1939 and 14 August 1945, 47,293 lost their lives in operations carried out by Bomber Command. Six thousand four hundred and forty aircraft were missing from 199,091 sorties over Germany. Bomber Command dropped a total of 955,044 tons of bombs of all types. Coastal Command played a crucial role in winning the Battle of the Atlantic. During the war, aircraft of the Command sank 184 U-Boats and destroyed more than 478,000 tonnes of enemy shipping.

The Red Army

The Army of the Soviet Union, the RKKA (*Rabochekrest'yanshi Krasny*, the Red Army of Workers and Peasants) with its tanks, its artillery, its air fleets and its million of enduring infantrymen, was the stone on which the military power of Germany was broken. Without the Red Army holding the line in the winter of 1941, Hitler would have dominated Europe and without the destruction of the main body of the enemy on the Eastern Front from 1942–45, there would have been no way for Anglo-US power to intervene decisively on the continent.

The Red Army nearly caved in in 1941. It had already been terribly weakened by Stalin's purges – its most able commander Marshal Tuchachevsky had been executed in

1937 and a quarter of the whole officer corps arrested. Thirty-five thousand were executed including three out of five marshals and 13 out of 15 Army Commanders. The NKVD, the Peoples' Commissariat for Internal Affairs which had been the instrument of home grown terror, controlled the police, frontier guards and a 150,000 strong armed security force and would follow the Red Army in retreat and in victory, stiffening resolve in the way it knew how.

In the first months of the German attack launched on 22 June 1941 the invaders' advance seemed everywhere irresistible; an army of three million in western Russia could not stop them and vast numbers of prisoners were captured, cut off and surrounded in huge pockets. New commanders, new equipment and above all winter arrived in time for the Germans to be stopped before Moscow. The huge German offensive of 1942 into the Caucasus ended in the disaster of Stalingrad and the defeat of the great armoured attack on the Kursk salient in 1943 marked the end of the German strategic initiative on the Eastern Front. The Red Army prised the Germans' grip off Eastern Europe and pushed them back to Berlin. In August 1945 the Soviet Army overran Manchuria in a matter of days, brushing aside the Japanese Kwantung Army.

The Red Army of 1945 comprised some 500 divisions, a colossal land force, deployed from Germany to Korea.

Soviet Air Force

In the first days of the German invasion, the Soviet Air Force (*Voenno-Vozdushnye Sily*) was all but wiped out on the ground. Within a week the German High Command proclaimed the destruction of 4017 Soviet aircraft for the loss of 150 German. It was aircraft rather than aircrew that were lost and, despite continuing heavy losses, the VVS was able to stave off total defeat, aided by acts of individual heroism (Soviet pilots for example took to ramming enemy aircraft) and by the appearance of new fighters such as the LaGG 3, Yak, and MiG 3 in large quantities.

Between July 1941 and January 1942 up to 2000 fighters fought in the defence of Moscow, more for example than were engaged in the Battle of Britain. Scale continued to mark the Soviet Air Force's operations as the Luftwaffe lost its original dominance, worn down by technical and supply problems, Soviet numbers and by operations such as the supply of the Demyansk and Stalingrad pockets in which vast numbers of vital supply aircraft were lost.

In 1942 'air armies' were established, each to support an army group on a designated front, expressing the overwhelming emphasis on tactical airpower. Aircraft such as the II-2 Shturmovik proved a formidable anti-armour weapon, swarming over the battlefield at treetop height in regimental groups of up to thirty aircraft.

By 1945 Soviet dominance in the air was almost total with over 18 air armies equipped with the latest aircraft. The Sixteenth Air Army, formed to defend Stalingrad in August 1942 for example with just over 300 aircraft, numbered over 2000 by the opening of the Battle of Berlin, in 1945 more than what remained of the entire Luftwaffe.

In spite of producing some significant prototype long-range aircraft, the Soviet Air Force's strategic bombing arm, the *Dalnaya Aviatisya*, was never able to mount more than pinprick attacks on the enemy heartland. The best medium bomber was the Pe-2 which was as good a combat aircraft as its German or Allied equivalent.

The Soviet Union received almost 20,000 aircraft from the USA and Great Britain including P-39s, P-63s, P-40s, B-25s, A-20s, P-47s, C-47s, PBY Catalinas, Hurricanes and Spitfires.

The Soviet Navy

The Red Navy was as decimated by Stalin's prewar purges as the Army had been and was unprepared for war in 1941. By the end of 1941 what remained of the Baltic fleet was bottled up in besieged Leningrad and in the Black Sea the German drive into the Crimea had the same result denying the ports of Odessa and Sevastopol. The use of naval crews as infantry, where they fought with great gallantry, further depleted the availability of trained manpower. The Red Navy lost a battleship and three cruisers to air attack and 38 destroyers and torpedo boats to bombs, mines and torpedo attack. No new ships were laid down during the war.

In step with the general 'Russification' of the Great Patriotic War in 1943, Soviet warships which bore the revolutionary names *October Revolution* and *Paris Commune* reverted to their old Tsarist names *Petropavlovsk* and *Sevastopol*.

Special Operations Executive

SOE was established on 16 July 1940 in a brave spirit of defiance with the Germans still poised to invade Britain, to direct and supply resistance organizations in occupied Europe. The SOE operated in the Balkans, in Italy, in Scandinavia, in Central Europe, Holland and Belgium and especially in France, wherever in fact there was a resistance movement to motivate and direct. The SOE's war was coloured by a particular kind of individual heroism, with the threat of capture, interrogation and death at the hands of the Gestapo ever present and the degree of success linked to the effectiveness of the resistance movement itself. In Holland for example, geographic conditions made a partisan-style resistance impossible and by 1943 SOE operations had been completely penetrated by the Gestapo. Over twenty-three thousand Dutch men and women lost their lives as members of the resistance. In the mountains of Yugoslavia by contrast full scale partisan warfare was not only possible but militarily highly effective.

The cost was higher in France. Of 200,000 French men and women killed in concentration camps, 75,000 were of the resistance and 20,000 more Maquisards were killed in action. Nearly all the captured SOE agents, over 200, were massacred in two distinct waves of executions in September 1944 and March 1945. Only around 30 survived.

United States Army

The US Army of 1939 was tiny, numbering only some 174,000 men. By the time of Pearl Harbor, with the inclusion of reservists, it had reached 1.4 million. By 1945 the US Army mustered eight million men and the United States was the world's first global superpower, with a total of 15 million men and women mobilized and vast military power projected victoriously many thousands of miles from the continental United States.

The US contribution to the destruction of Axis power was at the cost of substantial battle casualties but the US civilian population did not suffer as their European or Asian equivalents. In the 'Atlantic' (western) theatres the US Army suffered 765,751 casualties, 177,100 dead. The Pacific fighting claimed 169,635 casualties of which 57,137 were deaths. The overall total was 936,259 (234,874 dead). Total personnel captured were 124,079 and 30,314 were reported missing (of which 24,000 were later accounted for). The Army Air Force component of this total was 115,382 (52,173 dead).

United States Army Air Forces

The US Army Air Corps (USAAC), so named in 1926, was a component of the US Army reorganized on 20 June 1941 along with GHQ Air Force under a single unified command with Major General H.H. Arnold as first Chief Army Air Forces. In March 1942, the Army Air Forces became a co-equal command with Army Ground Forces and Army services of supply. The peak wartime strength of the USAAF was 2,411,294 men and women and casualties 115,382. From July 1940 to August 1945 the US Army accepted the huge total of 229,554 aircraft. It became the United States Air Force in 1947.

US Marine Corps:

Greatly expanded through the first year of the Pacific War and committed virtually entirely to that theatre to number

314

six divisions by the end of the war. Marine Corps aviation meanwhile grew from 10 to 129 squadrons by 1945. The USMC lost over 18,000 dead and 70,000 wounded in some of the fiercest fighting of the war from Guadalcanal through the Gilberts and Marshalls.

US Navy

The US Navy had begun a massive expansion programme before Pearl Harbor with the Navy Act of July 1940 laying down the requirement for a 'two ocean navy' – which is just what the US fleet had to become as the instrument by which America's vast industrial and military power could be brought to bear thousands of miles from her shores. Construction priorities shifted as operational realities did in the Pacific or in the battle against the U-Boats in the Atlantic. Between mid-1940 and the end of the war, the US Navy accepted no fewer than almost 75,000 warships, the overwhelming bulk (66,055) of them landing craft, and including ten battleships, 27 aircraft carriers, 111 escort carriers, 47 cruisers and 70 destroyers, 504 escort and 217 submarines. Over 75,000 aircraft were delivered to the US Navy in the same period and the US Navy mustered over 60,000 pilots at the end of the war.

Ultra

Not an organization but a security classification (the very highest) given to intelligence gathered from the fact that the British had broken the military codes used by the Germans with their Enigma encryption device. Enigma was an electro-mechanically operated computer which generated apparently random number groups and seemed to the Germans totally secure. However Polish intelligence had got a captured machine to the West in 1939 and at Bletchley Park the British gathered a concentration of academic brainpower and a huge secretariat to tend 'Colossus', an equally primitive but effective electro-mechanical computer

315

which could decode the Enigma encryptions. 'Ultra' intelligence helped the direction of the war from its early days but could not by itself win campaigns. It was of great material assistance however in the Battle of Britain, in the naval war in the Mediterranean and in the crisis of the Battle of the Atlantic. It was important too in judging enemy reaction to the deception plans which were so crucial to D-Day's success, but it failed to predict the German Ardennes offensive.

People's War

The Civilian Experience In World War II

The symbols of suffering in the Second World War are not military cemeteries. They are the names of places where the civilian population – men, women and children, suffered and died. Names like Auschwitz, and Oradour, Coventry and Belgrade, Hiroshima and Hamburg, Leningrad and Warsaw sound the litany of total war as much as Alamein or Arnhem.

The Germans behaved with extreme brutality to the peoples they subjected. The Japanese were brutal overlords and treated POWs abominably. The Allies used strategic bombing of the German and Japanese civilian populations in an attempt to extinguish the tyranny of their governments. The most perverse expression of this tyranny, the attempt to exterminate European Jewry, accounted for six million of the total of thirty million civilian deaths in the systematic programme of industrialized mass murder coyly dubbed the 'final solution'. The revelation of the extent of the Nazi war on the peoples of Europe swept away any moral qualms as to the means of overthrowing Hitlerism.

And yet 'civilian' life went on. Millions of people lived a fairly 'normal' life within the economic stringencies and constant dangers of total war. Germany for example never became mobilized for total war, rations remained high and taxes comparatively low. Women were not drafted for war work en masse, and consumer industries kept going. In 1943 for example, German industries still produced 13,000 tonnes of wallpaper while the great bombing attacks, such as those on Hamburg, by demolishing restaurants, hotels and cinemas in fact diverted workers in Germany's service industries to war production. Britain in contrast became a siege economy with an unprecedented degree of state and social control to wring every bit of useful warlike capacity out of the fabric of the nation. The continental United States was untouched by military operations yet mobilized manpower and industrial muscle on a fantastic scale.

The Soviet Union was ravaged by war, vast tracts of the country being overrun, scores of cities being blasted to rubble and an estimated 20 million killed, and yet it managed to outproduce Germany and German-controlled occupied Europe in war production.

One of the most important operations of the war was not directly military – it was the uprooting, moving and re-erection of Soviet war industries with their workforce out of reach of the invader. It began almost the moment the invasion began and, as the Germans were snapping their panzer rings shut around vast chunks of the Red Army and important industrial centres such as Minsk and Riga, the Soviet leadership decided to evacuate all the great industrial areas of western Russia, the central and eastern Ukraine, the Donbass and the industrial areas of Leningrad and Moscow itself. This transplantation of industry in the winter of 1941–2 ranks as one of the greatest organizational achievements of the war and was to prove crucial to its outcome. It was an epic too of human endurance, with workers toiling up to 15 hours a day living in hastily built camps scraped out of the Siberian tundra. Many died or were lost to the Germans and the workforce dropped from 31,200,000 in 1940 to 19,800,000 in late 1941. Meanwhile the State Defence Committee was laying down the production targets for total war: 22,000 aircraft and 25,000 tanks to be produced in 1942, and they did it.

The fate of those left behind to the Germans was far worse. Red Army political commissars were shot on capture. Russian soldiers, derided as subhuman Slavs, were not treated like other POWs and millions died of starvation in brutalized POW camps or as slave workers. The same went for the Russian civilian population, exploited as *Ostarbeiter* (workers from the east) until they dropped, while the Reichskommissars of the conquered territories answerable to the Ostiministerium in Berlin obeyed Hitler's own principles for the government of a colonial east – 'First conquer, second rule, third exploit'.

The Final Solution

The Jews however were simply to be exterminated. Hitler's was one, and the most fearsome one, of a string of anti-semitic regimes in Europe. Tsarist Russia had invented the 'pogrom' and Jewish discomfort continued under Soviet rule. In prewar Poland the large Jewish population was persecuted if not physically molested. But the Nazi takeover of Germany was founded on anti-semitism and suspicion of the enemy within and would institutionalize persecution of the Jews on a terrifying new scale. The Nuremberg race purity laws of 1935 forbade sexual relations between Jews and 'Aryans' while the prominence of Germany's 600,000 Jews concentrated in cities (one third of them in Berlin alone) allowed systematic petty persecution to flourish. In November 1938 came *Kristallnacht* ('crystal night', so called because of the smashed windows of Jewish shops) which moved state persecution of German Jews onto official footing. By 1939 three hundred thousand Jews had been bullied into leaving Germany, but as yet the Nazis, with an eye perhaps on world opinion, did not have a programme of mass killing to murder the rest systematically.

The conquest of Poland brought three million Jews into the Nazis' thrall. At first they were herded into ghettoes and, from 23 November 1939, forced to wear a yellow star. While in the winter of 1940–41 the Polish Jews began to die of hunger and epidemics, those remaining in Germany were subjected to further proscriptions which ranged from the brutal to the bizarre. They were for example forbidden to keep pets or use electrical appliances while a branch of the SS Race and Resettlement Office was working on a plan to use the Vichy French colony of Madagascar as a dumping ground for Jews.

Things changed with the invasion of the Soviet Union. Hitler had orally charged Himmler in March 1941 with the elimination of Bolshevik commissars, gypsies, political enemies and 'all Jews' in the forthcoming invasion. On 31 July, Göring gave Reinhard Heydrich, head of the RHSA, a written order charging him to 'take any steps necessary towards a general solution of the Jewish problem in areas of German influence in Europe'. On 20 January 1942 Heydrich convened the so-called Wannsee Conference where the fate of European Jewry was plotted. 'The final solution' [*Endlösung*] to the Jewish problem in Europe will be applied to about eleven million people. The Jews must be transferred to the East under close surveillance and there assigned to forced labour . . . a great many will be eliminated by physical deficiency, the remainder, the most resistant, must be dealt with accordingly'. The minutes of the Wannsee Conference survive and are one of the most damning documents of the war.

Mass executions began in Russia where the so called 'Einsatzkommandos' travelled in the wake of the German Army. These units, made up of SD, police and *Waffen-SS* volunteers, simply gathered up Jews in their villages and shot them, down to the last child. In the larger cities such as Kiev the Jewish population would be systematically rounded up, forced to dig a grave, then machine-gunned or shot in the nape of the neck.

It was messy and it was hard to cover up. When the Germans retreated in 1943, slave workers were forced to dig up and exhume the mass graves the Einsatzkommandos left in their wake and burn the evidence.

In the summer of 1941 gassing was tried instead of shooting. Victims were herded into a van and gassed by the carbon monoxide exhaust fumes. Inspired by the 'euthanasia' operations of 1940–41 when death by gassing had been applied to the mentally ill, 'Zyklon B' was the chosen method, a crystal that on contact with air would release deadly prussic acid fumes.

The Wannsee Conference spelled out the process in bureaucratic detail – how it would be administered and carried out. Extermination factories were set up in Poland, at Chelmo, Treblinka, Sobibor, Stutthof, Belzec, Maidanek, and at a huge twin camp site at Auschwitz-Birkenau. A network of concentration camps for non-Jewish enemies of the Third Reich was already established throughout Germany and occupied Europe – but it was eastwards to the extermination sites the trains would roll. First the Polish Jews, then the Jews of western Europe, the Jews from Italy and the Balkans and lastly the Jews of Hungary fed the gas chambers and the crematorium ovens.

According to authoritative figures, the Nazis killed 2.6 million Jews from Poland, 750,000 from the Soviet Union, 500,000 from Rumania, 40,000 from Bulgaria, 60,000 from Greece, 58,000 from Yugoslavia, 700,000 from Hungary, 60,000 from Austria, 60,000 from Czechoslovakia, 104,000 from Lithuania, 70,000 from Latvia, 180,000 from Germany, 65,000 from France, 9000 from Italy, 40,000 from Belgium, 104,000 from the Netherlands, 100 from Denmark and 750 from Norway. The exact death figure is unquantifiable but outline figures suggest that 300,000 Jews managed to escape from Germany before 1939 and that of the 8.5 million living in occupied Europe, between five and a half and six million were exterminated.

The concentration camps and extermination camps were allied to the slave labour system. By April 1943 Fritz Sauckel, Plenipotentiary General for the Allocation of Labour, could report to Hitler that 3.6 million foreign workers had been pressed into German industry and that 1.6 million POWs were also employed. Some 40% of armament workers were forced labourers held in concentration-camp like conditions and worked to exhaustion.

The most fortunate forced labourers were those allotted to land work on farms. The worst conditions were endured by those singled out at Auschwitz-Birkenau for a few weeks of work at 'Monomitz', the network of satellite camps run by concerns such as Siemens and I.G. Farben and specially built to exploit death camp labour, charged out at a rate of eight marks a day payable to the SS main economic and administration office. Auschwitz commandant Rudolf Hoess testified at Nuremberg that the 13 major concentration camps in German occupied territory controlled some 900 subsidiary labour camps.

At the end of the war, armies of near-starving, liberated slave workers joined the vast columns of POWs, refugees and other 'displaced persons' in seeking succour from their liberators and some sort of passage to what remained of home – if there still was one.

Home Front: Britain

Of the 57 nations that took part in the Second World War Britain and the British Commonwealth fought from start to finish. The war began for Britain on a note of weary resignation, unlike 1914 when the country went to war with flags waving and bands playing. There was a note of relief that the illusions of the appeasement were at last over, coloured by a geniune fear that the country would soon be blanketed with poison gas and mass casualties from bombing, but the machinery of war for a population under siege was ready. Conscription and a register of reserved occupations had been introduced shortly before the outbreak of war. The Munich crisis had been a signal for the digging of air raid shelters, the issue of gas masks and a militarization of the country. When war came on 3 September 1939, the plans were ready. Evacuation of children began immediately and one and half million were moved under the official scheme, in a matter of days. By January 1940, when the bombs had failed to materialize half of these official evacuees had returned home while at least two million other children were unofficially dispersed. Some children were sent to Canada and South Africa until the sinking of an evacuee ship tragically ended this privileged form of flight to safety.

The blackout was also introduced right at the beginning, plunging British cities into inky darkness. Heavy curtains hid lit interiors, street lighting was extinguished and motor vehicles groped about with pencil thin screened headlight beams. Gas masks were issued to everyone including children and babies and it was obligatory to carry them. Gas attacks were however never made.

The period of 'phoney war' ended in April 1940 when the Germans struck north into Scandinavia. On 10 May Chamberlain's Conservative government gave way to a coalition government headed by Winston Churchill, which took office as the panzers drove into France. One of the government's first acts was to pass an extended Emergency Powers (Defence) Act giving the government sweeping powers to sequester property, censor the media and the mails, and order the lives of individuals in service of the war effort.

The new mood of reality matched the hour. France fell and the British Expeditionary Force came back beaten from Dunkirk, but at least they came back – along with a ragbag of Dutch and French, Czechs and Poles, Norwegians and Danes – governments in exile with remnants of their armies now wearing British battledress along with the rest. The whole nation it seemed was in uniform. With the threat of invasion imminent and especially of a descent by parachutists in May 1940 'Local Defence Volunteers' were called on, at first a motley collection of old men and boys armed with pikes and rook rifles – later (the name changed to Home Guard in July) a well armed militia taught at least the basics of street fighting and tank hunting. Service in the Home Guard gave many citizens a sense of really being in the war effort and of direct defiance to Hitler, as did service in other paramilitary volunteer organizations that proliferated such as the ARP (Air Raid Precautions), later renamed Civil Defence, the Auxiliary Fire Service, the Womens Voluntary Service, and so on.

The military aspects of the first German air offensive against Britain have been covered elsewhere. Although the 'Blitz' was designed as a military softening up before invasion and as an extension of the U-Boat campaign by attacks on ports, a key target was the British people's morale. How close did it get to succeeding?

When an area was severely bombed for the first time, morale took a dive but the dire pre-war predictions of mass slaughter were not borne out. After the first shock, morale knitted together and the routine of the air raid warning, the scurry to the shelter and then the all clear took over. 'Keep calm and carry on' was the propaganda message – but in a sense it was true.

A Home Office memorandum of October 1940 judged

325

the effects of the raids to be 'transient'. 'London people lost much sleep and suffered anxiety and discomfort but there was no panic and no mass evacuation' it reported.

In fact in the first years of war the most serious threat to Britain's survival was not air bombardment but the U-Boat campaign which, if successful, would subject the country to slow starvation. Rationing began in January 1940 with bacon, sugar and butter. Through 1940–41 the number of basic foods on ration increased, meat in March, tea in July, margarine and fats, jam and marmalade in March 1941 and cheese in May. Overall however rationing worked; food was monotonous but it was there while the 'points' system introduced in December 1941 allowed 'exotic' foods such as rice or canned fruit which had an arbitrary points rating attached at least to be had, if infrequently. Under the scheme each ration book holder had 16 points to spend as they wished at any shop which had the items they wanted.

The Ministry of Food provided well meaning nutritious menus and exhortations to try for substitute dishes such as the famous Woolton pie and carrot tart while pressing American Spam or whalemeat on a suspicious public. Whalemeat was the one item the British public could not stomach. The gravest shortages were of imported fruit such as bananas or oranges, supplies of which simply dried up, and of eggs because chickens had been slaughtered either to eat or because there was no feed for them. The average was one egg a fortnight with none at all for long periods. From June 1942 dried eggs began to appear, again greeted with suspicion but remorselessly pushed by the Ministry of Food. Milk distribution was controlled from November 1941 with every family allowed a tin of dried milk once a month. Full cream 'National Dried Milk' was available for infants, who, overall, got a level of care unheard of in the years of the depression.

The Second World War was the first in which the electronic media played a part. The BBC had a fledgeling television service which was shut down on 1 September 1939 but the wireless was both the most important influence on morale and the most important channel for government information. On the outbreak of war the BBC was geared to broadcast dour news bulletins interspersed with solemn music but this just frightened people. What they wanted most was entertainment (it was the same with sports and leisure facilities such as dance halls and cinemas which, after initial restrictions, were reopened and enjoyed record patronage). But the wireless was the focus of the nation in crisis, used in a masterly and inspiring way by Churchill and the nightly nine o'clock news was listened to in silent reverence. It was also the disseminator of (censored) mass entertainment. The comedy ITMA (It's That Man Again) starring Tommy Handley was a phenomenon on its own, made up of catch phrases which may seem indecipherable to another generation, but 'Can I do you now sir' (the refrain of Mrs Mopp), 'Dis is Funf' (Funf was the German Spy), 'Ta Ta for Now', and 'I Don't Mind If I do' (Colonel Chinstrap's reaction to any offer of alcohol) entered the public imagination as much as Churchill's exhortation to fight them on the landing grounds.

Politics did not sleep through the years of emergency power control. Parliament remained in session, by-elections were fought and after the invasion of the Soviet Union, the far left embraced the war wholeheartedly (the Communist newspaper, *The Daily Worker*, was shut down for a time in 1941). The Labour Party consolidated its position from within the coalition government with Clement Attlee as Deputy Prime Minister and Ernest Bevin as employment and production supremo. From 1942 all young men of eighteen called up were given the option of going down the mines instead and when the response proved thin it became a matter of ballot. In all 45,000 'Bevin Boys', as they were known, went down the mines.

The war years were marked by a political questioning of the economic abuses of the 1930s and the promise shown by wartime central direction, egalitarianism and state welfare. The Beveridge report of December 1942 on the future of the state's social responsibilities insisted that 'organization of social insurance should be treated as one part of a comprehensive policy of social progress', while the

327

Britain at War; some social indicators

	1939	1940	1941	1942	1943	1944	1945
1) Strikes: working days lost (thousands)	1,331	9,41	1,077	1,530	1,832	3,936	2,847
2) Deaths by violence	26,139	51,516	50,502	27,908	25,153	31,010	23,644
(a) suicide	5,794	4,950	4,052	3,770	3,893	3,792	3,985
(b) homicide	189	194	210	294	235	196	292
(c) motor accident	6,168	6,961	7,445	5,523	4,319	4,717	4,157
3) Civilian deaths dur to war operations	82	22,428	22,350	3,884	3,140	9,372	2,433
4) Executions	8	14	13	12	10	7	4
5) Persons found guilty all offences	787,482	803,721	802,999	689,238	569,825	500,488	467,700
(a) drunkeness	56,797	48,863	43,778	29,778	29,314	24,910	22,188
(b) blackout offences		299,260	210,934	154,080	109,757	73,831	17,594
6) Divorce							
(a) petitions filed	9,970	6,915	8,079	11,613	14,887	18,390	24,857
(b) grounds of adultery	4,989	3,931	4,781	7,116	9,513	12,006	17,091

(Divorce petitions peak in 1947 at 47,041 with 31,482 on the grounds of adultery – hidden fallout from the war).

Butler Education Act of 1944 ensured for the first time that secondary education would be received by all children.

People's memories were long and patience short. In spite of Churchill's enormous prestige as war leader, when Britain went to the polls in July 1945, the Labour Party won with a big majority. They seemed to promise the radical change for which the war had created a demand, not just among traditional working class voters but among the middle class. The people's war, it seemed to some, could be turned to a people's peace.

Britain at War: Social Indicators

Almost six years of war put the social fabric of Britain under maximum pressure. Yet the pattern of behaviour evident in bald Home Office statistics reveals some contrary trends to those that might be expected. Crime for example, expressed as persons found guilty of various offences, fell dramatically from a 1939 total of 787,482 to 467,700 in 1945 (see below). Suicides fell as did legal executions while smoking increased, especially among women, drafted en masse into factories for war work. Motor accidents in 1943, in spite of restricted private car use, caused one thousand more deaths than enemy action. Strikes increased, reaching a peak in 1944 with three times as many working days lost as in 1938. Some diverse social indicators are given opposite –

Index

Index

Index

Index

Index